A Brief History of

MW01169840

Mathew Varghese

A Brief History of Creative Work and Plutonomy

Rethinking the Modern Thought-History of Work and Life

 Springer

Mathew Varghese
The Hajime Nakamura Eastern Institute
Tokyo, Japan

ISBN 978-981-15-9265-2   ISBN 978-981-15-9263-8   (eBook)
https://doi.org/10.1007/978-981-15-9263-8

© The Editor(s) (if applicable) and The Author(s), under exclusive license to Springer Nature
Singapore Pte Ltd. 2021
This work is subject to copyright. All rights are solely and exclusively licensed by the Publisher, whether
the whole or part of the material is concerned, specifically the rights of translation, reprinting, reuse of
illustrations, recitation, broadcasting, reproduction on microfilms or in any other physical way, and
transmission or information storage and retrieval, electronic adaptation, computer software, or by similar
or dissimilar methodology now known or hereafter developed.
The use of general descriptive names, registered names, trademarks, service marks, etc. in this
publication does not imply, even in the absence of a specific statement, that such names are exempt from
the relevant protective laws and regulations and therefore free for general use.
The publisher, the authors and the editors are safe to assume that the advice and information in this
book are believed to be true and accurate at the date of publication. Neither the publisher nor the
authors or the editors give a warranty, expressed or implied, with respect to the material contained
herein or for any errors or omissions that may have been made. The publisher remains neutral with regard
to jurisdictional claims in published maps and institutional affiliations.

This Springer imprint is published by the registered company Springer Nature Singapore Pte Ltd.
The registered company address is: 152 Beach Road, #21-01/04 Gateway East, Singapore 189721,
Singapore

For the fond memory of my father who worked hard for finding work for others

Preface

When reexamining, the contemporary history of thoughts relating to "work and life," we can clearly find that there is a steady decline in appreciating the significance of creative work in comparison with the earlier periods of our current civilization. The natural bond that existed between human "work and life" is now being threatened by plutonomy in the twenty-first century. Plutonomy means the control and rule of the financially wealthy, whose wealth is being appreciated and valued as the supreme against every other human attribute, especially work and life. The thought-history of "work" shows that the makeup of creative work is, a unique human trait, helping humans to build up the civilization in the present form. We can see that whether we revere or not, our "being" in the world is supported by certain cardinal ethical virtues. Those ethical values are the reason why life in the world is appreciated and valued for the last few millenniums, where humans could have lived with a sense of being protected in the world. Nevertheless, with the incursion of plutonomy—the rule of the wealthy—into all aspects of life is offsetting the protection of ethical and moral values that we have taken for granted since the dawn of our present civilization. Here, I argue that the developments of those ethical values are directly connected with human intelligence and rational faculties formulated out of *creative work*. Anthropologists claim that current human species, the homo sapiens, incidentally developed a *complex body-brain system* that helped us to behave differently from other living beings in the world. We can see that when we create things, we use a complex and delicate mechanism of *hand-brain faculty*.

Now we have technologically enabled systems controlling, watching, constraining normal human activities by installing fear and scare in an unprecedented level. If the current trend continues, our mere expectation that we could find eternal solution to all human problems by creating huge financial assets would land us in a world, where we may not be pursuing any of the cardinal ethical values founded on virtues of truth, goodness, harmony, consciousness, being, unity, etc., influencing dynamically our lives. Contextually, we may only use them as talking points. The protective structure of those values is founded on a deep respect for the nature's providences. Homo sapiens could build the present civilization by using the faculty of intelligence. This special human trait should have formed out of using creative energy by imbibing knowledge from creative work. The conception of metaphysics and ethics of Aristotle should have originated after valuing *creative work* and how creativity shaped up our intelligence (*nous*), and the logical, rational and linguistic faculties (*logos*). The virtue ethical system that we value as the foundational value is formed out of *creative work* imbibed from a system of *body-hand-brain complex*, which Aristotle conceived as *eudaimonia-arete*. However, now we disregard the value of creative work as being alluded in the original Aristotelian philosophy. Aristotelian philosophy is the foundational thought behind our political, economic, and sociological systems, where Aristotle used *eudaimonia* and *arete* to explain the purpose of life from the individual perspective to all other levels of collective systems such as community, nation, etc. The virtue-based ethical practices we uphold are directly connected with creative work, because the creative energy we harnessed through work helped us to pursue life even with all difficulties with the help of ethical virtues.

Aristotle's ethics on virtues is not instructive but happens innately when activating the internal ability of the human soul to generate spiritual flourishing (*eudaimonia*) through virtuous actions—creative work (*arete*) that would lead one to the realm of heavenly virtues. The complex system developed by millenniums of evolution of the body-brain system (hand-brain faculty) enabled humans to survive successfully by challenging the odds of the living world. Such a faculty that could experiment the odds of nature, and find solutions by using intelligence is not available for other living beings: Animals should submit to the adverse forces of nature, because they have neither a faculty of intelligence, nor a faculty for logical thinking. The fundamental human trait to use *episteme* (knowledge) and *techne* (craftmanship: artistic skill) emulated from the effective use of hand-brain faculty.

But today, the ghost of plutonomy is chasing us into some unchartered territories. Since the life of a human personality is not eternal, we cannot outstretch ourselves beyond the limits set by the nature, we can use intelligence to live within those limits as living beings. Nevertheless, our expectations, under the sway of plutonomy are unexplainably unrealistic and outrageous. Under plutonomy, we are allowing a small portion of the wealthy—plutocrats, for dominating the wealth of a nation with huge and astronomical sums of monetary wealth, and at the same time, denying majority of people to earn a living by utilizing their creative skills. According to Aristotle, the wealth of a nation belongs to the smooth conduct of the lives of all its citizens; that is why we created ethical value-based legal and societal systems to support the smooth conduct of life and taught people to follow them with due diligence. In the ancient world, systems were created for protecting the ethical values of truth, goodness, being, etc. The constitutional foundation of our political systems is founded on virtue ethics emanated from *eudaimonia and arete*. Now the political system is not founded on the constitution of ethical values, but making those constitutional values to be controlled by a financial system created under plutonomy for watching and supervising the entire system of civil administration. It is applicable to all systems such as democracy, communism, socialism, constitutional monarchies, constitutional republicanism, or tribalism. The monetized and financialized wealth has a magical power to attract anyone into its gambit. Now under plutonomy, there is plutocracy instead of democracy, plutocrat control wealth instead of traditional capitalists' or socialists' control on creation of wealth and its management. And now we have precariat workers who do all kinds of jobs as part-time contract workers, by brazenly declining the rights of creative workers who could have enhanced their life by activating the *hand-brain faculty*. The changes in perspectives have happened because of the mechanization of everything that has been happening since the modern period (circ.1800). Plutonomy now propagates that human involvement with work is not necessary that AI-controlled systems can create things abundantly for everyone to enjoy life as much as they could. I attempt to discuss how human life may struggle to find a place under such a system.

This book followed Aristotle's philosophy on how humans use reasoning and intelligence for formulating thoughts that could discern eternal ideas from empirical sources, and Aristotle cleverly conceived knowledge from the form of thought, with a deep understanding of humans' abilities. Thought formation is our single most significant ability. We can construct thoughts on the basis of true propositions to understand our true "being" that is naturally designed to be unified with the "qua-being". We normally call that as God that is ruling over all the cardinal virtues available in the world. We can understand only the ethical virtues through our thoughts and at the transcended realm God should be the "thought thinking itself". And the transcended virtues are eternal like the eternal thought of God. The transcended virtues controlling our thoughts are the virtues of truth, goodness, beauty, consciousness, etc., which is also known as God, Brahman, Dao, etc., for the last few millenniums of our present civilization. Because of the deep beliefs in to the doctrines of virtues ethics, we could live as humans, much different from our prehuman existence. We could challenge the traces of that prehuman species that used to appear as hate, anger, violence, avarice, greed, etc. It is very important for us to rethink on the thoughts that helped to create our civilization founded on ethical virtues.

As being observed by anthropologists that the present human species should have gone through millions of years of evolution to reach to the present form, from various other prehuman existences. According to neuroscientists, the human consciousness has evolved through 200 million years of evolution to reach to the present level of maturity. It is argued that *creative work* played a significant role in the development of human consciousness and the neural circuits that developed through the participation of creative work systematically. Our human nature is directly connected with creative work. If we decline the natural ways of brain performances by not allowing it to create a particular kind of neural circuit that defines one's personality, we may lose our human nature. We otherwise may instill fear, worry, and ignorance. If we deny creative activities, we may lose our logical and reasoning faculties and may be controlled by emotions and should be instructed for doing everything. We may, in future, have to accept an AI-controlled systems to instruct and manage everything for us. This would be a very fateful situation for us.

But, we can find solutions, if we reread classical philosophical thought that have appreciated creative work and the virtue ethical system helping us to survive as humans. This fact can be explained well, using Aristotelian philosophy on creative work that goes through four stages or causes, where the final cause is metaphysical, yet leading to greater insights and discernments about the transcended virtues: truth, goodness and being, and the contours of which cannot be described by language; whereas, the other causes: material, efficient, and formal causes can be explained. Man (efficient cause) works on materials (material cause) based on an idea (formal cause) that is internally conceived as it is the property of the soul and tries to make the best usable products to protect us from the adversities of the natural forces. The formal cause is the thought that enables a person to create a thing which makes his life worth living as being conceived in *eudaimonia* and *arete*—by achieving virtuous existence with an evocative flourishing of spiritual feeling, for example, the spiritual flourish that a parent imbibes on seeing the faces of own children and the accelerating joy when one feels on accomplishing a task. Through the accomplishments of creative potentials, one receives *eudaimonia* which is the foundation of ethics in Aristotle's philosophy. When we work efficiently with the inherent abilities that we are born with, we could further the knowledge in the form of thought and connect us with the eternal thought of the God—the thought thinking itself. In other systems of classical philosophies, creative work is duly revered like the Indians on Karma, Chinese on Dao, etc. I used those classical views on creative work together with contemporary understanding on the development of consciousness in creating a contemporary narrative on creative work in this book.

When we accept mechanization as the next stage of progress, we are not only declining people's right to do creative work, but also creating problems in energy production by replacing human energy with the created artificial energy systems for doing works, leading to huge energy crisis around the world which would upset the natural energy balance of the earth, which is now coming out in the form of climate crises and also in the form of constant human struggles with the forces of nature. We are forced to live our lives without virtues and moral values. The present human civilization is protected by the contours of virtue ethics, but today, the sway of fear taking over our lives, leading to destruction and mayhem.

This book has two parts, one describing the sociological and economical aspects when we discard creative work as the method for keeping the social fabric of a society and give complete implementation of automation systems using artificial intelligence (AI). The second part is a review of the aspects of creative work that should have helped humans to exist within a virtue ethical system of being protected continuously. The first part tries to unpack the historical situations that has been developed since the advent of industrialization of the world that followed the methods of technoscience. This is based on the Marxian thoughts on the historical progress on "work and life," from the preindustrial and industrial world order to the contemporary times. The postindustrial culture is again divided into Industry 1.0, Industry 2.0, Industry 3.0, and the progress of which into the Industry 4.0, would remove, the aspects of creative work from our lives, where the call is for the development of complete automation using AI technology that works on big data and nanotechnology.

The second part is a philosophical review of human civilization from the pre-human species to human world of *work and life*, where work played a significant role in shaping up the entire world civilization. And cogently argue that the denigration of human work could damage the human mind-brain complex which is the basis for humans to use their brains. Basing the neurological studies on this aspect, I tried to revisit the philosophical perspective on *creative work* from the perspective of classical Greek, Indian and Chinese philosophies where creative work and completion of it are the purpose of protecting the spiritual makeup of human life.

The working class under plutonomy is precariat—the working class who can do only part-time works or such unattached works with any enterprise. They are unorganized and hired on the basis of short contracts where the human rights for work and life are hugely denied. It is estimated that nearly 70% of the work force today live in precarity. In order to address the anomalies of plutonomy, this book offers no agenda or program. But the subtext of this work clearly says instead of forming policies aiding huge investments and interest-free supply of money for the plutocrats to run plutonomy, the people and governments should take policies that enhance all opportunities to do creative works, and then the society resurrects by itself from the draconian control of plutonomy and artificial intelligence. How that is to be done is a constant challenge before us. We also should understand techno-sciences are just a method that may aid us, but applying that everywhere is suicidal, as humans are not machines working on big data and artificial energy.

As I am not an economist nor a businessman, I had to receive relevant input from people who are, in the field of business, having direct knowledge in dealing with the current developments in the field of finance, economics, banking, manufacturing and production, etc. I was immensely helped by my longtime friend, from my school days, Prashant Sankaran who is a business consultant and activist who promotes employment generating ventures with young entrepreneurs. This work is deeply indebted to his ideas and suggestions. The wealth of information I received from various personalities about the current situation in the field of business and finance is what made me to think about "creative work" seriously for discerning it philosophically; to mention a few: Mizugu Fukuroi, Loren L. Bundt, Toshitada Matsui, Hiroyuki Osumi, Willy Toko, Prasad Menon, Walter Kasmer, Patricia Oliver, Anil Thekkepat, Marie Helene Lacroix, Gyorgyi Kolossvary, Paulson Mittathani, Eve Silvester, Nishiyama Keishiro, Hybeen Thomas, James Kurian, Tamiko Hanaoka, Naoyuki Ogi, and Vinu Prasad, who spend their valuable time sharing their thoughts with me by discussing various connected issues with "work and life" in our contemporary times. I wish to thank my wife Yuko Fukuroi for keeping me together all these while with her matured and clear thoughts and my deep thoughts of reverence to my mother who was my first teacher and guide. The seed thought that has grown into this book form was sown by my father Varghese Mittathani who showed me with his own life, how work can shape life for himself and for people around him. I also wish to thank my senior colleague S. R. Bhatt, a very erudite scholar who helped me greatly in my academic career and also in publishing this book. I also wish to thank Satvinder Kaur, Leana Li, and Flora Wu at Springer for generously helping me with this work.

Tokyo, Japan   Mathew Varghese

About This Book

Plutonomy today is upsetting the synergic relationship that existed between wealth creation and wealth distribution. This book argues that creative work should be used to re-establish that synergic balance. The wealth distribution gap that exists today is making almost everyone with no access to wealth. And significant majority are living in precarity that of not having enough employment and enough income. In the dialectics, between plutonomy and precarity neither could achieve any virtuous purpose of protecting life well. The use of artificial intelligence would further complicate this situation. As for humans creating things using the complex *hand-brain faculty* is a gift of nature, like dogs use the faculty of superior smelling, bats depend on the inherent superior listening, or elephants have the powerful protecting trunk. We humans built our present civilized way of living with the expeditious use of the complex *hand-brain faculty*. Metaphorically, plutonomy of today is a black hole that could swallow up everything into its deep obscurity.

Part I discusses the historical dynamics of plutonomy—the norm of the wealthy where an active dialectic is being developed between plutonomy versus precarity—being in a state of insufficient *work* and income to support *life* where the work of artificial intelligence is the synthetic unity.

Part II discourses the paradoxical plutonomic world system from philosophical perspectives for reexamining the importance of *creative work* in creating an organic system of ethical and moral virtues. In the postmodern world order, that system is getting replaced by the norm of the plutonomy.

Introduction

Creative Work—Hand-Brain Faculty and Plutonomy

Doing work by hand with a control regime of the mind-brain faculty should be the main aspect that helped the development of our civilization supported by ethical values. *Creative work* helped us to continue following a definite culture and tradition for the last few millenniums. The natural development of a hand-brain faculty should have developed and prospered, when humanity learned to use hand tools for creating things using inherently formed and flourished creative skills. This had organically enhanced the mechanism of body mind involvement through a unique system—the *body-hand-brain complex*. And this faculty matured into a system that helps humans to think and use knowledge. Because of the *hand-brain faculty*, humans learned how to survive by making usable things and also learned how to use the faculties of knowledge, intelligence, and reasoning. This ability is uniquely human. With the efficient use of such a faculty, the humanity has generated a system of values that we revere as ethical and moral virtues for being protected safely with our life on earth. We naively thought that those virtues are given and being controlled by some transcended "divine providence," existing at a higher dimensional realm, watching and controlling, and always protecting us. But, we also know that such an all-pervading providence would have a deep subjective side, reflecting the transcended heavenly virtues in our inner being as consciousness—the inner knowledge. The *inner being* is supported by ethical virtues, and by following virtues we could connect with the *qua-being* understood as the dominion of gods.

But the knowledge about such a system of virtues is revealed to us through *creative works* by appreciating the creative skills embedded within us. The human nature is founded on knowledge based on virtues—the true knowledge, acting as the inner light, removing all human ignorance and fears, giving us a feeling of goodness, truth, harmony, being, justice, etc., and helping us to live harmoniously by agreeing with the forces of nature. The creative skills—*techne*; the ability to use intelligence and reasoning to form knowledge structure—*episteme*; and the synergies of these two inherent abilities should be celebrated as the foundations of our present civilization. The ancient Greeks venerated creative skills, *techne*, highly: the inherent human faculty enabling us to be artistically creative—the craftmanship. We can argue that such artistic skills are evolved with the complex functioning of human *hand-brain faculty*. The history of the complex hand-brain faculty and the importance of creative work are worth reviewing for understanding the problems of the twenty-first century. We discard those skills as worthless when we use techno-science indiscriminately everywhere.

The prehuman life should have struggled to survive in a world that was enclosed with deep darkness of ignorance and fear. That virtueless existence prompted humanity to function under a different regime of the mind-brain faculty that prompted the feelings of hated, angry, fear, revenge, etc., leading to violence that was aggressive and deadly for own survival. Thus, the prehuman kind should have obliterated under the sway of ignorance and fear. The homo sapiens, that makes the entire human species of today, had a fundamental trait that used brain creatively with the agile and calibrated functioning of the hand-brain faculty. When humans learned to create things, they created a virtue ethical system understood as truth, goodness, unity, consciousness, harmony, justice, etc. The homo sapiens built our contemporary civilization by using the hand-brain faculty. We today consider those virtues as the God's true being and revere and appreciate them highly. We believe our internal faculty, soul, is controlled by the virtues of heaven—the world of Gods. We understand about God only through the discernment of those ethical virtues in our living world. But, now we do not appreciate the role of the hand-brain faculty as much as we did before and also the knowledge developed organically for protecting our lives with the cover of ethical virtues, since the beginning of our human civilization. Unlike prehuman species, humans have another inherent ability to use knowledge (*episteme*) from sense perception. It is like *techne* (the artistic skills) worked in a synergic manner that helped humans to create a unique system of living, where we value and appreciate virtues that is supported by knowledge from creative skills.[1] Indians call this as the realm of *karma* (*techne*) and *jñāna* (*episteme*) that make human life different from other living beings. And the Chinese use the term, *Dao* to revere the synergic relationship, for showing its inner dynamics.

Notably in the twenty-first century with the emergence of plutonomy and the use of fully automatized AI systems may obliterate, our natural ability to do creative works. The demotion of the hand-brain faculty makes us to decline the importance of the cardinal virtues of truth, goodness, being, consciousness, etc., the values that protected our lives comprehensively thus far. We discern today the realm of those virtues as the "providence of God," or "providence of nature," which we can discern only through *techne* and *episteme*, and by establishing its synergic unity. If we fail to appreciate creative work, we may not be able to survive as humans by

---

[1]See Essay on Techne and Episteme in Stanford Encyclopedia of Philosophy https://plato.stanford.edu/entries/episteme-techne/.

receiving protection from those cardinal virtues. As a result, we may be pushed back to live in the kind of prehuman existence or to live in some kind of virtueless scary pitiful life style of some kind of posthuman dystopia.

Wealth Distribution Through Creative Work

Today, people may wonder why China made an 8851 km wall (including ruined parts the Great wall of China is estimated to be originally 21,196 km long);[2] or why Indians in ancient times built such artistically elegant temples and structures like Ajanta caves or even the Taj Mahal in the midlevel India; or why the cathedrals under the Holy Roman Empire, or the mosques in the Islamic world were all made by appreciating human creative work as the fundamental trait. What was the purpose of such extravagant display with the cost of huge spending of wealth and manpower? We think today that our ancients feared some trivial things, and out of their blunt resolves to eradicate those fears, they created those mammoth structures, on the basis of faith, not on the basis of a rational understanding about the true being of the worldly life. They would have ruined wealth and drained the valuable resources of a country that should have been used otherwise for improving the lives of the people. We also think that willfully an elite class manipulated the people's ignorance and fears to alleviate their own fears. And, we take today the ancients' view of life as an example of the idiosyncratic attitude that was the trait of life in the ancient world order.

But when we observe such acts carefully, with a non-judgmental mind, we may find a different kind of sound reasoning that substantiates all those acts. Such activities should have a strong economic side that our ancients have used for evolving prudent systems for dividing the nation's wealth by offering work to everyone, so that everyone can earn a living by appreciating and enhancing their inherent abilities. This would further help to generate more wealth for providing better and richer lives to all. Appreciating and respecting the "divine providence" are the duty of each individual and when each could do creative work by activating the hand-brain faculty, which is the best way to keep people happy and contented. And a system for the division of labor developed for dividing the wealth of a nation to the different layers of society. Otherwise, people who do agriculture, or those who make cloths and utensils, or those who make houses may have some work occasionally, but unless their skills are not updated and appreciated, nobody can use their services fully well. A large section of people may not do any work at all, and therefore no access to any kind of wealth. If such big projects are not available, the wealth created through agriculture, trade, etc., would not reach to a large section of people. Unless people have not given opportunities to appreciate their creative skills, they may not be able to realize the spiritual virtue, *eudaimonia*—happiness,

---

[2]See Article on Great Wall of China in Encyclopedia of Britannica: https://www.britannica.com/topic/Great-Wall-of-China.

human flourishing, etc. The Greek philosophy is founded on virtue ethics with the conceptions of *eudaimonia-arete* and can be realizable through engaging in creative work. And if the works are monotonous, repetitive, boring, and lacking any kind of creativity, people may lose intrinsic interest to live a life. The reasoning should be that by encouraging creative work, a ruler could distribute wealth justifiably, reasonably and sensibly, in order to benefit everyone, and also could generate enthusiasm and motivation to people to live their lives well with the flourishing of virtues everywhere. The major duties of the ruling systems should be to find a way for a justifiable distribution of wealth and to help everyone to live a happy and prosperous life.

The 21,196 km-long Chinese Great Wall was built over a period of nearly three millenniums by different dynasties for protecting the borders from the invaders. And those walls are huge structures, using substantial manpower, built by using technology developed over such a long period of time. In other words, those were huge infrastructure projects that did provide jobs to millions of people and helped to ensure the distribution of wealth justly and sensibly. Because of such efforts, various other developments in technological innovations had happened that aided human creativity substantially, making Chinese civilization a marvel in the ancient world. In the ancient times, wealth creators were a few farmers, artisans, and traders, but the created wealth is normally being stacked up with those who had close proximately to the process of wealth creation and control; and the others were disenfranchised and should have remained poor and died in poverty and deprivations. The excess wealth also was given as tax—protection money to the kings, who ensured smooth creation and protection of wealth in a particular country, but that wealth never would have reached to the entire population. In order to keep the people's life being protected with wealth, distribution through a justifiable way was necessary, the rulers who created big projects had ensured the same, so that everybody could get an access to the wealth of a nation.

The creation of a temple ensured prosperity for a king and his people who built such magnificent structures in ancient and medieval India, because the building process that lasted for over a period of time ensured wealth distribution to the rest of his population like sculptors, metal workers, masons, carpenters, traders, healers, etc., who formed a large part of the population. And since the wealth distribution was ensured, the wealth creators could get more enthusiasm to produce more as the market for the produced goods was guaranteed due to higher purchasing power of the entire population under the rule of a king. The ancient society showed due reverence to human labor and appreciated it greatly where work was rewarded in different ways. Though some kind of social security was ensured for the most disadvantageous section of the society, the rulers always discouraged what may be termed as rights for getting access to social security as a fundamental right. But every able-bodied man was encouraged to do some kind of work, which a prosperous kingdom carefully creates in the peace times. The systems in the ancient world order were based on an agricultural-based social systems prospered with an industrial economy supporting it. The circulation of money was also minimal but the produced wealth and services moved around organically. A kind of division of labor existed in all ancient societies that ensured wealth distribution to almost everyone. The caste systems, that existed in the regions that followed Chinese and Indian cultural space, were meant to ensure such an organic distribution of wealth. Nevertheless, due to the constraints in ensuring wealth distribution, caste system was discarded during the advent of modern industrial economy.

Demotion of Creative Work in the Techno-Scientific World Order

Human involvement with creative work using the hand-brain faculty began to change, since the time of Eurocentric scientifically motivated industrial revolution started to find a domineering place in the human society. This phase of human history replaced creative work, phase by phase with machines, for making production in huge quantities to support a growing population. As a fall out, creative work that had highly appreciated human *hand-brain faculty* got demoted substantially leaving humans to do work only for money. Progressively replacing the natural hand-brain system with machines was the foundation of the industrial revolution, and at different phases of industrial revolution, human creativity had been devaluated from doing work, for making machines to do most of the work activities. The machines exactly copied the creative procedures of the human hand-brain faculty and executed work quickly and efficiently. This method helped to mass produce goods in huge quantities. This phase of human history revolutionized life significantly leading to a new kind of understanding about human life on earth. The new era that started has reduced the importance of human *hand-brain faculty* in the creative process in the production of goods and services. The human hand become an appendage to a machine-dependent work culture. Human hand only helped the machine to perform well, where the human creativity remained dormant and unused.

Since human hands become a mere addition for making the machines to work properly, human brain-mind—consciousness becomes inactive and fallen incessantly into the grip of fear and ignorance, as no knowledge discerned from creative work that supported one to find a virtuous life through spiritual flourishing and happiness. However, the efficient methods of science and technology helped to make big market and high returns to a few countries that engaged in manufacturing of goods using mechanized systems. This production method left behind a vast number of people in poorer part of the world, not only just unemployed but creatively worthless also. The countries that engaged in high quantity production using machines received high returns and unusual prosperity for its people. The division of haves and have-nots created a very difficult situation in the world that lead to revolutions, wars, etc. And also, industrialization together with colonialism flourished immensely as industrialized countries needed resources for their manufacturing centers to grow in production as well as new market for the mechanically manufactured goods to the native populations in the colonies. People who followed the tradition of receiving wealth coming to them by the way of work became slaves of machine-controlled systems and had to live in poverty of being in scarcity of not having enough, which is known as *precarity*. People learned to depend on charity if they find no work. Social welfare schemes based on charity from the governmental or non-governmental sources are now spoken about, in a world where mechanization using artificial intelligence (AI) is becoming a huge reality.

At the time of first industrial revolution, those western monarchies like Britain and France could flourish due to the availability of cheap resources and labor from the colonies and could again resell the manufactured goods to those workers and others in those colonial countries. As for the colonies, the postindustrialized world order was a period of darkness with reprehensible control and repression that left a vast majority into poverty, social decadence, and precarity. The colonies were administrated by trading companies, similar to the British East India Company, with a military and logistic support from the UK. The military not only had engaged in trade, but had also created a structure of domination that vehemently controlled the civil administration of each colonial country with a kind of draconian control through the military garrisons, for feeding fear and scare in the colonies. At the same time, the economic system that existed in those colonies had to compete with the western industrially manufactured goods that made the ancient manufacturing system to fail miserably. This was true for India, China, and many other parts of the colonial world. For example, in India the traditional handwoven cloth industry was replaced by machine made cloths from Britain. That was the demise of the traditional systems that survived based on valuing the *hand-brain faculty* helping humans to survive living good lives for millenniums. In such traditional industries creative work, with the support of the hand-brain faculty was the core of production method supplying sufficient goods to the local population, where such systems survived giving a kind of purpose and meaning to life.

Science coupled with technology began to control almost every aspect of life. Techno-sciences were the strongest weapon that has used for destroying all kind of traditional local economic management systems around the world. Poverty ensued in countries where colonialism thrived. But colonial system ensured high paying jobs to some who could control the wealth in the colonies. They measuredly suppressed revolts and uprisings by the use of excessive military force. Colonialism and techno-sciences destroyed economic systems that existed in the colonies especially in the non-western world. In this period, the wealth distribution become corrupt and illogical, and a lot of people lost their economic freedom even in the colonial countries leading to violent revolutions. The replacement of human hands in production with machines had made sure that the system would follow a regime of unequal distributions of wealth. Colonialism made the First Industrial Revolution possible, and also it gave rise to a society which was unequal in more than many ways, opening a huge highway for the communist movements and other revolutions. The inordinate accumulation of wealth into the hands of a few had led to wars, especially the European wars, ended in World War-I and World War-II.

The Second Industrial Revolution after the World War-II, used active mechanization, and high value production became the norm for all human activities; various systems were developed on the basis of this norm. Philosophers and thinkers almost accepted scientific knowledge as the only acceptable form of knowledge and all other systems of knowledge were ridiculed and relegated into the status of the primitive subaltern knowledge, against the high performability of the western scientific knowledge. The western philosophers truly thought that the scientifically literate would be inching toward perfection in all aspects of life and that intellectual strength could liberate the entire world of humanity toward more freedom. So, they brazenly promoted, their methods and thoughts, to everyone around the world. But, the scientifically minded philosophers and thinkers, following the views of the classical thinkers, especially from Greece, thought a single theory (thought) to explain everything can be made using the scientific rationalist methodology, but they could not find any one theory—a theory of everything—in this regard yet; instead there are innumerable number of theories vying for filling the place of a single theory. In the Greek classical tradition, Aristotle defined God as the "thought thinking itself".[3] Here it is clear that with the available sources in the world, we cannot make a thought that is equal to what is implied by Aristotle as God, which is transcended, so the form of it is unclear. The philosophers and thinkers then turned into creating ideological systems to replace the supremacy of God—the thinking of thinking.[4] The ideological systems that have developed since the modern period competed with each other to fill the single thought in the philosophy of Aristotle.

The ideological systems needed control on the people, so that they fall into the strategy of following the singular system that implicitly act as a theory of everything or the thought that represents the transcended God. In the modern world, the optimization of the control mechanism became so prevalent everywhere using scientific methods or applying scientific reasoning. It was similar to the time of the Holy Roman Empire in Europe or of the Islamization of Asia and Africa, either accept the authority of those ideological systems sanctioned by the religion, or face severe wrath and impervious isolation. The modern scientific systems also started to propagate scientific reasoning and judgments as solution to face all the problems of the world. The world in the first and second industrialization period were run by ideological systems. All those systems, capitalism, socialism, communism, democracy, liberalism, and religious doctrines had created some kind of ideological space and exercised control on people. In this period, the use of hand-brain faculty in work was limited into some small pocket societies, in the remotest regions of some countries, where modernity had not yet reached. The value of their skill was not appreciated and should have to give way to the products made by high technology. A kind of struggle started between people of those regions, where colonialism and modernization devastated normal life due to technologization of

---

[3]Varghese (2020), p. 28.
[4]Aristotle (1941), p. 991.

everything. As a solution, instead of retracting, the world community reinforced more effective high technology for making life better for those people. A lot of people lost their access to wealth, because of the lack of opportunity to do some work to live a normal life. The common people from the poorer part of the world become a source for cheap labor for doing all kinds of works, in factories and construction sites of rich countries, at very low wages. During the second phase of industrial revolution (Industry 2.0), there was a mad rush for getting jobs and getting money for bettering the life situations. Money became the most effective driving force that directed human life hugely. Human creative work and the skills that are a product of hand-brain faculty's involvement in creative work become an object of analysis and study. Careful scientific study of creative work helped the postmodern world to create mathematical models and structures that made the mechanization process very efficient. The systems thus created have adopted Aristotelian logical tools to create theories, overlooking the fact that Aristotelian theories have transcended metaphysical connotations, but their effort to evolve a theory of everything—a theory of all the theories—failed miserably. A new kind of system began to develop around the world, which aimed at developing more and more wealth, so that the wealth can be distributed to everyone. The seed thoughts of plutonomy—the norm of the rich—began to take shape up progressively from this thought.

Plutonomy is a reinterpretation of capitalism that was founded on the doctrines of protestant Christianity, where a true Christian should act as an agent of the God almighty, doing the God's work of providence, by giving a kind of sustenance to everyone to live in this world. This was given as an impetus to capitalism in the agrarian cultures when Martin Luther initially introduced this ideology. The agrarian tradition could somehow accommodate hand-brain faculty's involvement in the creative process. But, when the industrial revelation stated with huge production systems, the unskilled—workers who cannot use technology got marginalized and neglected. In order to protect the rights of the unskilled proletariats—common unskilled workers—who could claim very little or nothing to live on in the hugely industrializing western world. This aspect of worry gave impetus to the rise of the communist movement with the adoption of Karl Marx's communist manifesto as the guiding document for the communist movement. Communist movement proposed the control of the wealth not by individual entrepreneurs or companies, but by the communities and the state. But, this ideological assertion was a direct confrontation with another ideological system, capitalism which promoted the values of entrepreneurship and the creation of middle-class values, for fueling a free market economy.

Both the systems followed scientific and technological mode of production, but on the distribution side, communism showed more leniency toward the poor working class; on the other hand, bourgeois capitalism brought skills from workers with little monetary rewards. But most of those skills were not by appreciating the hand-brain faculty and creative work, but by the ability to apply the technical skills. The countries that had high technological know-how began to amass a lot of wealth but a lot of other countries, which is known as the third world, endured huge poverty and backwardness. The industrial progress happened basically with the countries of the Organization of Economic Co-operation and Development (OECD), or the developed countries. The wealth began again to be accumulated in those regions of the world and they wanted to invest their wealth into the poorer part of the world, which caused the generation of a new industrial revolution (Industry 3.0) starting from 1980s. Notably, this period was dominated by information technological systems, which created a kind of magical spell on people especially concerning space and time. The systemic change helped the wealthy in the developed countries, to invest their wealth almost everywhere. A new class of wealthy people began to appear under the system of plutonomy, which redefined the entire system with financing, began to act like an industry replacing the existing systems strictly based on production and consumption. Soon the world economic control moved into the hands of the financiers away from the hands of manufacturers and distributers. During this time, manufacturing was only becoming a prospect and possibility for the financial industry to circulate the monetized wealth into places, where finance could find new avenues for use. The financial industry began to form its own course, which required more areas for investments, and now it used up all avenues to flood their money, and it is inevitable for that industry to have new avenues for investments. And we are now in the beginning of Fourth Industrial Revolution, where we are expecting to use artificial intelligence and automatons fueled by big data, to displace all human involvement with work and the use of hand-brain faculty in production. The erstwhile bourgeoisie in the capitalist world order is now being replaced by plutocrats in the plutonomic world systems. The democratic movements in the capitalist system are insignificant and can be used in the nominal sense, but the real controllers of the political systems are the plutocrats, and plutocracy is what is going to rule the system effectively. And precarity of human labor would become the norm for the working class. Precariat or part-time or contract workers are the ones who do almost all the works. And together with economic insecurity hand-brain faculty's involvement with work has become irrelevant and insignificant today. In executing a work, one needs not to use *techne* (craftmanship) at all, but *episteme* (knowledge) provided by AI systems would be used everywhere. Thus, human direct involvement with nature is getting obsolete progressively and becoming less human gradually.

When the scientific revolution started, the world was looking for clarity and certainty through the methods of science. Everything in the conceivable phenomenal world was needed to be objectified for making its particular method of analysis workable. Pure materialism was possible only through proper adaptation of scientific philosophy in a rational framework based on the rules of science—pure objective analysis. Philosophy in the modern and postmodern world accepted only scientifically sourced objectivized knowledge and the source of knowledge and theoretic judgments. Pragmatism with the scientific analytical method had optimized everything, in the world of experience, to become the most acceptable method. And it is the center pillar of all philosophical and academic activities of the post World War-II era. Almost every aspect of human life had fallen into the narrative structure of *techno-science* and also into the structure and style of industries, such as production, marketing, distribution, and monetary returns. And the economy began to be taken over by the financial industry, where all economic activities were turned in to be a part of the finance and investment methods generated by *techno-science*. Securitization of all available wealth turns them into tradable financial products that can be sold in the market and gain high returns. As and when money supply increased, financial products began to attract high returns everywhere, and the new wealthy class—plutonomy—thrived by doing the trade of the financial products. The production system that should have been an important aspect of economy become strained hugely and also become an area where financial industry can use, as just another area for circulating and spreading their wealth. Wealth distribution that happened through work has hugely strained in many developed countries where globalization of production was the new norm. Since wealth distribution is so difficult through providing jobs, family, society, and country have to face new realities, where human creativity, in executing work and gaining some respectability, ceased to exist.

The world that followed the new normal of plutonomy—the norm of the wealthy —began to search for newer methods of wealth distribution, because human involvement is necessary for the wealth to gain some respectability, otherwise it may be insignificant like the huge wealth somebody gained at a casino. It can only be noticed when the casino gambler shows up his money in public by buying up things everywhere. Unlike the wealth creators at the time of First Industrial Revolution, who had complete control and knowledge about the wealth one owns or manages, the plutocrats have no clear idea about the invested wealth. And the quantum of their wealth is so profound that it is difficult to keep track on everything easily, even with a technologically enabled information system constantly tracking it. In the threshold of Fourth Industrial Revolution, the plutocrats may institute an artificial system run by data automatically directing a wealth management system that could control everything including individual persons and their emotions. The huge wealth controlled by the plutocrats under plutonomy may institute a system in the future world, where everyone could live without doing any kind of significant work, but everyone is expected to live under a systematized schema of social welfare.

It is possible to equate this situation with the ideals of communism where everyone will get a share of the total wealth according to one's needs and wants. Some modern thinkers, in our times, argue for an open society where there should be no expressive difference between each individual citizen. They are now thinking in the same line as the communistic ideals that could be achieved through technocracy, where everyone would be ensued the freedom to live a happy and prosperous life without any sort of social or political restrictions, as the system is managed by an automatic self-regulating system of interconnected machines. Unfortunately, those thinkers never discussed in depth about the importance of work using the hand-brain faculty and importance of creative work as the base values of life. But, they promoted for making various social security schemes as the way forward, thinking that money and material wealth could satisfy all the needs of the entire humanity. At the beginning of twenty-first century, the thinkers and philosophers less inclined to discuss on the issue of the incursion of techno-science in human life. That is been recognized and accepted as a natural progress of development as something, with which, we all should learn to live with, as it is apparently giving greater freedom to everyone. Most of them are hugely influenced by Aristotelian discourse of *Posterior analytics,* where the knowledge (*episteme*) discerned as the source for theoretical postulations and ethical paradigms, which is arguably a controversial method, as human beings are influenced not just by reasonings only, but also by emotions such as fear, anger, and greed.

But, in actuality the intrusion of technoscience into all aspects of life demolishes the chances of a human person to develop his skills and knowledge from work, because what needs to be learned through involvement and practice is given in the form of easy procedures that can be operated by anyone with basic education and training.

The wide spread belief is that in such a world situation, the human work with the help of techno-science would change the fate of humanity only for good. However, during this period a kind of financialization of all economic activities happened in tandem, where the creation of valueless wealth becomes a reality. It helped with the confiscation of all the creative aspects in all kinds of work to be transformed into digitalized data for to be run by computers. The aim of doing work was, to provide a good life with monetary benefits, being demoted hugely. Economics became a branch of techno-science, and wealth creation becomes a method to create financialized assets that can be traded globally, for achieving that, every aspect connected with business was suitably engineered. Human sciences become a part of the education system, which means social, political, spiritual, psychological, life of any individual should be explained in the norm of the techno-scientific methods; and everything connected with a person's private life be turned into data. The data then can be used for building systems having some practical value. And using data processing gadgets, such as computers, each individual can be categorized and profiled based on certain predetermined standards. The synergy that existed between *techne* (craftmanship) and *episteme* (knowledge) is now broken completely, letting it to be taken over by big data run on huge AI systems, leading to the birth of a kind of technocracy.

During the Second Industrial Revolution (Industry 2.0), in the political sphere, the so-called democratic values turned out that they should only be controlled by a kind of majoritarianism with some secular values, at the same time the majoritarian decisions were formed on the foundation of emotional choices not on rational decisions. And they found an easy enemy with the communist socialist bloc of countries that had ruled nearly half of the world, by alleging them as anti-God, anti-progress, etc. Those two systems were at loggerheads with each other for many decades doing propaganda justifying each's actions by lampooning "the other" nefariously. And finally, the capitalist democratic system won, because of their control over huge confiscated wealth through commercialization and consumerism aggressively. In fact, that had brought prosperity to the industrialized countries. But the others were deprived or disadvantaged of any benefits of industrialization in any manner. Due to huge mechanization, the wealth distribution remained as a difficult task, because wealth accumulation had happened due to the lack of distribution and lack of market for the produced goods, a new system needed to be developed to solve the situation. And it gave impetus to the generation of the Third Industrial Revolution (Industry 3.0) with the help of information technology. It redefined the usability of our individual knowledge and skills in executing jobs. Wealth control using information technology created many new avenues for investments. And we now are in the era of plutonomy, where a handful of plutocrats are controlling the so-called democratic systems because of their unusual access to huge amount of wealth. And, in the work front, most of the works are done by systems using artificial intelligence, but some works that require human involvement are done by using contract workers or part-time workers, who are paid very little. Precarity becomes the new normal in the work culture under plutonomy.

In the emerging world society, most of the works are done by machines or by part-time workers (*precariats*), where the creative part in any kind of work is done by AI systems ensuring unprecedented accuracy for high productivity. As a consequence, unknowingly, wealth began to collude into the hands of a few individuals and the world system now completely under the sway and control of plutonomy who normally control the finances. This word, plutonomy, is the formation of two Greek words: (*Ploutos*: = wealth, *norm* = rule), on interpretation, we can find semantics of *Plutonomy* as rule of the rich—the norm of the wealthy. Under plutonomy almost every aspect of creative work is executed by mechanized systems and everything connected with work is mechanized with precision for getting higher returns. It never would look at any aspect of human life beyond those dictums. In such situations, human hand-brain faculty need not have to be utilized at all. A kind of tyrannical situation is rampant in today's living environment, because the plutonomy dialectically opposes the human work involvement with production making *precarity*—no proper employment, no proper income, the new norm for the wokers in the postmodern globalized world order.

The Fundamental Philosophical Perspectives on Creative Work

Plato in his work, *Republic* termed tyranny as the worst form of civil administrative system, where humans will never get suitable situations to gain true knowledge or knowledge from creative activities. This is because humans have to live in fear and worries. And Plato also cautioned that democracy, which is the second worst form of civil administration, always tends toward tyranny. It happens when an oligarchy would control the entire democratic system. Tyrannical control begins when an oligarchy or some chosen people try to control the system on the basis of their whims and fancies, and when they use all possible means to manipulate the ordinary citizens' livelihood to fulfill their self-interests or to maximize their self-interests. The masses would have to live in fear and ignorance. They never be able to gain knowledge about the ideas (forms), so that one can use his/her creative instincts to gain knowledge, which leads to the realization of transcended virtues.[5] The plutonomy today is very oligarchic in its making and their fancies are managed by automatized AI systems.

Plato had written about this in the context of the city states in the ancient Greece. Contextually, our democracies are experiencing the oligarchic control in the form of plutonomy today; instead of a democratic system managed by a constitution and legal system that would function on logic and reasoning, it is now working as an extension of the plutonomy. The super-rich plutocrats can use their wealth accumulated through activities that can supersede the logic and reasoning ensured in the constitution and in the legal systems, and institutions created to protect the interest of the state and its citizens. One of such common interest is the right to live a virtuous life where one can live and flourish individually and collectively. As per the teaching of the ancient Greeks, the purpose of life is to live by realizing *eudaimonia*. Eudaimonia can be translated as the inner spiritual flourish that one receives when one lives a virtuous life. According to Aristotle, such an inner flourish will come only when one executes his given duties—*arete* with full potential excellently. Through *arete*, one can inculcate *techne*. The meaning of the word *arete* is attaining excellence in virtue. It means—If you are a parent, you should excel at raising your children; if you are a doctor, you should excel at healing people; and if you are a philosopher, you should excel at gaining knowledge and wisdom, and also excel in teaching about wisdom to others; and if you are a business man, you should work to enhance the self-interest of your customers and the society at large by providing goods and services, at a mutually beneficial way where one would be receiving money for the rendered services.

In the world order of today, humans have no way to find *eudaimonia* and have no opportunity to excel in any of the activities truthfully and justifiably to realize goodness and wisdom. It is argued here that we need to find the core values that helped us building a fully functional system, which is now under the threat of the oligarchic power of the plutonomy. It is difficult to destroy plutonomy in any manner in the modern society. A violent revolution would breed deep fears in human society and then the redefined system would follow the whims of plutonomy further. We could only reinvestigate the value of hand-mind faculty in providing *eudaimonia* to each and every individual person and should build a system that revere human *creative work* wholeheartedly.

---

[5]Plato discusses four systems of governance which cannot provide virtuous living for citizens in a state they are: timocracy, oligarchy, democracy, and tyranny. He argues that when a society loses its soul by not following the virtuous living for its citizens, it will decay and pass through each form of government in succession, eventually becoming a tyranny, the most virtueless and unjust regime that work only under the whims of fear and ignorance. (Republic, Book-VIII).

Human nature is such that we always tempt to believe in an authority that protects our life in the world, but according to classical philosophical views such protection mechanism is internal and self-actualized, not externally controlled. In India, the conception of *Dharma-Karma* explains the religiosity, where one needs to execute own duties (*dharma*) with the most benign manner. And when one does own *dharma-karma* with the most excellent manner, one could get what is known as *mokṣa* (liberation), in the form of happiness, flourish, wellness, etc. In the classical Chinese Daoist teachings, when one executes his duties (Dao), he/she would receive happiness, a flourishing feeling (Dao), a feeling of co-existence (Dao), with one's life where one lives to reach to the ultimate (Dao) that provides one a feeling of spiritual flourish (Dao).

This book investigates the classical philosophy's fundamental tenets on creative work and how it has influenced, in shaping our present civilization, where the hand-brain faculty played a significant role, for creating things. In the last century, Mahatma Gandhi promoted the true accentuation of the hand-brain faculty, when he championed the Indian resistance movement against the British colonial rule using spinning wheel as the symbol of resistance. He spoke against mechanization that was being promoted as a sign of prosperity in the modern times. But in reality, the work culture of today is different as humans are completely subservient to machines, and with the implementation of artificial intelligence systems, the ability to use hand-brain faculty has completely been denigrated now and systematically being eradicated. The concern is that we humans might be forced to live in the subhuman existence without realizing the core values of being human. I argue here that the human values are fundamentally founded on the complex functioning of a *body-hand-brain faculty*.

The Declining Value of Creative Work and Hand-Brain Faculty in Plutonomy

Part I of the book mainly discuses on how plutonomy flourishes under the current trends of using mechanization with artificial intelligence and also on how it rede-fines the importance of "creative work" by forcing the humans to play a much minor and minimal role in all kind of production activities. In the world that is moving toward the Fourth Industrial Revolution, the importance of hand-brain faculty would be ignored fully, even though that created the human civilization, as the way we live and experience today. To understand the topic better, I used a narrative form of discussion with life experiences of some fictional personalities. Here, I explain how far we moved away currently from "creative work" in deter-mining the destiny of our lives. The body-hand-brain complex helped humans to use the rational and logical faculties effectively, to live peacefully and naturally. Humans engaging in work are not just to produce goods and services for everyone, but to help everyone living well out of the created wealth. Work also meant that those who engaged in production should live well by experiencing the "divine providence" of nature (God). Humans are creatures evolved in the nature, and our needs are provided by the nature's forces. Our hand-brain faculty is the implement given by the nature for living well. It is like a dog uses superior smelling skills for finding things, or a bat uses sound for traveling from place to place, or an elephant uses its trunk for moving about by protecting its huge body, etc. The superior ability of the hand-brain faculty would enable humans to do creative work, and it should be taken as the only conduit that we have, to integrate us with the nature's forces, and to its providences. This work tries to understand the development of the present human civilization and what role work has played in it. Here the attempt is to develop three narratives about the thought-history of "human life" and its relation to "human work" in three distinct periods of time. The first period is the preindustrial life of common workman (artisan) and agricultural labors in the mainly agriculture-based feudal systems, where the feudal oligarchies were the wealth controllers. The second narrative is on the industrial and postindustrial baby boomer, salaryman, factory worker-based capitalist systems, where the bourgeoisies were the wealth controllers. The third narrative is on the globalized world's millennial part-time workers—*precariat*, and AI systems-based plutonomy, where a few plutocrats are the controller of the wealth.

Human Life and Creative Work

In Part II of this book, I revisit the thought-history of creative work by reviewing the philosophical thoughts that upheld creative work and a deep appreciation of the body-hand-brain complex in the ancient world, and try to reflect these thoughts with the contemporary neurological studies on consciousness. The modern consciousness studies, using the scientific methods of analyses, clearly agree with the ancient views on *creative work*, which say that with the formation of neural structures when one engages in creative activities, one also develops the consciousness (awareness), by the creation of a personal self-model—*ego tunnel*. It means one uses his brain and hands in a creative activity, and it is instrumental in creating a conscious space representing the personal self-model—own personal identity. The concept of hand-brain faculty is formulated out of the *body-hand-brain complex* that works when one engages in learning by using creative activities.

In the classical Indian view on Karma, the hand-brain faculty in creative activity is clearly expressed, and on reviewing the Karma theory of the ancient Indians, we can explain human life as a process and progress in Karma. Mahatma Gandhi by introducing the ancient art of hand spinning using charka (spinning wheel), and by hand weaving of own cloths that helped Indians to understand the importance of the hand-brain faculty and its significance in shaping up human life, even under the sway of industrialization and huge mechanized manufacturing systems. Gandhian way of living and Gandhian socialism is fundamentally based on the appreciation and reverence to the involvement of hand-brain faculty in the execution of one's own karma (*sva-karma*).

As we have already noticed, the Ancient Greeks had structured their philosophical systems on the foundation of *eudaimonia, arete, logos,*, etc. That otherwise would emphasize that a meaningful human life with human flourishing and steady happiness need excellence in executing work (*arete*) that may happen in the precinct of human reasoning and logical thinking. In other words, human life would find its meaningfulness with ethical virtues, if they do not self-engage with creative work using the hand-brain faculty, for developing the inborn ability to develop *techne*—craftmanship and artistic skills. Aristotle in his ethical works and studies on economics reiterates *eudaimonia-arete* as the conduit for total welfare of the community and society starting from the level of individual, to the society and then to the state. Almost all classical Greek thinkers agreed with the concept that work is the only way to engage with the God given forms (ideas), and thereby one could develop knowledge—wisdom and an ownership with one's own life.

And the ancient Chinese defined creative work as the way of Dao, the purpose of one's life, Dao is the way one needs to follow, Dao is the possession one needs to protect for a good life, and one needs to engage with Dao, creatively to make it move forward. On the other hand, if one loses Dao, he/she loses the purpose of life. And for being creative, one needs to use the body-hand-brain complex actively and find ways to use it organically. For, we can only have harmonious existence in/with/for Dao.

The significance of creative work is a much-neglected topic in the academic as well as in the thoughts of the discerning general public, yet all are being confused about the emerging unprecedented situations, in the emerging world order of plutonomy. Strong disappointments and distresses are a common feature of life everywhere. As we depend uncharacteristically on digitalized mechanical systems, we could not use any of our natural creative skills, and because of which a kind of intellectual sluggishness is dominating our lives. It must be understood that the nature has provided enough vital energies to humans for living and surviving in the world, but when we use machines within our control we may upsurge and accentuate those inherent vital energies. But when using the machines beyond a limit of ownership of helping that accentuation process, we limit ourselves in using those nature (God) given vital energies. That is seen here as a daunting problem for humanity to confront. In the all-pervading use of artificial intelligence, we in effect under utilize our intellectual and physical energies; at the same time, we are forced to create artificial energies for all intellectual and physical activities. The created system of hand-brain faculty through thousands of years of complex maturation might be deteriorated and destroyed the gains that humans have achieved thus far. And now the focus is to create artificial systems to support even to move within our living spaces, even against our own volitions, could further deteriorate the chances for us to experience eudaimonia—happiness and wellness.

Upsetting the Energy Balance of the Earth

The huge production and utilization of energy could upset the natural energy balance of the earth, which would further deteriorate the worsening environmental situations through climate changes and finally destroying the entire human living environment. At the same time, we will be forced to ignore the human physical energy that is absolutely free and irreversibly helping the nature to conserve its energy balance. When we use the intellectual and physical energy harnessed through the effective activation of the body-hand-brain complex into a faculty that is under our complete control, we get a feeling of living through our lives with a sense of purpose and completeness. On the other hand, a new kind of plague is spreading around the world as an aftermath of high food production due to industrial agriculture, where high food production with artificially enhanced nutrition would upset the balance that existed between production and consumption. The fast spreading disorder of obesity and other such eating disorders are rampent today spreading with irreversable consequences. The poor quality, high nutritive food made available for everyone to eat with less cost. Eating tasty food becomes a habit for many around the world. Another aftermath of these development in the globalized world is the lack of movement of hand in all kind of production activities, which lead to less natural brain activities. This would multiply the malady of obesity further and to ward off mental distress people may resort to eating cheaply available food. Nowadays, people have no way to realize the spiritual flourish—*eudaimonia* by using the hand-brain faculty, that would lead them to fall into the grip of cheap entertainments or seek happiness from drugs. Obesity and drug abuse are already identified as problems without any easy solutions.

The futuristic expectations of a human society where individuals engage in less activities in creating things by directly connecting with nature, while living in a home bound existence with a lot of free food and lots and lots of entertainment sources might lead to a kind of life that may go against the tenets of the history of the civilization that developed and prospered on the basis of creative work, where true human freedom and human flourishing were revered. The ethical doctrines of Aristotle which says the foundation of all economic activities should be there to help humans to achieve *eudaimonia*—spiritual flourishing and *arete*— excellence through creative activities leading to the acquirement of ethical virtues. But today that necessity is on the decline, due to the rolled-out net of *plutonomy* into all aspects of life.

Distancing from its fundamental doctrines, the scientific model of modern economic system destroyed the total flourishing of human societies, with wealth that has no meaning to human life, because the lessening opportunities for human "creative work" would destroy the very existence of human life with self-destructive consequences. The phony convenience we may achieve would be our biggest inconvenience in conducting normal lives. I present this as a huge social philosophical problem of the twenty-first century to a discerning community of thinkers. The production of food in factory farmhouses uses huge quantity of artificially created energy, which was not the case with farms run by farmers who use systems that needed less energy. This underutilization of human energy in agricultural production has double whammy effect of the health crisis due to lack of physical activity, and of the necessity to produce equal amount of energy artificially by running power plants, and the resultant environmental damages.

It is very important that we need to re-establish the synergy between wealth creation and wealth distribution by enhancing the opportunities for doing more "creative work," or bringing in a synergy with hand-brain faculty in utilizing our vital energies for helping us to live in agreement with the nature. We need to bring unity and harmony with wealth distribution and creation through creative work, so that we may live a life naturally respecting human values. The myth of wealth creation as the way for achieving providence of nature (God) provided us with plutonomy (the norms of the wealthy) and plutocracy (the oligarchical rule of the rich), and plutocrats (the superrich entities), and precariat as nominal workers who do only part-time works on contract basis from hourly to a few years long contractual agreements. We may reverse the relegating tendency if we use the norm of *creative work* as the way it was practiced in the Eastern civilizations, where wealth distribution created an organic method that ensured the progress of life for millenniums, in which case *hand-brain faculty* played an all-important role of sharing the "providence of nature" that could benefit everyone is the ideological structure of both capitalism and communism. But today, such ideologies are no longer valid or already served its purposes, set in the seventeenth and eighteenth centuries with Industry 1.0. that is now invalid at the time of Industry 4.0, because plutonomy is not capitalism. It is the ghost of capitalism; same is the case with socialism it is the ghost of communism but now controlled by plutonomy. In our post-ideological era, i.e., twenty-first century, all the ideological systems, including traditional religions, are only serving as "taking points" amounting to irrelevant conclusions.

Wisdom of the Great Wall

When we conceive the idea of the Great Wall, we can see various facets of ancient Chinese wisdom. The wall should have been meant to resist the alien tribes from attacking the mainland. When such attacks would happen, there should have happened huge losses of life and wealth, and also normal citizens had to live in fear of being attacked every now and then. Such loss of wealth and life would, in general, be ended in confusions and sufferings. When the Chinese emperors built such walls to protect themselves from the enemies, they also helped to build silk road to connect with other civilizations around the world; this has enabled them to connect with people and cultures to propitiate trade and commerce that kept an air of stability and peace everywhere. Now, the alien tribe of plutonomy is attacking and nefariously destroying wealth everywhere; we also are falling into the sway of fear and confusion similar to that happened in the ancient Roman Empire. The

Romans never had built something similar to the Great Wall of China, for they had to spend huge quantities of wealth in order to engage in constant wars with alien tribes from everywhere. The Romans, on the other hand, had to colonialize and plunder wealth form the Mediterranean region and North Africa to feed those wars; their spiritual attitude was an inordinate appreciation to valor, heroism, bravery, aggression, chivalry and propitiating Gods that may instill heroic images in their minds, for hating "the other" as enemy.

Notwithstanding, the globalized plutonomic world like the ancient Romans worshiping wealth and money with a regime similar to the Trinitarian conception of God, where the total wealth (the father), individual wealth (the son) and money (the holy spirit). The plutonomy today uses interest-free money to harness entire wealth of the world. And now we force ourselves to forget our existence as human beings and neglect our limitations and try to forget how we reached to this stage. We also forget the values of using and appropriating our innate skills (*techne*) through creative work by activating the body-hand-brain complex faculty, which helped us to generate intelligence by building up an individual conscious space in the form of *ego-tunnel*—the personal self-model, which the ancients considered as soul—self-being. For achieving that end, we need to build a Chinese wall against the incursion of plutonomy into our present civilization. The entire human civilizations have been built differently from that of the prehuman species by using effectively our inner intellectual faculties for resisting fear and ignorance. By cultivating fear through technological systems, we are just enabling the prehuman existence, where fear and ignorance destroyed life completely. The wealth is the problem for both plutonomy—now a few individuals and "the rest"—more than seven billion people: the one hoard too much; while "the other" have no wealth to live on. This anomaly has seriously worried philosopher Alain Badiou: "After all we must recognize that, today, 264 people possess as much wealth, inheritance and income, as the 7 billion others who make the rest of the world!"[6] This is a genuine worry and being shared by all right-thinking people: Why this kind of anomalies happen in the world that has taken immense pride of itself on its social cultural and technological achievements bluntly.

References

Aristotle: Metaphysics (Book-12, 1074b). In: McKeon, R. (Trans. and ed.) The Basic Works of Aristotle. Random House, New York (1941)
Badiou, A.: Trump. Polity Press, Cambridge (2019)
Varghese, M.: Nāgārjuna and the Art of Negation. Sanctum Books, New Delhi (2020)

---

[6]Badiou (2019), p. 9.

Contents

About the Author

Mathew Varghese works on Middle Path philosophy of classical Buddhist thought. He ingenuously uses the Buddhist critical investigation method of employing negation in his philosophical writings. He follows Middle Path philosophy, where we can explain the worldly experiences using four-value logical system (*catuṣkoṭi*) more clearly than systems that use binary logical interpretations. He is a textual scholar and has published three books. He works as a research fellow at The Hajime Nakamura Eastern Institute and teaches philosophy at Aoyama Gakuin University, Kanagawa University, and Wako University in Tokyo.

Part I
Historical Thoughts on The Dynamics of Plutonomy

Artificial Intelligence—Plutonomy Versus Precarity

Chapter 1
Precarity and Millennial Apathy

If the youngsters of today in their twenties and thirties were asked about their aims and aspirations of living life, mostly, all of them would answer with a blunt statement: "I don't know"; or would express their inability to think clearly on this. Certainly, most of them could not have any idea on how to plan their future with hopes and aspirations. The emerging precarity in the globalized world is adversely influencing their thoughts seriously. But, this disinterested and apathetic attitude of the postmodern millennials would worry, startle and perplex their parents' generation deeply, who made their dreams and aspirations through hard work in their twenties and thirties. There are no direct answers to the worries, of the post war, baby boomer generation. Some may call, the millennials, as the lost generation; or for some others, they lack strong determinations; or for some others, they lack religious, moral and ethical virtues. However, what are the real reasons for the dispirited and apathetic views of the youngsters? Unlike the earlier generations, in some aspects, it is certain that life is more comfortable and trouble free in the twenty-first century. The millennials have almost everything at their fingertips that their earlier generations never could dream of. Some thinkers conclude that the world order now emerges, is the end of all historical struggles. The postmodern world would create an organic open society that would end all historical struggles. Now onwards, we can live freely as the way we want to. But! Have we reached the freedom of choice in absolute terms? Then, instead of being ecstatic and hubris, why the millennials are so dispirited and apathetic? Why hard work doesn't matter anymore? In actuality, the historical struggle has taken as a new dialectical framework between plutonomy versus precarity. Plutonomy—the norm of the wealthy: against precarity—being in a state of insufficient *work* and income.

Millennials are those who born after 1980s and are to live their lives in the twenty-first century. They are in possession of various freedoms, and are able to do many things that the earlier generations couldn't even have fantasized about, because technology makes them to live a new kind of life of ease and comfort. Besides, all the goodies that the millennials have, they have to face a different sort of inconvenient challenge that is present and clear. It is of living and competing with the rapidly

© The Author(s), under exclusive license to Springer Nature Singapore Pte Ltd. 2021

M. Varghese, *A Brief History of Creative Work and Plutonomy*,
https://doi.org/10.1007/978-981-15-9263-8_1

emerging world of Artificial intelligence (AI). The widespread uses of AI make technological unemployment at every aspect of our lives. This aspect calls for a rethinking on the significance of human *work and life*. Are we able to live a life without doing any work? Does work mean earning profit and economic freedom only? Does human creative work enhance satisfaction and happiness in one's life? How should we deal with the faculty of body-hand-brain complex that helped us to formulate the present civilization? The incursion of AI systems in the globalized world arises several such fundamental questions.

We can find several narratives explaining these issues. As the twenty-first century globalized world order has many faces and façades; normally, this unique system of world order is overhyped and expressed according to the fanciful whims of narrators and interpreters, who act as thinkers and philosophers today. And most of those narrations overhype the future expectations, but never address the issues relating to the declining opportunities to do "work" or to find steady employment. The youngsters are being faced with a new reality that is historically new. In the globalized world, the youngsters are called the millennial generation, who need to face severe life situations especially in finding *creative work*.

For the baby boomer generation, those who were born after the post-World War-II period in the 1950s and 1960s; the millennial apathy would be a deeply worrying aspect. The name baby boomer generation was given based on the fact that they were born in a time after the World War-II when large number of children had born into the war ravaged, depopulated world. This period after 1950s and 1960s, was a time for prosperity that had happened through hard work. Those who could work sincerely and honestly were also could be the big-time achievers in the post-World War-II world order. The baby boomers' world order was, an era of strong dreams and aspirations, realizable through "hard work". Plenty of opportunities for finding "work" were a part of this period as it was also the period of wide reindustrialization of the world, factories were made almost everywhere. Education and hard work were the main mantras that motivated everyone in the baby boomer generation. After the war, reconstruction and new construction had happened together with reindustrialization around the world, therefore proper education and hard work were highly valued everywhere. They thought that having dreams and great aspirations should be a part of life, and accomplishing them should be the sole purpose of life. Thus, all could live in a more equitable, just and egalitarian social systems by aggressively and passionately pursuing such dreams. In the post-world war era, the main thought was that science would reveal all the truth about everything, and following those scientific methods are the best possible way for living a good life. However, we experience a different kind of reality with the life of the young generation where science and technology dispirit and trouble them, because the overuse of technology deter them from engaging with any sort of "creative work". AI systems that are profusely being developed demand humans to exist in subordination.

Since eighteenth century, science began to shape up aggressively our thoughts in a big way. Scientific methods and procedures were highly regarded as the most dependable and acceptable systems for the modern world to pursue. The post-World War-II reindustrialization achievements, further heightened this dependability on science and technology. As for the baby-boomers' re-industrialized world order, a lot of young men and women entered as the work force to empower the re-industrializing world. And as for "work" that was the golden period. People could work hard and shape up their lives socially and economically as well. This was also the booming era of modern political ideologies of communism and capitalism. The capitalists and the communists dreamt the dream of the newly booming reindustrialized world order, where the workers at different levels would soon share the wealth created as rewards for their hard work. And for the capitalists the "smart ones" get more and the lazy ones get less, but both could survive by depending on each other. On the other hand, in the communist countries, the wealth should have to be divided according to the need, not according to the greed of the "smarter ones". In the reindustrialization world, the spat between capitalists and communists became so intense and hostile. They effectively divided the world into two. The capitalist countries focused on the efficiency in production with a presumption that the wealth created would be trickled down to the lower levels of society, on the bases of various trickled down processes, such as, direct employment, indirect employment, increase in retail sales, etc. In this period technology had taken over the position of pure science, especially in education. A new era of education of technological sciences became in vogue, because using technology in manufacturing and other service business would increase the efficiency and profitability. And the machines steadily replaced human work progressively. And today, we aggressively pursue the infinite possibilities of technology disregarding the limitations that we understood by the learning of natural sciences. The aim of science education is to help us knowing about the world; while technology is to help us manipulating the world order to advantage us. But the postmodern education of technoscience makes us ever more manipulative and aggressive.

However, even after being educated on the successful methods of science, the aimless attitudes of the youngsters, of today, would be a cause of worry for those, who brought up in the (baby boomer) re-industrialization –industry-2.0, period, who could dire to dream and pursue them. Even with the use of technology, the re-industrialization—industry—2.0, period people could engage in creative work using their hand-brain faculties, as technologization needed new ideas. But, in the era of globalization—industry-3.0, the millennial youngsters have to face what is known as technological unemployment. High technology swallowed up most of the "works" with an accelerated use of automatized techniques. It essentially declines the human involvement with creative work, but wealth creation and profit making happened without human involvements, and also without *creative work* and the use of the complex hand-brain faculty. As work declined, the divisions of wealth too became constrained. Even though the wealth creation happened at a very fast phase, the trickling down of it happened in a very slow, drop-by-drop, phase. The hope of progressing with one's own wellbeing by doing a work is least possible today. The chances for doing *creative work* have diminished, and instead of wealth creation, wealth confiscation is happening progressively, from the lower levels to the top levels. These all happen in the backdrop of the sudden disappearance of the communist socialistic ideology, where wealth distribution with the involvement of the working class, was the main method for ensuring equality.

In the early period of industrialization, there generated the ideology of communism with a model of the socialistic state-controlled system, which had dialectically opposed the ideology of capitalism and free-market economy based on consumerism. The doctrine of capitalism would have manifested as aggressive individualism, with a ferocious urge to pursue individual choices and self-interests. Capitalism thrived by promoting the kind of self-interest maximization of an individual as the motivational thought, for production and consumption, where creating wealth was the key and the distribution of the created wealth happened only through "work". On the other hand, the communists promoted planned economic management and effective distribution of wealth that also happened through work, for it was meant to benefit the poor and the disadvantaged more; but it hadn't worked well because wealth creation was very slow. For the capitalists, making profit against all other considerations was the prime method that was forcefully being followed in the re-industrialization (industry-2.0) period.

The shines of prosperity became too apparent in capitalist countries ever since industry—2.0. The good life was defined as a life with abundance of goods, a lot of free time to enjoy, and a life centered on achieving fullness by the maximization of all desires of an individual. There was a kind of passionate enthusiasm to adopt the capitalist method, which could provide almost everything in abundance. Accordingly, copying that kind of ideology was considered as the way forward for the entire world. One should have to aim for the big, happy, dreamy Western way of living as the bench-mark of prosperity that had again been propagated through mass media and pop culture that influenced the communist bloc countries as well as the other non-western countries, in Asia and Africa. Because of this unilateral propaganda by the capitalist western media, the dream of industrial prosperity began to flourish in the minds of many everywhere. The counter propaganda by the communists failed in their mission, because wealth creation was very slow and cumbersome under the order of the ideologically constrained communist regimes. Romanticism with materialism and capitalism caught the imagination of everyone around the world. Communism got destroyed in the western world due to the ideological constrains and rampant corruption that has eaten away the deeply ideological structure of communism and its social, economic, cultural and political dispositions; while in China communism got imbibed into the Chinese native culture and tradition of Confucianism, evolving a new kind of socio-political-cultural system, which is unnoticed or bluntly discarded by the ideologically constrained democratic capitalist world order.

The ideology of capitalism worked as a superstructure to guide our thoughts. The capitalist propaganda became the perfect one, when an over hyped narrative on Japan was created as a great success story of following capitalism in the reindustrialization period, as "the other" non-western, non-Christian example that followed capitalism against the failure of communist China under Maoist model of socialism. Such propaganda got huge acceptance around the world with the understanding that not just the modern western world, but even an ancient civilization like Japan following Eastern values, could make capitalist methods to work magnificently. This had generated a feeling that capitalism and free market economy should get universal appeal and recognition as the world should be progressed in capitalist lines at any cost. On the other hand, the methods of communism were relegated as antidevelopment and unprogressive. The socialist model that developed after the European enlightenment began to collapse with the sway of capitalism.

The capitalist countries, in the re-industrialization—industry-2.0, period, were also followed, Christian (protestant) way of living and thinking, Japan in the same period of baby boomers, was an exception to those Western countries, as it followed Eastern thoughts and culture. An exclusive narrative on Japan has happened in the baby boomer world to show that any other culture could also be able to make great economic development if capitalism was followed expeditiously. At the same time, during industrialization period-industry-1.0, before the War, Japan was pictured as a backward leaning antidevelopment, unprogressive country run by feudal oligarchies. The shift in propaganda narrative made Japan a notable country, which thrived on ingenuity and hard work. Patronization of Japan in this way made capitalism an acceptable world system to be followed by all others in the developing world in Asia, Africa and South America.

In the so-called developed world, the motivating mantra for good life, at the time of industry-2.0 period, was that of gaining proper education and training in scientific methods, with the ex-factor of "hard work". A successful man who might reach to the higher echelons of richness, power, freedom and prosperity, the limitless sky is the only limit. The ex-factor of "hard work" is the secret of all successes. A significant shift happened in the life style of a huge majority of the baby boomers in a few countries. As a consequence, almost all aspects of life were determined by money and economic prosperity. And therefore, the world systems created in the capitalist countries were prompted by the persuasive idea of "self-interest maximization" as the most powerful motivational mantra. The ideal man was defined as the one who holds a visceral affinity to maximize everything through "hard work" and who would visualize the world with infinite possibilities as the focus of the maximization of his self-interest through hard work. Such individuals with self-centered individualistic attitudes were venerated hugely everywhere. The world as a creature by some external agent became stronger in the Industry-2.0 period. And the capitalist superhuman agent, on earth, can make the being of that creature better.

On the other hand, the communist countries discouraged self-interest maximization, but encouraged the concept of "collective interest maximization" as the motivational thought, but together encouraged the concept of "hard work" in the spirit of an Epicurean living style of frugality and the virtue of co-operation and sharing. People find least enthusiasm in following collective interest maximization of the society, so the value of the ex-factor, hard work ironically declined. Since the aggressive individualism of capitalism had categorically opposed the ideology of promoting frugality and collective sharing, they promoted gratifying individual desires through aggressive consumerism. Maybe communism failed because of that shift in focus to frugality and sharing. In the controversy between self-interest maximization and collective interest maximization, capitalism won especially in the baby boomer generation that was based on following soft human instincts of desire, pride, greed, etc. not on any assumed benign ethical values. Communism never promoted any conception of world as a creature by an external agent, but considered it as a part of the co-evolving evolutionary act dependent on material causes and conditions.

However, for both the capitalists and the communists, the protestant Christian ideology of sharing the "divine providence of nature" was the foundational thought. The process of wealth creation and distribution should be there for benefiting everyone, as God (nature) created everyone, with varied abilities, that the able entrepreneurs should create for to benefit everyone, by providing work and a living wage. For capitalists, those entrepreneurs should be independent; whereas, for communists they should be under the state control. But in both cases, the idea of providence directly should oppose the basic principles of greed and self-interest maximization. And that idea of providence of God soon became obsolete in the baby boomer world order. Then the secular humanist values had replaced it, though ideologically sound, these values were soon shifted to where money and wealth had concentrated, and it is now replaced by the traditional conception of the "providence of God". The idea of "providence" works in the working doctrines of communism, but without the superstructure of God as in Protestant Christianity, yet they implicitly followed the Epicurean conception of heaven detached from the world. Communism adopted secular humanism instead of God as the controller of the virtue ethical values. The shift in perspective was possible mainly due to the easy availability of "work" and a continued demand for new workers in the rapidly reindustrializing world after the World Wars-II. So, the baby boomer generation found lots of opportunities to better their prospects in accessing money and wealth. The ideals of globalism and universalism began to flourish under the religiosity of secular humanism. Capitalism, gradually, discarded the Protestant Christian values of providence of God. Wealth and the power and control of money began to fill in the emptied space left behind by the ideals of the "providence of God".

Nonetheless, today for the children of the baby boomer generation, the creative work opportunities are on a steady decline. It is not possible for them to better their lives by accessing to wealth and money. And, for the millennial generation of today, such aspirations are not fueling their imaginations as much as it did for their earlier generations. They have no passion for neither, "self-interest maximization" nor "collective interest maximization". For them those are obsolete ideologies. In fact, today they experience a new world situation, in which a kind of lethargy is sweeping along. The new perspectives on materialism and secular humanism are very weak to protect them ethically and spiritually, and they tempt not to believe in any superstructure controlled by God and also tempt to reject any ethical authority as any superstructure other than the national law. The values based on the idea of providence and charity that made Protestant Christianity as the motivating religious view for the capitalist system is redundant today in the Western world. It only acts as a metanarrative, for lots of different kinds of narratives in the entire world. It may be because they don't foresee any role in the emerging world situation to dream something and achieve it through "hard work" as much as the entire earlier generations could do since industrialization. Even if they are educated, the kinds of jobs available are not able to fire any kind of enthusiasm or creative skills, but are mere repetitions, where they have nothing to do creatively using their *hand-brain faculty*.

1.1 AI Systems Versus Hand-Brain Faculty

Today, at the wake of industry-4.0, the world is preparing for huge automation using artificial intelligence (AI). When this happens the value of hard work of a common worker would be declined substantially. In which case, the providence doctrine of capitalism is also getting degenerated, but actively remaining as a talking point in the public domain. The common workers are now taken out of the chain of active beneficiaries, that they don't have any contributions to make, and that the jobs are barely earning them the living wages. Mechanization also has already declined, a worker with any opportunity to engage in any kind of creative work using the complex mechanism of hand-brain faculty. Because of which, a worker could not earn any satisfaction from doing a work, since appreciating creative skills should have generated happiness, human flourishing and spiritual wellness. The satisfaction and happiness by using *hand-brain faculty* is what one gains from all kinds of creative work activities. Besides, the mechanization with the introduction of Artificial intelligence (AI) challenges him to compete with the machines, where a human person is sure to fail at various level of executing the work. The AI systems are run by data with the help of high-speed processers that the hand-brain faculty of an individual never could compete with. Slowly but steadily, the process of wealth creation is happening without any active human creative work contributions. Technologization has reached to such a level that most of the common jobs that were available, for human creative work, during the re-industrialization period are not available now, as robotic machines with enhanced precision and productivity replaces those workers. The application of artificial intelligence actually helps the businesses to maximize the profit to its highly maximized levels. And now companies are running after to implement it. Humans simply cannot race against the high performability and precision of those robotic systems, but can operate them minimally where one needs not use any of the creative skills. A worker's hands may be used, but not his brain. The hand-brain faculty should be understood as a complex system perfected through thousands of years of evolution. The inherent human ability to use intelligence, for formulating thoughts out of sense perceptions, should be understood as the organic functioning of the hand-brain faculty.

The younger generation of today could not find any place in the world that is moving so fast. We have no idea how the world would evolve further in to the future. The charters of Protestant Christian values, centered on the conceptions of providence that had hugely influenced capitalism, with the moral outlines of prudence, honesty, truth, integrity, and goodness, are no longer valid today. Though communism reinterpreted those values in their conception of secular humanism and materialism without the conception of a God watching over, as an all-knowing entity are also no longer valid. In the reindustrialization period that moral framework acted only as a metanarrative, but in reality, the Christian values were replaced by money, power, wealth, with a naïve conception of secular humanism and freedom as the framework. The religiosity of secular humanism is inexplicably vague. Secular humanism might have adopted the ideas of "providence of nature", from Stoicism and Epicureanism—the classical materialistic philosophies, where the heaven's supremacy is replaced by the providential laws of nature.[1] In fact, those classical philosophical systems have influenced enlightenment movement in Europe in the modern times.

And the ideological framework of both capitalism and communism has weakened further due to historical reasons. Nonetheless, for the baby boomers, creative happiness from work provided them with a feeling of goodness, happiness and virtuous living, as they could use their creative skills to create and work with the mechanized systems. But in the globalized world order, for the millennial generation, of today, happiness from creative work is completely absent, or happiness from monetary benefit is also completely lacking. They could only do part-time works that provide them neither. The total absence of creative happiness from work could be the possible reason for the millennials' apathy and dullness towards seeking virtuous life. However, it is a complicated issue to be reflected upon easily, as there are many other reasons to be reflected upon. Yet, on the dialectics between machines and humans, the machines would win by providing humans everything connected with material prosperity, but the social and cultural life, we experience today are formed in to the present mode only through creative work with the active involvement of the hand-brain faculty. Historically, in the last 70,000 years, it is only through "creative work" that humans have grown intellectually and rationally, not otherwise. Lack of creative work would destroy life's inner essence and the inner urge for seeking wellbeing, human flourishing, and happiness. The ancient Greeks considered it as the inner essence of human life to seek *eudaimonia* (human flourishing) and *arete* (excellence in a creative activity). But today we vastly distanced from those core values that our civilization is founded on the essential values generated out of being creative and seeking happiness from creative activities.

Reference

Cicero, M.T.: On the Nature of the Gods. Brooks, F. (Trans.). Dodo Press, London, 45 BC (2008)

---

[1]Cicero (2008), p. 75.

Chapter 2
Creative Happiness Versus Power of Money

In the preindustrial period wealth creation was closely linked with human work, both physical and intellectual actively involving the hand-brain faculty. A synergic relationship should have been existed between creative work and good life, through the activity of wealth creation and wealth distribution. Work had created wealth that again distributed though work with a system of wages that benefited a lot of people directly or indirectly. The pivot of this system was based on the spirit of wealth distribution, not on wealth accumulation. Almost all those involved in, either as the receiver or the provider of work could have got a fair share, thereby, would have participated in the "creative work" either directly or indirectly. The profits and creative works were appreciated by providing the benefit to everyone in a family or in a society; thus, almost everyone else who had, involved in and connected with the system of work in the preindustrial world order, also benefited. This aspect of happiness from creativity and from monetary benefits more or less continued in the industrial period, but a shift in the purpose of work towards monetary benefits happened steadily afterwards. In those days, the "self-interest" of a worker was to support this synergic relationship and to make better the "collective interest" of family or society.

Notably in the preindustrial world order, all works required human involvement. Human work and intelligence—hand-brain faculty—operated in tandem to create things that could be used for making human life more comfortable and convenient. Fighting against inconvenience had determined the characteristic feature of creative work using the hand-brain faculty. The creators would always think about how to use, the objects around them, to support normal human lives. They learned and exchanged ideas to create more effective and efficient things. In this way, there existed a natural synergic relationship between the user and the creator. A creator should think and reflect upon the demands and concerns of the user and how one could use it to enhance the comfort and wellbeing. For a creative worker, the user's requirements were the prime concern. The creative workers always had creative challenges ahead to be accomplished with each aspect of the work. One should design the form (idea) of the thing before creating it, where he could learn and relearn about it constantly. He

© The Author(s), under exclusive license to Springer Nature Singapore Pte Ltd. 2021
M. Varghese, *A Brief History of Creative Work and Plutonomy*, https://doi.org/10.1007/978-981-15-9263-8_2

involves with the object to make the best usable, comfortable, and salable product. By involving with the form of the object, the carpenter should make the best cot, table or chair for his customers. His "self-interest" ought to be seen both as the satisfaction he would receive from accomplishing the creative challenge of involving with the form of the object, and also as the money he could receive, for helping him and family to live on. It never appears to him to create something and force it on a user to use it through persuasions, allurements or inducements. For example, the artisan carpenter with each created object, he should learn about the requirement of the user before making a usable thing. He could get some new knowledge, with each object that he should create, and that would enable him to create another product more efficiently in the future occasions, by inculcating a feeling of fulfillment with the new knowledge received. He would continue creating, learning, and teaching others in his work life. New knowledge made creative worker always happy, thriving, exciting and flourishing.

One the other hand, despite heightened prosperity, the knowledge one could receive from work be much less, during the industrial periods, and progressively on a sharp decline, when mechanization prospered further, and it is, now, almost non-existent in the fully technologized and globalized world order of today. Learning something new from work is absolutely non-existent. The focus of production is, now almost, shifted to the creation of profit only in the globalized world order. The individualized learning from work that has given the worker a special position in the society, has deteriorated in the industrialization periods due to the extra stress given for aggressively increasing production, and it has steadily begun to decline and now reaching to zero, as the technologization of production progresses using AI. And today, the workers only need to implement some kind of knowledge given to them from the "works manual" for executing a work. Mostly the workers do work only for monetary benefits. The synergy between work and satisfaction has broken subsequently.

But the feudal oligarchs, under feudalism of the pre-industrialized world, exploited the workers that the wealth created was distributed minimally and the workers had no bargaining power due to the lack of demand and other such social constraints. The profits should have benefited the feudal oligarchy more than the workers, so they never could be financially well off and never would be the active consumers in any manner. So, in the Western world, a kind of resentment generated towards preindustrial world order and feudalism. This resentment was the reason for the shift in focus for high wealth generation through huge production in the industrial periods. When the consumer base enhanced by creating more demand, wealth distribution become more, and the assumption was that it would move towards the lower levels by creating more job opportunities. So, the working classes become active consumers as well as wealth creators, and they began to demand more. Now with the aggressive production methods using AI enabled wealth production methods, we can create things and profits abundantly without any sort of active creative inputs from the workers. This aspect substantially has lessened the direct demand from the working classes. As the demand for the workers contribution has weakened, the consumer demand, too started to wane out substantially. The synergies that existed between wealth creation and wealth distribution has got broken. The acquisitions of some sort of self-interest from work also have taken a paradigm shift. Instead of feudal oligarchy, we have plutonomy controlling everything, with least acknowledgement for the workers' rights and requirements.

In the industrial period, an artisan carpenter could use machines and tools to enhance the efficiency in production. The demand for production and for huge consumption increased with the world that began to use a lot of products for to achieve comfortable life for everyone. Economic activity had increased with the availability and circulation of printed money. Access to money helped to create a world order where monetary wealth had taken the central stage. And it became the prime motivation. Consumerism began to flourish in the industrial periods. Consumerism acted as a pivot for production. As the job opportunities increased, the worker could get better monetary compensations. There also had a shift happened with regard to the rewards from work. The satisfaction factor from, doing a job as well had shifted to, for getting monetary compensation and the prosperity thence followed. The workers maintained some sort of bargain power because their work mattered hugely for high industrial production. But eventually the creativity factor had slowly and steadily monetized. The expert workers could demand more than the common workers. They began to be known as professionals.

In the industrialized world after the eighteen-century, a newly rich class of industrialization, which Marx called, as the bourgeoisie, who exploited the work of the skilled worker's labor by purchasing their skills, making them a part of the emerging middleclass. But the unorganized workers he named as the proletariat, were payed very little.[1] The period of industrialization had seen a shift in the control of wealth. It shifted to the control of bourgeoisie from the feudal oligarchy. A part of the same class of workers who formed the erstwhile serfdom that served the feudal oligarchy, in the industrial period, had become bourgeoisie and their middleclass accomplices; the rest become proletariat. In the post industrialization periods, the abundant opportunities helped a new group of people to occupy the position that had already been vacated by the erstwhile feudal oligarchy. On the other hand, the workers who were not lucky enough to get into the middle-class culture of the industrialization, became the marginalized proletariat relegated into a pitiable existence; and as industrialization progressed their number started to increase. In short, the same neo-feudal serfs had become bourgeoisie and proletariat. The bourgeoisie, in fact monetized the value of all creative works. Professional workers who monetized their skills began to flourish in the industrial world. During this period money began to control all human activities including human relationships. The huge circulation of printed money and other financialized products did a magical trick to accentuate and enhance the power of the bourgeoisie class. The common working class had been subjugated by the world order of the industrialization, where unequal distribution of wealth made a lot of people to live in subhuman existence, and due to mechanization, the creative work skills became redundant. Monetary benefit became the pivot of all activities

---

[1]Communist Manifesto (2016).

connected with life. Happiness from doing a work had taken a huge beating. Yet the world of entertainment kept them to forget their problems.

Creative work, by emphasizing the hand-brain faculty, involved both physical and intellectual aspects that made human societies to progress well. Nonetheless, in the pre-industrialized feudal world, though badly compensated, the society revered and respected the creative workers, where the compensation was not only the monetary compensation that helped them to live a life, but also the happiness drawn from doing creative works had helped them to live better. Happiness from doing creative work was highly being revered and appreciated. The monetary compensation by the way of materials helped everyone in the family and community. One of the reasons for this aspect of distribution of wealth between a begetter and his community members was that of mutual dependence, as the begetter could not store the income, which was in the form destroyable material goods such as food, etc. that would be destroyed in the course of time; unless, the income was in the form of solid assets like gold or silver which could be stored. Thus, the income of the begetter should have to get distributed to others at the soonest possible duration. But the honor and respect from the work should be the sole property of the worker, not of the employer. Doing creative work was a God given gift, because God was considered as the source of all creative activities who gave us the opportunity to use hand-brain faculty to experience the divine grace.

The workers, using creativity in work made them free by keeping them closer to goodness through learning and knowing. With the widespread use of money, in the modern times, made the creative professional workers to shift their focus for earning money as the sole self-interest, giving least care for creative happiness. The fruits of work became the sole personal possession that could be deposited in the bank and also be made into financial assets. As the mechanization progressed, all kinds of wealth became monetized more and more, and the consumer market began to flourish more and more, the efficient skilled and smart workers and those who involved in creative work began to form the new oligarchy that matured as the bourgeoisie, and abundance of wealth control made them a kind of shadow ruling elites, who acted behind all societal decisions. The rich oligarchy and their kind of crony capitalism began to flourish exponentially. But by monetizing workers' skills and recreating those skills to run the automatized artificial intelligence systems, thus the plutonomy has evolved from the crony capitalism. Today the superstructure of plutonomy controls everything, with plutocrats replacing bourgeoise, plutocracy replacing democracy, precariats replacing the common working class—proletariat.

The workers in the pre-industrialized world found a kind of spiritual satisfaction in earning and sharing. They found that sharing with others in the family or community was the most fulfilling part of the life. And the major religions promoted it as a part of their religious life. One should experience life that is within him to its fullest form, which could have been unleashed through creative works. But poverty due to lack of distribution of wealth was a real problem. Making creative work was a part of that effort to attain satisfaction, and the philosophers promoted it also as a method to distribute wealth since antiquity. The challenge at this period was lack of production, and those things scarcely produced, were grabbed by the feudal oligarchy by relegating the real producers of wealth into meager valueless consumers who could get only the lowest share. And without any kind of effective commerce and transportation, the creative skills of the workers were the sole property of the feudal oligarchy and that they owned the workers, yet the creative skills had a special place and with it the workers could earn higher social status. The feudal oligarchy controlled the workers' rights, to make only complicated situations into their favor, and instituted various cultural and religious restrictions to keep their control on the wealth including the creative skills.

Different communities did different kinds of jobs and the combined efforts pooled into an organic whole. This was true to the Eastern cultures since ancient times, especially in the Asian region where Indian and Chinese philosophies were influential. The caste system in Asia could be viewed from this perspective. But the workers' lowest position in the cast hierarchical system, both in India and China explains how the workers' rights were exploited. But at the same time, creativity of the worker was hugely respected by the society at large. Since money was not in active circulation, the workers' compensation had a different level of appreciation and reorganization: The creative skills were appreciated highly everywhere in the pre-industrialization world order, even though they were badly compensated. The young people in that period had competed with each other to learn and master a creative work fully, not for high compensation, but for earning respect and reorganization in the society. In the industrial period, they had a higher status, compensated better, and could be traded their professional skills to earn more money, albeit the unskilled were marginalized, compensated badly, and given least value for their work. Yet, in the globalization period, another curious thing is happening. Creative work happiness is negligible but monetary wealth accumulation is easily possible if the workers know how to sell their skills as professional skills. The normal workers are all now, equal to the unskilled workers, and are growing hugely as the precariats (part-time workers) who live in a kind of precarious lives by not getting neither respect nor monetary wealth. And this kind of working class is now growing exponentially high as the installations of AI controlled mechanized systems surge. The precarious and perilous existence of those part-time workers, hired on jobs, contracts, are unorganized, and in a micromanaged existence; the precarity of the working-class population should be a matter for worry for every right-thinking individual.

Reference

Communist Manifesto: The original text at: https://www.marxists.org/archive/marx/works/1848/communist-manifesto/ch01.htm#007//. Retrieved on 17 July 2016.

Chapter 3
Technological Unemployment

The term technological unemployment signifies outsourcing of works to low-cost centers, trafficking of workers to multiple work locations globally, using of AI Robotics, and neglecting domestic workforce and their rights, etc. In the globalized postmodern world order, where unemployment is being created due to the uncontrolled use of technological systems spreading almost everywhere. The purpose of life in this period should be seen as an effort to achieve freedom by creating more and more wealth, using any means possible. The methods have an unquestionable authority as long as it supports the economies through the distribution of the created wealth. But today unemployment due to the extraneous use of technology destroys jobs and therefore the distribution of wealth is getting paralyzed. And the unutilized wealth moves in as the resources for financial industry to work, creating super-rich entities who produce no wealth at all. And plutonomy works as the superstructure controlling everything possible.

An unintended consequence of huge mechanization should be that it would be a huge strain on the energy balance of the nature. Now the pursuit of humanity is moving in the direction of maximizing profit using technological systems by replacing human work purporting it as redundant, unprofitable, and huge draining on the system. On the other hand, technology is reliable, highly productive, vastly dependable, not creating any redundancies on the system, when comparing to the high performance performability of AI controlled systems, human hands are less efficient, and human intelligence is not steady. But for the technological systems to be functional, it needs energy to run it properly. And the needed electrical energy is to be created in huge quantities, and huge quantities of resources are required for making that. When people are left unemployed, it means their physical energy would be left unused and be replaced by artificially created energy for running the AI run support systems. And when human physical energy is unused, it would lead to huge physical and mental health crisis, like the spread of obesity, depression, drug abuse, suicides, etc. It must be understood that human life is dependent on the energy balance of the nature and upsetting that may result into the formation of certain shocking consequences.

© The Author(s), under exclusive license to Springer Nature Singapore Pte Ltd. 2021
M. Varghese, *A Brief History of Creative Work and Plutonomy*,
https://doi.org/10.1007/978-981-15-9263-8_3

But when High technology would assure high profits, it also ensures unemployment everywhere. Technological unemployment is defined as the redundancies of human work due to the implementation of technology for gaining high profits. It is unemployment created in a nation state by shifting of jobs to another geographical location through sub-contracting, or using trafficked migrant workers who are being transported legally and illegally from other geographical locations, or arbitrarily using AI enabled systems instead of human workers. These activities would generate only an uncomfortable situation to human *creative work*, and are done on one declared purpose that is to increase profits and to increase investment opportunities for the plutocrats. In short, the system should be shifted to be AI run to enable plutonomy to thrive and flourish.

Under plutonomy, there is a concerted movement to denigrate the rights of workers, in all of the world systems, that are being developed in the twenty-first century. Workers' rights mean not just earning a livelihood, but to work and improve their internal faculties as being humans. All aspects of work-related benefits, to human workers, are atrociously denigrated in the postmodern globalized world only for making high profits. In the highly technologized world, the production of goods has taken over by automatized artificial intelligence systems, or using systems like offshoring of jobs, or using the cheap labor of migrant workers, or using part-time workers (*precariats*). This happens because of, some naïve hopes, working as the super structure to all our decisions. We presume with an expectation that the worldwide consumer community with its ever-increasing needs is an ever-increasing phenomenon, and maybe one day, we all could live without doing any work at all. We all may be able to live happy lives with all enhanced facilities in an equalitarian open society, where everything is provided according to the wants and needs of an individual.

But in actuality, the globalized world has completely over stretched in all rational considerations on wealth creation and its distribution through human work. What happens now is wealth creation without distribution. The highly automatized systems could make products in huge quantities cheaply, and the produced products are being marketed anywhere in the world to costumers for gaining enhanced profits. But, it is to be shared through various financial activities based on various kinds of investment methods. People, instead of participating in any economic activity, simply invest their money in stock market, bond market, etc. to gain higher incomes. Financial industry is a postmodern world system that will work only on postmodern relationships. Yet, in reality, it can help to benefit only a minuscule part of the population. The workers' rights to bargain for better compensation are being reduced substantially in the postmodern globalized world order, because of the use of artificial intelligence and the highly leveraged activity of the financial industry. And the rights for better life are slowly narrowing down to zero, and becoming like precarious situations for common workers to earn living wages. In short, for a worker earning a decent living wage is difficult now. The erstwhile activities of sharing of work and compensation are almost extinct now. The labor-intensive jobs are often being offshored neglecting domestic workers. And the "creativity part" of work is completely taken over by artificial intelligence (AI) systems; the workers' role become acting as being a part of the machines, and only a little money in the production activity is being shared with the workers, and a major part of it would go to resource the financial industry. The precarious life of a modern-day worker is a theme that now worries, all right-thinking people around the world. Nobody can properly discern the tectonic reverse shift happening in the field of "work and life", where human hand-brain faculty is not at all revered and appreciated. That decline is now moving faster with an accelerated speed.

Almost all the manufacturing activates are done in a few outsourced centers situated in a few geographical locations for catering to the global demand; ironically, all companies use the same manufacturing facilities for their product requirements, but use different labels before selling them; the Chinese manufacturing systems hugely benefited by this method of production. And the wealth distribution happens to those who invest in those businesses, and not with the workers' labor participations. With the increase of those newly rich people, we today have plutocrats who control the wealth created through aggressive technologization that destroys the contours of "work and life" of normal workers. Lack of creative work opportunity will seriously damage the complex mechanism of the inherent human *hand-brain faculty*. The postmodern plutocrats—the superrich class of industry-3.0, effectively replaced the bourgeoisie of the industrialized world of the industry-2.0. In the globalized world, the norms of the industrialized world are no longer workable. It is the value of financial products that determines the distribution of wealth. But those who invest in those products are very few and again the high performance performability of AI systems controls all investments and also the business of financial products. It should be a worrying factor for everyone who engages in investments and finance businesses. The plutonomy of today is infested with the ghost of AI.

In the new era of plutonomy, there is a qualitative difference between a plutocrat and a bourgeoisie: a plutocrat may be a business owner but mostly he is an investor doing investments and trading of financial products. He may not know who is the real owner of the business into which he is investing his money. He invests in many financial products and makes lots of money by trading it all around the world. And with the use of AI, one could make immense amount of money. According to a report recently published by Paul Buchheit, 93 American individuals own nearly 60% of the country's wealth.[1] These statistics is applicable to various national and international situations. Investments are the foundations of the newly rich community of plutocrats. Their wealth grow at epic proportions as the investments are controlled by algorithmically programmed Artificial intelligence systems managing their wealth with the high-performance precisions of the Nano-technology. Eventually, there will also be epic proportions of "dead wealth" that would get flooded everywhere. The unused dead wealth is engulfing and destroying the economic world order created in the industrialization periods. The accumulated huge wealth would go around the world confiscating the value of wealth around the world. The plutonomy of today

---

[1]Published on Monday, February 09, 2015, by Common Dreams: "New Evidence that Half of America is Broke" https://www.commondreams.org/views/2015/02/09/new-evidence-half-ame rica-broke.

thrives on the gaming logic; what is in fact happening in the financial market is a postmodern way of financial gambling. The gambling managed by algorithmically programmed systems that function on the phantom of big data with the precision of Nano-technology.

The millennial workers are those who are precariously drawn into an economic destruction mode of the postmodern world order, following the gambling rules of the casinos. The precarious existence of workers becomes so rampant when nearly 2 billion transnational workers become available, at any time to be used as cheap labor after globalization, into an ever-shrinking domestic labor market. The competition becomes so intense and overproduction due to cheap credit becomes a problem for everyone. Oversupply of cheap money from the investment banks and the cheap labor from the international labor market contribute to the phantasmal world of postmodern economic systems that creates economic chaos; the businesses are controlled by the fancies of the investors, but those fancies are determined by AI systems and big data. Since the availability of interest free money is so wide spread, busting those economic bubbles is not easy, because interest free money can inflate that bubble to astronomical limits. As the resistance of that bubble become stronger due to AI and big data, the economic insecurity for normal individuals is on the rise, and consequently an unseen deterioration of human life happens everywhere.

But the expectations of the rich in the OECD countries were that the opening up of market in Asia and other regions would bring newer opportunities and demand for their investments. But the expected boom in the Asian countries was centered mostly in the big cities with the activities of the plutonomy there. The villages are largely unaffected by the consumerist investment culture as people won't desire for more than what they used to have. So, the plutocratic system exploited the cheap labor especially from China and India to make the production of everything cheap generating technological unemployment a big reality that is difficult to reverse.

On the other hand, the outsourced production activity created a new stress—a new struggle on the domestic labor market in those countries that used cheap labor of China, India, etc. As a product that required labor were outsourced to low cost manufacturing centers in Asia, Africa, etc., the common domestic worker/consumer became insecure and redundant and only being used as means for selling cheap products. For example, a shoe maker in India can make a shoe for less than $5/, but if the same shoe is made in any of the OECD developed countries, it could cost the manufacturer $ 50/, but the shoe will, in either way, be sold in the open market for $125/. The profit margin for the branded marketing company is huge, but it also makes the local shoemaker unemployed and he could act only as an ineffective consumer. Since the manufacturer/marketer could show huge profit, she/he can attract interest free investors' money for further business expansions. The system now functions with the help of artificial intelligence effectively to show profit for the investors' money. Financial industry is a major industry today in the erstwhile-industrialized countries. Investing in the financial industry is the best way to make money today at the time of plutonomy. The problem of undistributed wealth is the problem that plutonomy faces today.

The unemployment/underemployment among young graduates around the world are alarmingly high. The jobs they can find are only part-time works mainly in-service industries. They are underemployed that they can work only on calls basis by the labor dispatch companies. The wealth and properties their families may have had are all financialized, that earns nothing, as the interest rates are nearly zero, and in certain cases it can only fetch minus interest to their bank deposits, bonds, etc., which are increasingly getting lower day by day. Most of the young people in the millennial generation are to compete with transnational workers, for to be a part of the work force they have also to compete with the ever expanding technologization. Most of them travel to other countries to find work by becoming a part of the international cartel of trafficked workers. Millions of Africans and Asians are becoming a part of the trans-national trafficked workers. These trans-national workers are a kind of *precariats* who would compete with the domestic workers in matters relating the wage and other such compensations. The accent on monetary profit from all economic activities is doubly emphasized and the distribution of wealth is much worse comparing with any other time in history. Technological unemployment, in the postmodern globalized world order, and the changes that it brings in to human life, is a subject that is being vastly overlooked today. The world order under industry-3.0, is hugely obscure and it is turning out to be of deception and deceit. The question now is for whose benefit the plutonomy functions. That leads to speculations and formations of speculative conspiracy theories. But philosophically it is a typical situation when human nature is controlled by emotions of greed, fear, passions, etc. not when controlled by rational faculties or common-sense understandings. That may be the reason why the intentions of plutonomy are increasingly getting obscure and worrisome.

Chapter 4
The Millennial Precarity and the Herd of Precariat Workers

According to Marx, the class conflict of the preindustrial world was there between the feudal oligarchy and the serfs, but after the first industrial revolution, the class struggle was between the bourgeoisie and the proletariat. In the reindustrialized world, industry-2.0, too, the opposition of bourgeoisie and proletariat continued minimally, but the gap began to reduce with some promising out-comes for better distribution of wealth had emerged. In all those cases anomalies, wealth distribution was the major issue and was centered on the dialectic between rich versus poor. But, in the postmodern globalized world, industry-3.0, under the budding of plutonomy this antagonism is largely between *plutocrats versus precariats*, furthering the dialectic between rich versus poor that the rich become the absolute, leaving the poor insignificantly behind. This happened because the large portions of the work force are the new herd of part-time workers who live their lives by shifting between unemployment and underemployment, for finally not getting any economic security to formulate a steady living situation with family, etc.

The term precariat is meant to explain the "life and times" of the marginalized workers in the globalized world order, who in order to survive have to compete with various aspects of the technologization that are being brazenly used today to support plutonomy. The Marxian term proletariat is insufficient for explaining that situation as it has evolved during the (modern) industrialization period where workers' rights were denied but their works were a required factor for economic progress, so ignoring worker' contributions would not be possible. But today in the postmodern globalized world of industry-3.0, human work is the most expendable and least appreciated thing, while profit and money power are over-appreciated benefiting only the plutocrats. The oligarchy today is neither feudal, nor bourgeoisie, but is the plutocrats who largely would act as investors and as administrators of the financial industry. It is expected to become more lethal in the upcoming era of industry-4.0. Maybe the new world system would generate a new kind of mechanized workforce, where human work contribution is not at all necessary.

Most of the *precariats* are the young men/women in the globalized world, the so-called millennials, who are to live in a world of high technological advancements and

© The Author(s), under exclusive license to Springer Nature Singapore Pte Ltd. 2021

M. Varghese, *A Brief History of Creative Work and Plutonomy*,
https://doi.org/10.1007/978-981-15-9263-8_4

who are to compete with the Artificial intelligence and big data. They are to live by appreciating the digitalized world, where AI is displacing, all the available jobs that used to be done by human workers for now using the technological appropriation of creative work skills. The creative workers' thoughts are now transferred into digitally exploitable data that can be processed and be implemented on mechanical systems using Nano-technology. At the time of industry-2.0, the creative skills were human, though the implementation was mechanical. So, the millennials have to rise against the efficiency and precision of the robotic systems for doing any kind of work; or they may have to compete with the technological systems for to be successful. Competing with artificial intelligence systems in executing works, human work would fail miserably. Therefore, they can only act as helpers to the machines in a network of machines. Moreover, the work environment is so polarized that one has to compete against the high precision of robotic systems, and also against trans-national workers, where the competition is on the basis of undercutting wages. And another un-noticed and worrying aspect is that a precariat (part-time worker) could not learn anything new from his work-life except to help operating the machines. He never could get an opportunity to create anything and could also get some new knowledge, or ever to activate the complex *hand-brain faculty* in any manner. As discussed, the composite system that developed due the constant activation of body-brain complex made the human ability to use intelligence leading to creative skills. A worker's contribution, is nearly zero as the artificial intelligence systems would prevent him from giving any sort of individual contribution. The programmers who created the AI system have imaginatively created programs that restricted any creative contribution from a worker as big data is available to be processed. The programmers' ability, to use algorithms with huge amount of relevant data to create systems that would automatically self-check and correct all possible mistakes have destroyed the chances for a worker to learn something new by executing a work independently. There is no need for any human inputs, and a worker's skills would not matter anymore. A worker, therefore, can be replaced easily with another one who can read an instruction manual for making an AI system functional. And that is also becoming minimal progressively as self-validating systems are gaining importance in the industry-4.0.

The accuracy of technological systems made it possible to make human work to be servile to it. From a CEO to an ordinary worker, the employees of a company are hired on the basis of contract for a specified period of time with some specified responsibilities; whereas, the governing board of directors who work on behalf of the investors would make the executive decisions as being directed by the AI systems after processing all relevant data, would work only on the basis of gaining monetary profit. The financial interests of the investors work as the lead for all decisions. The investors' community is the core of plutonomy that nowadays could make societal decisions with substantial political power. Plutocrats appropriate all the wealth of the world into their control. A significantly large majority of work force today is part-time workers who earn much less than what is required for maintaining a family, etc. Maybe we as humans have to sacrifice everything that is being valued, thus far, for making plutonomy to work progressively.

Unlike in the earlier industrial periods, the part-time workers of today are not attached to any labor unions or any such organizations that could provide any collective representation. The precariats are absolutely independent, as they are being hired only on demand basis: It can be for a few years, few months, few days, few hours. The part-time workers of this sort are called "precariat workers", a term invented in the globalized world under plutonomy. According to John Nicholas: "a new category beneath the traditional working class. This precariat referred to a hodgepodge of part-time and freelance jobs where the workers had no rights, security, or benefits, and generally not much income—hence their precarious material and psychological state of existence. Members of the precariat are often educated and qualified for far better employment but are unable to find any positions".[1] Economist Gay Standing coined this term in his well-known work: *A Precariat Charter: From Denizens to Citizens.* Mostly economists are well aware of the Marxian term proletarian, the common workers; and bourgeoisie as the wealth controllers. Philosopher Karl Marx introduced these terms, nearly 200 years ago, when he had spoken about the inequitable distribution of wealth at that time. The epoch-making text: *Communist Manifesto* that he wrote, became the policy document for the communist movements in Europe and other parts of the world. The workers' movements under communism made quite a storm in the life history of workers in the industrial world, both positively and negatively.

Karl Marx, in the *communist manifesto* had briefly mentioned about the ordinary workers precarious life situation, when to live in a highly mechanized world where the creative inputs from an individual worker would completely be declined and his creative energy would be wasted comprehensively. Curiosity, the word *precariat* may be related to that precarious life situation, mentioned in the *Communist Manifesto,* where machines would challenge the creative potential of humans wickedly. Marx feared work without creative satisfaction is being in a kind of precarious existence; where, humans may lose the enthusiasm to live on in such subjugated situations. Human society at large would become highly machine minded and might imbibe it emotionally and rationally. Today under plutonomy, a very few numbers of plutocrats could replace the bourgeoisie of the industrial world. And now there is a kind of dialectics is being developed between precariats (part-time workers) and super-rich plutocrats. Unlike the bourgeoisie, the plutocrats of today depend on wealth confiscation, not on wealth creation. They mostly are working in the field of financial industry that are mainly run on artificial intelligence. Which helps them to engage in a kind of organized loot powered by technology.

Therefore, unlike the industrial workers (proletariats) of the nineteenth century, the Millennials of the globalized world are to live in a world of technological unemployment where the youngsters of today need to confront directly with the superior efficiency of the machines, where machines are certain to be dominating—or replacing—the human "creative work" contribution by the networked, self-learning, algorithmically controlled mechanical systems. To face this situation, humans are

---

[1]Mcchesney and Nicholas (2016), p. 16.

not adequately educated or trained. On the other hand, the society pushes the millen-nials into the highly technologized, globalized, and networked world systems that are made using highly intricate and complex technological systems run on huge amount of data and being processed in Nano-seconds. Such a kind of time and space is unper-ceivable for human consciousness. The ultimate beneficiaries of such systems are largely unknown to a participant of such systems.

Since the time of industrialization scientific systems had helped humans to ratio-nalize human thoughts in a systematic order; therefore, compared to traditional systems, mostly based on convictions and beliefs, scientific systems were hugely appreciated. Scientific rationalization helped human "creative instincts" as one could understand the logic behind everything which somehow made the human *hand-brain faculty* more effective. But, in the globalized world, the AI enabled systems are more complex and intricate and beyond the parameters of normal human under-standing. So, working with mechanized systems would not give any creative satis-faction of creating something, as it did, when creating with the hand-brain faculty. In the industrialized world, there existed a relationship between machines and man; that is redundant today. It is like, when computers were introduced people had to write programs using machine language based on *bits and bytes*; but today nobody uses the machine language to write programs from the primary level of coding, but the newer systems are built over the already existing primary systems created by program-ming of bits and bytes (the *machine language*). Today when one writes a program, the *machine language* self-programs on the basis of the already existing primary codes. The knowledge and application, of machine language are unconnected, to the real time systems of today that could decode normal human language and would execute intricate programs. Now, that is activated further with the user interfaced self-programming systems that when the user input his requirements, the machine self-programs, which would be the main feature of the fourth industrial revolution. Nonetheless, the computer can understand only the machine language working only on the basis of bits and bytes, likewise humans can only understand the activation of *hand-brain faculty* when doing a job. So, when we depend on machines, unlike the computers, such an activation never happens. Since our intellectual and reasoning faculties are directly founded on the complex activation of *body-hand-brain system*, the efficacy of the intellectual faculties would diminish and would be replaced by fear and ignorance, instead of insightful knowledge; if hand-brain faculty is not effectively deployed.

However, notably relationships in human life have been hugely affected by the technological systems of today. Humans need not interact with each other. And the creative inputs from the workers can be substituted by self-programmable systems, which use neither human intelligence (brain) nor activity (hands). The notion of an owner paying a worker for doing a work is now getting obsolete. The idea of "divine providence" has also become redundant, serving only the purpose of acting as talking points. We have no idea who controls such systems under plutonomy. Yet, the plutonomy is only the beneficiary of the newly created systems. It has created a few pseudo oligarchic entities that presumably act as the owners of those systems with minimum responsibility. It means the oligarchy of those who control finances only. The financial systems are run by algorithmic controls with self-programing networks, automatically forming the system of Artificial intelligence, which can displace human intelligence easily.

The nineteenth century industrial revolution needed human labor. And the bourgeoisie, who could have survived only with the labor of the proletarian, had accumulated all the wealth for satisfying their greed for money, leaving a very meager share for the survival of the workers. The struggle between bourgeoisie and proletariat was real and a dialectic being developed thence. However, today for the millennial precariat do not have any such issues of confronting any bourgeois owners, they have to live without seeing or knowing who the real beneficiary of their works. The artificial intelligence manages the system, and the profits from business are divided promptly into the pocket of investors, who live in some other geographical location, who directly would part-take neither any responsibility, nor any effort. The capitalist bourgeoisie, in the form of an identifiable authority as the sole owner of a business enterprise, is largely insignificant now. The CEO etc. are contract employees for the company. And the AI systems are considered as legal entities equal to individual personalities. Technology (AI) has taken the place of the bourgeoisie. Technology tells the precariat what to do; where to go; when to work, and what payment one would get for the works done. The dialectics that existed between bourgeoisie and proletariat is completely broken and become extinct today.

But with the lack of understanding of the contemporary situation, we try to understand the situation mainly using Marxian conception of the bourgeoisie control over the systems. The horrendous transfer of wealth moves into the hands of a few plutocrats cannot be explained, where the wealth they confiscate are mostly unused. We must recall that the main purpose of huge wealth generation during the industrialization period was to have sufficient wealth, so that it could be distributed properly to the satisfaction and happiness of everyone that would act as an effective system for market expansion. This act of "divine providence" is no longer happening anywhere in the era of globalization. Under capitalist system various conceptions of the divine providence were infused in to enable a justifiable way of wealth distribution.

In the preindustrial world, wealth was created very scarcely, but the distribution was somehow done as it was the necessity of the time. All the people followed a kind of religiosity-based beliefs in matters regarding human life. Providence of God or nature was imbibed into "work and life" situations of the normal individuals. The explanation given about this period is largely based on how the midlevel Christians viewed the world and life. World systems, since sixteenth century are based on the Christian—Protestant—values. So, from the modern historians' works, we have very scanty report about the life of people in the East—especially from China and India. The world trade at that period was focused on the products from the East. So unlike Europe the East should have had better wealth management systems. In the East, there existed an organic caste system that ensured production and distribution of wealth through work. But the norms of which was unacceptable to the world of rapid industrialization where caste system should have created a major impediment, because workers never should identify any other identity than the industrial working-class identity. It is mainly based on the norms of economic management system that is founded on the Protestant Christian values and the values of European enlightenment.

The period of rapid industrialization was an economic method adopted by the West in the modern times to create wealth, so as to distribute it to benefit the entire community. And as Marx explained, it changed the social order from the oligarchic control of the feudal system to the system of the bourgeoisie, which was based on greed. It was the time of the newly created rich upper middle class (bourgeoisie), who began to control all the benefit of work of the common workers (proletariat) by nefariously controlling them by denying them the substance of life justifiably as being envisaged in the "divine providence" conceptions. The newly rich middle class created a new set of values based on "freewill and freedom" following Hegelian doctrines, since eighteenth century, that urged everyone to have a dream and should realize that dream of prosperity though hard work. The conception of "divine providence" acted only as a talking point in the post Hegelian era. The religiosity of the preindustrial world had declined during this period. Morality and ethical behavior began to change substantially, to the fanciful thoughts of an individual, notably based on his whimsical fantasies. The religiosity of the past had substantially changed for acquiring power, richness, and freedom. The capitalist in the post Hegelian era could use his dialectical method of double negation to subjugate the ordinary workers maliciously. Yet the capitalist system was built on the conceptions of the "providence of God" in the Protestant Christianity, where an individual's dedication to the society is the most impotent ethical act. But under the industrial bourgeoise, this divine doctrine helped them to negate every class under them, which could be the reason for the origination of nationalism (national socialism); fascism (regimentation of society); and all sort of brotherhood movements around the world, for each to find a significant position in the world that was suppressed by bourgeoisie control.

In the globalized world order the dialectics between plutocrats versus precariats, replaces the dialectics between bourgeoisie versus proletariat, making "hard work" meaningless. Work acted as the synthetic unity at that period. The aspect of morality and ethical behavior based on divine providence, of the past has further deteriorated. It is now based on following the rules and the constitutional authority of the nation states to decide on what divine providence is? Almost everyone is looking up to the governments as the way the medieval Christians looked at, to the church for moral direction. In the precariat's globalized world, the values of power, richness, and freedom of the industrialized world order are lesser and lesser important. In the preindustrial and industrial world, family and community played an important role in shaping up the views of an individual. But individualism in the globalized era since 1980s makes him less sensitive to familial and societal commitments. At the same time, a marginalized worker (precariat) is scared of everything around him, as he has to face life situations alone and also to face self-extinction due to the lack of opportunity for creative work or for not being activated his hand-brain faculty.

Reference

Mcchesney, R.W., Nicholas, J.: People Get Ready. Nation Books, New York (2016)

Chapter 5
Joe's Story: Precariat's Life and the Alt-Reality World

One of the attractive sides of technological developments in the twenty-first century is that people can have lots of free time for themselves. If someone has a minimum income he may be able to live comfortably with a lot of time for entertainments, as cheap and free things are available to satisfy the basic needs. One needs not have to toil hard in factories or in farms.

A young worker (millennial) of today lives in a world, which is, due to artificial intelligence, unimaginably sophisticated and perfectly organized; for example, the supermarkets of today are perfectly functional without any human workers' active involvements, the banks are doing almost all businesses online without any direct human interface; finger print readers and surveillance cameras are supposedly keeping every shop and shopper safe from attackers and burglars. Online purchases are gathering momentum, and products and services are following the perspective customers though the networked advertisement systems. Retail shops are managed by highly sophisticated networked management systems. Speed is what matters today. The smartphone could read your mind and follow you up to various products. When a purchase is made using an online marketing system, the company should also make sure that it would reach to the buyer at the shortest possible time. Many companies are planning today to deliver the goods though automatic delivery systems such as drones, or any such AI controlled delivery methods, and so on. Each business activity is being encouraged in using less and less manpower, while being encouraged for using more and more Artificial intelligence enabled systems. Being connected with the rest of world through the cyber space is what is actively being encouraged in the case of postmodern globalized world systems. Every man/woman walking on the streets is expected to be followed by, a surveillance system, based on the phantom of his/her past actions, the data of that, are being collected through various data collection platforms and providers which everyone uses regularly.

The emerging world of precarity is what I could find in the typical instance of Joe. To me Joe is a typical kind of millennial youth who lives in the world of alternative reality. Joe spends most of his time in the world of cyber space. His living world is like existing inside the matrix of cyber space. He works to make the artificial intelligence

© The Author(s), under exclusive license to Springer Nature Singapore Pte Ltd. 2021

M. Varghese, *A Brief History of Creative Work and Plutonomy*,
https://doi.org/10.1007/978-981-15-9263-8_5

supported systems as his living space, which quickly enslaved him. In that alt-reality world, all that he does would help to remove human work systematically. Earning a life and economic freedom by doing a work is unbecoming and redundant for him in these days. The identity less individual like Joe never would starve to death, even if he does nothing as a regular worker. He can get almost everything, using online shopping at home. He is an individual who can live on any sort of income and if no income is forthcoming, he can ask for assistance from any of the available social security schemes either by the governments or the schemes of private charities. If the new emerging world systems would be perfected into a reality, then we all will be controlled by a singularity, a technologically driven singularity that would perfectly be controlled by a network of artificial intelligence systems run on huge data that would follow each of us everywhere like a phantom. But, Joe is the man of today competing with/against artificial intelligence, yet sure to be overpowered by the futuristic world of technological singularity run by AI run systems. So, there is no enthusiasm to challenge anything. We can see them in almost all OECD countries (developed countries) widely and soon enough, we will be seeing them in other underdeveloped and emerging countries.

The precariat-lifestyle is almost similar to the life style of the unorganized daily wage laborers in the developing countries. It is estimated that nearly 70% of human work force are some sort of precariat workers, who work on short contracts and are increasing steadily by adopting all sorts of working population into the system of precariat working class. In the Japanese society they are known as *firitta*, meaning freelancers; in the context of India, they are *coolies* (daily wager); in the western world they are *gig workers*. In the case of a daily wager, he is uneducated, and belongs to the lower strata of the society, and also used to live with the family and community even with such low earnings. But in the case of precariats of today, they are highly educated, well trained, yet being rejected and being taken as unsuccessful individuals, with neither family nor community supporting them. Precariat like Joe's life is typical. He lives in alt-reality world; whereas a daily wage worker lives in the real world with other humans. The precariat workers of today are isolated individuals from family and the society.

Joe lives in a world of constant connectedness, where the final consumer is identified and the products or services are delivered with minimum of expenses, and thus Joe may feel the uselessness of his existence. He lives in a world of alt-reality and alt-space, no aim to be accomplished than becoming a part of a network of part-time workers through a dispatch company if he needed to work. He does not know who the final beneficiary of the part-time works he does, as he changes his workplace on the temporary basis. He only follows the requests of the online agency on where to go to do his allotted part time jobs, only for a stipulated period of time. "Work" for him is the only way to find a means to survive his daily life. Unlike a daily wager, he has no reason to be concerned about the beneficiary of the work he performed. And he is not concerned about it at all. The people, whom he knows, are all going to work at the online-networked workplaces where nobody directly controls a worker. An automatically networked system controls all human workers. The idea of an organic community is replaced with a networked system of constant connectedness of a different sort. Joe earns only a little money that could help him to live on for a few days only; and then he has to work another few days for another period of time; or when he has no work, he can seek helps from the social security programs of various sorts, like monthly allowances, food banks, free food services, etc. He, however, never could find a steady job with a regular income and a family and an organic community of his own.

Most of the young people in majority of the OECD countries are living in a kind of self-isolation from the normal traditional living environment of family, friends and community. They are hugely apathetic and vastly unconnected to everything that is going on around the world. They switch in and switch off between the real world and the alt reality world, in which they continuously exist most of the time. The work satisfaction through knowledge generation by doing a work is unknown to people like Joe. He is not alone; there are millions like him. The community he belongs is an extension of a technologically enabled online alt-community. The Internet provides him constant entertainment and a feeling of continued connectedness. When he goes home he can see various reality-shows on TV that depict some kind of home life inside his lonely home. One program that can be seen in Japan and elsewhere, at the prime-time TV programs, is the food preparation program (kitchen variety entertainment) where popular stars sit around a table, chat together and eat food together. Joe, who brought his food from a convenient store, or a fast food place, eats the food together with those famous TV stars. Even though he doesn't have any family or community of his own, he could create a virtual community of famous people around him, because the natural sense of living with a community is still alive and kicking deeply there in the depths of his consciousness.

Joe is a typical precariat who could live on one part-time job after another. In all these available jobs, he works on without knowing anything about it well, as he needs only to follow the instruction manual sincerely. In this case, a worker's opportunity to learn from his own mistakes is nearly zero. Therein, what is been denied to the young generation of today is the opportunity to live with a robust consciousness, a brain that constantly engages with work related activities; or one never get an opportunity to use the complex *hand-brain faculty*, that helped humans to live a happy and flourishing life since the dawn of the current civilization. Classical thinkers like Plato or Buddha thought that creative work is what makes a man live well within one's lifespan. Denying creative work is like denying proper nourishment to a child, and letting it to grow up with some lifestyle health problems.

Chapter 6
Zero Citizens: Neither Citizens Nor Denizens

Zero citizen is a phrase that can be illustrated to explaining the future social status of most human persons in precarity, who do only part-time works and, therefore, unconnected with a nation-state. The modem term citizen of a nation state would have originated from a person's life from the subjective perspectives: One may belong to a particular family, clan, community, but finally an equal citizen of a nation-state. The nation-state should ensure the individual's right to exist in a community and it should be duly protected. In the nation state, citizenry is the foundation. Nation protects a citizen, and the citizen offers complete allegiance to the nationhood by mainly paying taxes for keeping the financial structure secured. However, Joe's story represents a typical situation in the life styles of the millennials. The world of today breeds an identity-less community, where one may be a citizen but the rights are that of a denizen. A citizen of a country enjoys certain rights of being so, but denizens are denied most of that. A denizen is treated as a guest in the nation-state. The expatriate-workers are guest workers in a particular nation; similarly, in the twenty-first century with the wide spread use of part-time workers, the statuesque of most of the population would be like that of expatriate workers. The good example of Denizens is the contract workers from south Asia in Gulf countries like Saudi Arabia. They can work there and earn money but could not enjoy all the privileges of the native citizens. A south Asian expatiate worker has a family in his native country and would do those insecure jobs to feed the family back home. But the case of modern precariat like Joe, mostly they are forced to live as single individuals as their incomes are insufficient to maintain a family. But the precarity of Joe is different. He has no family, or any of such support systems. He is working to survive for the day. He is the postmodern precariat, who can claim the status of neither a citizen nor a denizen. He is a zero citizen. He only could survive in precarity: in Aristotelian conception, a situation antithetical to the tenets of citizenship of a nation.

There are many like Joe who live as neither citizen nor denizen kind of life, as their earnings are like that of the denizens, and not bonded to neither a family nor a community. As the nation-state postulate that for every personality, those support systems are the preamble for meeting the emotional and spiritual needs. It is an

© The Author(s), under exclusive license to Springer Nature Singapore Pte Ltd. 2021   35
M. Varghese, *A Brief History of Creative Work and Plutonomy*,
https://doi.org/10.1007/978-981-15-9263-8_6

aberration to the very idea of citizenship in a nation-state. The spirit of living a complete life is almost dead for people like Joe. They easily give up and then disappear from the active social life. The fighting spirit and a willingness to survive at any cost is hardly seen with people like Joe. He does a job for money only; he would stop working after getting a little money. Joe can get a social security support, but once they learned to live on those support systems, they never seek to find any new employment. The duties and responsibilities of a citizen are redundant to them. Notably they are not willing to take a citizen's responsibilities, like voting in elections, paying taxes directly, joining any national security forces, nor any of such duties. They are neutral to any obstacles and challenges, never find any value in accomplishing any sort of challenges. If the technological unemployment goes on at this rate, Joe's case may be a commonplace case everywhere: The population of zero citizens, living without having any familial or societal responsibilities would increase exponentially. The people whose identity with the world is the amount of data they would provide to the AI system might increase, albeit the data engineered systems are meant to provide an equitable, well ordered, social and economic life to each citizen in the globalized world order.

The curious case of the life story of Joe is unique. Joe was born at an American military camp in Seoul, South Korea to a Korean Japanese (Japanese national with Korean descent) mother and an American soldier father. The marriage between his parents was temporary as his father disappeared first, and soon after his mother remarried and also had disappeared, from his life. As a child Joe was being taken care of by the Christian Chaplin of the camp, who, instead of pushing him to an orphanage, took him to his Grandmother in the USA. Joe now has citizenship of Japan and America and because of which he could travel and work in any of the OECD countries freely. He is a typical example of a Zero citizen as he can live and work in most of the countries without any apparent difficulties, but not particularly attached to any country or nation-state as his own. He completed his primary school life in the USA and college life in Japan. And now he lives in Japan and since his student days he has used the services of various dispatch companies for finding different unconnected part time jobs—from a watchman to a store clerk. Even after completing his college, he only gets calls from those dispatch companies on his smart phone for continuing his part time jobs. Above all, his work would be only to follow the instruction manual provided to him by the dispatch companies. He is not supposed to have any idea about the owners of those dispatch companies or from where those are being operated. And also, he has no idea who is the ultimate beneficiaries of the works he does. He only knows that if he makes mistakes, in executing, the directives of job manual instructions, he won't be called in for any jobs again. The dispatch company would blacklist him, and it may go into the data base center as a defaulting worker. There is no hiring or firing. They all have his data that has been manifested like a big phantasmal shadow ruling over him. The dispatch company sees only his employability. And the news about his carelessness in job would only decrease the chances for his employability seriously. As the dispatch company is specialized in services in various fields, he gets calls for different random jobs. It ranges from working in food industry, to cleaning toilets, to be as a barman, to be a storekeeper, to babysitting, to acting as one-day-husband for some random woman, to be a part-time lover, to an errand boy, to one-day-son, to one-day-friend, etc.[1] Most of those jobs are hired on hourly basis or at best on the daily, weekly, or monthly basis. He should follow the job instruction manual, word by word only, in each and every case. He should be thoroughly professional and should follow the instruction manual with care and concern. Various kinds of restrictions and controls are there in the "work and life" of Joe. He should not show any human emotions beyond the limits specified on the instruction manuals. He always should do his job like a machine or should imitate like a programmed machine. This is against natural human nature, which is organically evolving with emotional velocities, but always remaining anti-mechanical. In the precariat's *work and life*, such emotional velocities are denigrated and replaced with crude rationalism of technoscience—known as professionalism. One needs to fight against his natural human nature of being influenced by emotions.

As based on the systems that developed in the world of today, at least in developed countries, if one loses all opportunities to work, one can survive with social security support. So, people like Joe can survive on charity. In the USA, the government data estimates that there are around 50 million food stamps recipients. Using which one can purchase food and basic necessities from any of the designated stores.[2] This figure shows that nearly 1/5 of the American population live on direct government help. The average food stamp [SNAP] allowance per person for a month is around $ 125/-. These kinds of social security schemes were earlier given only to the most poor and disadvantaged sections of the society, are now being used by the ones who lose their jobs, such as, qualified professionals who cannot find any suitable employments, those who are underemployed and underpaid, those who do only gig jobs, etc. Such social security schemes are a part of European socialist tradition, the state or church provides for the disadvantaged. Under food security schemes, countries like India give free food grains and pulses to the poorer section of the society. On following these kinds of schemes aggressively, the next level of globalization and social development would be of helping people to live in a Jobless world. In which case, most of the population would have to live by depending on some kinds of social security schemes. Machines would do all the production activities. The charity-supported citizens are not real citizens of a state; they should be equated to zero citizens (neither citizens nor denizens) as they live without any rights as any normal citizen, who actively engages with all the activities of the nation state. The idea of a nation state and the notion of citizenry would be collapsed eventually helping the plutonomy to control everything.

The extreme use of such schemes widely by majority may startle and make a right-thinking person to contemplate hard. Why we work? Is the purpose of work only of earning money? If it is only for earning money then complete mechanization

---

[1] The rental companies that supply all kinds of relationship modules are flourishing in many developed countries. https://theweek.com/articles/631927/inside-japans-booming-rentafriend-industry. Retrieved 26/Jun/ 2016.

[2] This benefit is largely used by precariats but the income is insufficient to live day-to-day life. https://www.huffingtonpost.com/2015/02/28/food-stamp-demographics_n_6771938.html. Retrieved on 07/12/2017.

can be justified. But it is not so; various other life-purposes are served while one works on a job. When a person like Joe works in a proper job with a regular income, he loses his zero-citizen status and gains an identity. Economic independence is the mark of a modern civilized citizen. The conception of nation state is drawn from this concept. It also helps him to use his intellectual and physical energy that again helps him to grow creatively by using those faculties. He can use the natural human vital energies for making up his life creatively. This vital energy is the foundation of creative work accentuated through the *hand-brain faculty*. This aspect will reduce the dependence on other sources of energy, which is an irony today. The unused human physical energy makes one to store it up in the body that fattens one badly up, where one does eat and sleep only. Obesity is a worldwide pandemic and a huge health crisis in the postmodern globalized world order, with no sure cure at all.

However, one of the defining aspects of mechanization is that any working method can be proceduralized and then digitalized into actionable data; and every method is carefully studied and analyzed and transferred onto the programing language of the computers where programmers create software that replace human labor from those programmable digitalized data sourced from human behaviors. Those procedures would run repeatedly and can be copied, and can be adopted to support other procedures. A network of such procedures could function as a system, giving a feeling that an artificial intelligence system works like an automaton with an intelligence comparable to the human intelligence with superior results. The AI systems are systematic and perfectly rational, but normal humans are not perfectly rational, but also are being controlled by emotions and feelings. The conflict between rationality and emotions consequently makes humans weak and behave in an erratic manner. Humans therefore could not compete with the rational systems that are always functional and now those are algorithmically self-programmable. That may be the reason why people lose interest when working together with AI, as failure makes humans unenthusiastic to do something. And since the humans are not making any direct individual inputs onto those systems, replacement of a worker with another one is simple and easy. Creativity and creative satisfaction from work is denied to the precariats, who does only part-time jobs that would not use the hand-brain faculty at all. Those who have no access to wealth may disappear from the active life. We may see in the future that the zero citizens of today may evolve into trans-humans, in which case humans may behave like machines or people who live with zero emotions and who live only on the scientific rational paradigms decided by machines run on big data. Fear of the data from one's past mistakes would make one to behave mechanically. The phantasma of big data driven surveillance would destroy natural human freedoms. Almost everything that happens in and around you would be there to haunt you, even the data of someone related to you or connected with you.

Contextually, the creative work culture, traditionally in Japan, is centered on two methods, first one is learning from the books at schools; second is learning from seniors at the active workplaces. In the second method one learns to use his skills to develop one's own individuality. The second stage learning is now obsolete with the widespread incursions of AI systems. As a consequence, there is a wide disregard for human work, all kinds of education and opportunities for learning from onsite works are on the decline now. This aspect is directly forcing the world of zero citizens to fall into the zones of entertainments and comforts, because one cannot get any sort of satisfaction from actually doing a work creatively or enhancing the hand-brain faculty to the fullest potential. A Zero citizen would never know anything about creative work as it is redundant for him.

Chapter 7
Life in the Comfort and Entertainment Zones

A precariat's life is mostly of spending in the virtual world where one gets free enter-tainments abundantly, because the jobs, a precariat could do, are non-entertaining, unfulfilling and uncomfortable. And one always searches for comfort zones for gaining quick gratifications with some immediate pleasures. The jobs of Joe have become repetitive and boring, as he needs only to operate various machines by reading the instruction manuals given at the job locations. He was being instructed for everything that he did, and he had been monitored everywhere for collecting data; thus far, this was the experience of doing all of his short contract jobs. The saddest part of his suffering and confusion is that he couldn't understand the reasons for his rather dull life even though he was working almost every day on those repetitive jobs. He was largely scared and a kind of unknown fear had gripped him, generating perpetual stress and depression. Today by using technology, one can get any sort of help with the click of a button. And most of those helps are in the form of instruc-tions, mostly—dos and don'ts—when operating a machine run by the interconnected artificial intelligence systems. He cannot understand the meanings of those expert opinions. He knew that technology takes care of all those difficult issues. From the media and other similar social narratives, he could understand that the rich are getting richer at the expense of the poor by using some unknown fraudulent methods beyond our understandings. And since nobody can stop that easily, the world has only one direction to follow and accept that one direction, that is our fate. So, we must agree with the technologized world even with poverty and with a decadent life. The social narrative also taught him that seeking "freedom" by using "freewill" is everything in life that one must passionately aspire for. He always sees various scary views by experts and thinkers on losing "freedom" and its violations on the media, because freedom is the supreme spiritual merit for one to pursue. This freedom narrative supersedes all other narratives on human life and existence. But millennials like Joe do not follow the freedom discourses with any sort of enthusiasm because he doesn't understand what unfreedom is?

Unlike their parents' generation, the millennials of today mostly stop listening to those narratives, because that create a kind of discomfort and a deep uneasy

© The Author(s), under exclusive license to Springer Nature Singapore Pte Ltd. 2021
M. Varghese, *A Brief History of Creative Work and Plutonomy*,
https://doi.org/10.1007/978-981-15-9263-8_7

feeling. They continually look for entertainments that could shortly help them to forget immediate worries and discomforts. But the self-consolation, they hold on, strongly is that they are not poor in the conventional sense, unlike the other miserable people in Africa and Asia, shown on the media, reeling under pain and suffering due to lack of proper eating. Today media narratives are the best source of knowledge, even replacing school education. Joe considers himself as a lucky one, for he creates a self-narrative of himself becoming rich, powerful and to be completely free by accumulating a lot of money sometime in the near future. The media narratives put him into a fictitious imaginary world, where imaginative thoughts result in discomfort and uneasy feelings for seeking more comfort. Now as for Joe, he could get food just by ordering it through his smartphone, and it will be delivered at his doorstep. This aspect, for him, is an instance of progress and development that is accepted as the purpose of human life: eating and playing only. If he has some social security support, it is automatic. He now began to be sucked into a sort of comfort zone of a couch or a bed.

In the cyber world in which he exists today, he could feel self-sufficient, without any enthusiasm or drive to live on. A kind of fear began to grip him; fear is a negative emotion; yet, it is considered also a natural protection mechanism. Scholars and academics think that the reasons of fear should be revealed, so that one can self-defend and move in the path of freedom and democracy. Joe knows that it is imaginary and unreal, but that knowledge itself makes him uncomfortable. As a rule, anything that is comfortable is acceptable but if anything, that creates some kind of uncomfortable feeling, then humans can remove them by using the rational faculties. But, today the millennials would reject them the sooner, they caught up with any sort of discomforts. After all, those opinions and expert comments are focused on discussions for more democracy and for more "freedom", but nobody would ever discuss how freedom is relevant if unfreedom is no longer an issue, where mostly unfreedom is non-existing.

Joe could not understand what is unfreedom aired in those expert narratives on freedom, freewill and democracy. Freedom and freewill are two catch phrases of almost all narratives happening in and around the millennial world especially in the case of expert opinions. The simple inference that one can get from all those narratives is to get more freedom for getting more comfort and entertainment in a very short time, because life is short and it would end quickly. Therefore, the social aspiration should be there for achieving comfort and entertainment for everyone as the social responsibility of an organic society. The norms of the postmodern globalized world are centered on this aspect. Pleasure in the form of comfort and entertainment is the order of the day. So, freeing from the boring life, Joe entered into the world of entertainment and comfort. It is like a matrix, into which one may have forced himself to delve in.

7.1 Classical Hedonism Versus Postmodern Comfort and Entertainment

Aristippus, who belonged to the Cyrenaic school of classical Greek philosophy, had argued that normal human nature would be driven by immediate and naïve pleasures and achieving it "here and now" is what motivates one ingenuously. But he warned that if we would not be careful, the pursuance of pleasures be like one entering into a brothel for seeking various kinds of pleasures and might stay put there continually. The ancient Greek brothels were places for various entertainments and merrymakings. Cyrenaic philosophy is based on the ethical doctrines of hedonism—seeking of wordily pleasures, "here and now", as the way to achieve *eudaimonia* (human flourishing). Hedonists were against the schools that promoted pursuance of virtue-ethics as a way to achieve *eudaimonia* (human flourishing), like Platonists or Stoics who sought the virtue ethics of the transcendentals: Truth, Goodness and Beauty as a way to achieve lasting human happiness—*eudaimonia*. The Cyrenaic and Epicureans have promoted seeking worldly materialistic pleasures moderately as a way to find *eudaimonia*. Even though Cyrenaicism promoted seeking pleasure (Hedonism) as a way of life, they also warned against the extreme pursuance of pleasures could destroy an individual's life.

Once Cyrenaic thinker Aristippus taught his student at the gate of a brothel that "it is not the going into such a house that is bad but the not being able to go out."[1] It means one must be deeply aware of one's own mental latitude and should be prepared to get out from such places at a particular point of time; otherwise, one may stay put in that place indefinitely, by thinking that he can get the ultimate pleasure experiences later in the future. That future may never come, and one may be destroyed with that expectation of achieving perfect pleasure eternally. And that wait may continue unendingly till one's death. The world today should re-read the teachings of Aristippus on hedonism as the postmodern globalized world people wait for achieving the ultimate aims of life from comfort and entertainment. As we can see from the public narratives that the central thought of postmodernism is hedonism and the universalization of hedonist pleasures "here and now", because human existence in the world is short and determined by "space and time". This postmodern narrative on hedonism is widely accepted nowadays.

But the pleasure seekers (hedonists) of today lost all controls and limits, as it would come through various entertainment programs unabatedly. Though the numerous mediums are meant to keep one continuously entertained, unlike, the brothels of the ancient world, today entertainments would follow you everywhere. In the case of millennials like Joe, the feeling of comfort and entertainment comes out of eating tasty food and sleeping without any worry about the future. And then unknowingly stay within that world, expecting more. Now he can carry a networking instrument like smartphone or any such application that could continuously entertain him. He is now living like a NEET (Not in Education Employment or Training); now this

---

[1] Laertius (1828), p. 83.

acronym may also be used for describing people who would not go outdoors but stay only indoors. In Japanese such homebounds are called Hikikomori. A NEET individual self-creates a comforting narrative about him. In that narrative structure, he feels comfortable, powerful and rich.

Most of the narratives are created around the notion of "the other" that are in trouble, not us. This can be explained with the behavior of people who like to watch poverty and misery as the problem of "the other", even if they themselves are in deep poverty or in severe economic insecurity. The comforting narrative, one gets, in this regard, is that compared to "the others", I am—we are—much better. The persons who can write such narrative structures are the modern-day scriptwriters, journalists, politicians, strategists, business leaders, and so on. The narrative structures are, often times, been drawn from the naïve realistic feelings of an illusory social consciousness that needs to be protected, like the narrative of the capitalists are created around the notion of a draconian system of socialism and communism that dehumanizes life, which needed to be rejected as "the other". The concept of "the other" should be negated and be discarded aggressively. There are capitalist narratives, on the socialists; and communist narratives on Fascists, Nazis, Imperialists, Oligarchies, Totalitarians, etc.; there are narratives of the liberals on both nationalism and communism. All such narratives use "the other" to substantiate their own positions. People who follow such aggressive attitudes also are very active in the globalized world of today. Instead of following such narratives, the classical wisdom in this regard is that when one engages in some sort of creative activities, human flourishing and satisfaction (*eudaimonia*) emerges and thrives. All other activities give only temporary reliefs. Following social narratives of today is like the situation, when one who got caught up inside a brothel or inside a matrix, waiting and expecting for great miracles to happen.

But ironically, in the globalized world of the precariats such idealistic narratives are less influential. Any conception of "the other" is almost dead. It is not helping one to generate the same comfort zone anymore; instead, a kind of self-generated "fear" comes forth and that is what rules the social consciousness of the postmodern globalized world communities. And for Joe, the idea of "the other" is a myth. Nobody offended him; he got good care and help from all those who were a part of his life and also were good and kind to him: his grandmother, the Chaplin, his companions, his student day friends, the dispatch company that gave him jobs, etc. He never touched a woman other than the sex related part-times jobs he did for an entertainment dispatch company; in which case, he was following an instruction manual strictly. When he was small, his grandmother used to hug him lovingly, which made him much comfortable. He remembers that often. The possibility to negate "the other" is insignificant for him.

Once or twice he also used the women sex delivery service, but they also were following some instruction manuals. Delivery health is the name used in Japan to describe this kind of prostitution service, where women are delivered at your place on requests, mostly through smartphone Apps. The women who works in these industries are also precariats, who also live like other millennial precariats: not being able to find a way out, but only living on the edge—an insufficient employment and income situation. He knows that he is now being controlled by someone outside of his living world; and couldn't understand who, where, and why? One can see millions of people like Joe in the developed world. Joe's experience is a common feature of life for majority of millennial precariats. They lack attention and care from their family or their community. The parents normally allow the children to live in a well-structured rational world, which is emotionally neutral and based on certain secular humanist values defined with an exalted notion of "freewill and freedom" that is enshrined in the national constitution of the nation states in the postmodern world order. The narrative structure of those are same everywhere. It acts like a kind of postmodern religiosity for the secular humanism. The contours of such a view is that get well educated, get a great job, marry a woman of your free choice, and build a family. But those exalted ideas are now working only as a metanarrative in the millennials' world.

The religiosity structure of secular humanism works on the strict regime of scientific rationalism, which ruthlessly individualizes everything in the globalized world order. Essentially secular humanism rejects any conception of an eternal God of "goodness and providence", and therefore lacks focus and clarity. The classical philosophy and religions consider goodness, truth, harmony etc. are transcended eternal values that humans need to follow. On the other hand, in the globalized world, with the application of artificial intelligence that postmodern religiosity of "freedom and freewill" based on individualism gets solidified like a permanent matrix. It makes, the human ethical values based on truth, goodness, temperance, beauty etc., redundant. Everyone is petrified by fear, the fear of being watched, being followed and being controlled by an unseen force that is following one everywhere and collecting data. The postmodern matrix of existence is founded on aggressive individualism supported by a conception of "freewill and freedom" and realizing it "here and now" is valued more than a transcended conception of God, heaven, etc. centered on transcendental values of goodness, truth and beauty.

With the origin of the re-industrialization, since 1960s especially with the advent of modern liberalism, in the western democratic world, a kind of sub-narrative started to have formed, that blatantly rejects all human feelings and emotions and tries to create a new narrative structure on the basis of scientific rationalism for explaining the religiosity of secular humanism as "freewill and freedom". The application method of AI advances such a religiosity further. Rejecting the traditional notion of community, society, beliefs, and religiosity based on providence, the postmodern narrative created the ideology of secular humanism, where the notions of individual's free choices subsumed importance. The conception of secular humanism follows the contours of Christian humanism started in fourteenth century by Italian renaissance thinker Francesco Petrarch who was inspired by the works of Roman thinker and philosopher Cicero, who was inspired by the thoughts of Epicurious on society and religion. Thus by and large modern socio philosophical thoughts are hugely influenced by Epicureanism.

Nonetheless, in classical philosophy Aristotle taught that true happiness come in to being (*eudaimonia*) by following virtues of truth, goodness and beauty. Abrahamic religious systems reinterpreted it, by keeping their conception of one God in focus;

whereas, for the Eastern systems like Buddhism, Hinduism, Daoism etc. living a virtuous life is the only purpose of life. This essentially defines with the Sanskrit word *puṇya*, virtuous living by following the virtuous path taught by the tradition by organically integrating with the eternal virtues—in Brahman, Dao, etc. But such conceptions of virtuous life are denied in the globalized world of secular humanism based on aggressive individualism and AI systems. In the postmodern world the conception of virtue is defined as power, money and freedom to enjoy the goodness that material possessions could provide, because achieving hedonist pleasures "here and now" is the sole aim of life. There is a struggle happening in the minds of normal people to accommodate fully this new narrative on virtue ethics. Nonetheless, Epicureanism which is the source of secular humanism advocate moderation, temperance, a moral code on the basis of co-operation and sharing, thereby humans can match the wisdom and happiness of the heaven.

The classical hedonism of Aristippus and Epicurus was a strident criticism on the ideals of *virtue ethics* promoted by Plato and Aristotle with *hedonism,* yet they promoted only moderate enjoyment of worldly pleasures. The postmodern hedonism promoting "freewill and freedom" is a persuasive negation of the virtue ethics promoted by religions and also that of the classical hedonists and materialists. The one who seek redemption through "comfort and entertainment" is similar to the one who entered into the brothel (as alluded by Aristippus) and waiting there eternally for getting the perfect pleasure that would liberate him from all sufferings. The Hedonist of today is thoroughly confused; the one who enters there even want to forget that s/he would live only for a few years; one does all illogical things to establish himself, in a world that changes always inexplicably, through hedonism. It is important to read the confusion of this postmodern hedonism on a wider context and to see on how the ideas of power, money, freedom, are consistently failing to replace the framework of virtue ethics and virtuous living.

Reference

Laertius, D.: Lives and Opinions of Eminent Philosophers. In: Yonge, C.D. (Trans. and ed.). George Bell & Sons, London (first pub.1828), reprint

Chapter 8
Hillary' Story: Plutocrat's Life in the Alt Reality World

The life and times of a plutocratic millennial, Hilary who, unlike Joe, is blessed with abundance of power, money, and freedom, but like Joe, is dull and disinterested in, with the very act of living life. In reality she is extremely rich and is being called so by everyone, beyond which she doesn't understand the value of being rich, and also doesn't understand why she is so rich. She never worked or never earned anything by herself, but the wealth she owns, in her individual name, is there because of her being born in a postmodern superrich family. But her father, who no longer lives with her, is a successful investment banker. She was told he is investing on everything, everywhere around the world, and is a VVIP who can travel anywhere and everywhere and being often times received like a super VVIP guest in different parts of the world. She can get anything, she wants, that money can buy. She has houses servants, private jets, yachts, and can freely use all those state of art facilities that the modern world could offer. She gets information about her wealth and its growth on her smart phone. It always grows. Sometimes, it may crash but, at the end of the day, automatically recovers. She was told that all her investments had been protected by the support of high-tech algorithmic systems run by big data and Nano-technology that investors would use for protecting their investments. She doesn't know how it works. An executive from the investment company, told her, that the use of algorithmically programmed high precision networking systems would protect the investors wealth from all kinds of loses.

She only knows that she lives in the winner's world, albeit she couldn't understand what algorithm is, or how would high precision Nano-technologies work? What she knows about it, at best, is that it works like her Google page or Amazon page on the Internet. When she opens her Google page, the browser, chooses a page that contains her favorite site using the information from her search history, based on the data Google stored earlier; it would select relevant information for her to seek her interests further. To enable this, Google should have created a digital personality of her using the mathematical function of algorithm using high speed computing using big data and Nano-tech. Similarly, the algorithmic system used by the investment companies automatically choose shares and financial products, and would buy and

© The Author(s), under exclusive license to Springer Nature Singapore Pte Ltd. 2021
M. Varghese, *A Brief History of Creative Work and Plutonomy*, https://doi.org/10.1007/978-981-15-9263-8_8

sell them on her behalf without any direct knowledge or participation. When she is about to lose, the system borrows money from somebody—mainly from banks—and makeup the losses. Those activities are done without any involvement of the human intelligence, the AI selects and executes everything using big data, where the programmers imaginatively created systems to operate and self-manage everything.

But she has no enthusiasm to know how it works, as she carries no direct responsibility whatsoever. As for Hillary the AI controlled financial system is in the alt-reality world. She was also told that she could borrow any amount of interest free money, from some financial entities for doing any kind of investments. She is only a small unit that is being controlled by the superstructure of the modern financial industry. The algorithmically powered tracking tools keeps the share markets strong and steady with due internal resistance against sudden market crashes. The AI system that works behind is a highly complex and intricate system, and it is difficult for anyone to understand it fully. But almost all investment decisions are made for various entities by the AI systems without any active human involvement. That is why for companies—boom and bust—happen so frequently everywhere all the time, but the big investors' wealth always been protected.

Earlier, investing in stock market was a way for people to invest their extra money—savings—in successful companies and earn better returns as dividends from those companies. It was a way to generate extra capital for the companies' operations for making their performances better. But the investment economy of today works like an industry upsetting all cardinal principles of capitalism, as it is not the capital generated from the investors wealth, but itself is running as an industry where the commodity is financial products and financialized assets. Now interest free money and valueless assets are fueling this curious industry of our times. It works almost like a game and only those who understand the gaming theories and gaming logic applied in those systems, may manipulate it and gain high profits. Nonetheless, it now becomes a highly tricky and complex system, because of the use of the algorithmic high-tech networking system managed by AI, without any human interface, using gaming logic applied mechanically. The system of plutonomy is built on such a system. And, for Hillary, the working of plutonomy is like the working of an alt-reality.

In reality, Hillary is, like Joe, also practically retired from active life, a NEET (the acronym also applicable for disinterested and home bound youngsters of today). She has no enthusiasm in knowing about money, finance, wealth, etc. She is, like all the other millennials, dull and disinterested in life. Contexually, Joe is also a NEET (hikikomori), by this definition who practically lost interest in all aspects of living his own life fully. As per the sociopolitical narrative of our time, Hillary is a part of the 1% rich who control almost all wealth in the form of financialized assets; and Joe is a part of the other 99% who owns no cognizable wealth at all. How come they are the two sides of the same coin? In the postmodern world order, there is a kind of postmodern slavery reigns, where the perpetrators are unknown to the popular social narratives, and also not in the knowledge of the social consciousness. Are there any real controllers of the alt-reality world that we experience everywhere? Do some people secretly operate behind such systems? Could we punish anybody for that? No! They are not within the system; they are in the alt-reality world. This is a problem of the system, and all are a part of such a broken decadent system.

When comparing with the living situations of the baby boomers' generation, we can see the living situation of the millennials of today that almost everyone has almost of everything from the very young age. The millennials have the freedom and means to get anything that they want. They all have good people around, who support and encourage them, their parents are not so compelling or pushy like that of the older generations, yet they are unhappy, apathetic, disinterested, discontented, and lonely. Ironically, the social narratives around are based on pursuing aggressive individualism that promotes the fulfilling of the contours of "freewill and freedom" and achieving of those choices to become a part of the postmodern globalized world order. Nevertheless, the arguments of today follow the narratives of the baby boomer generation that prospered, because of pursuing the spirit of individual dreams and aspirations. But in reality, the idea that power, money and freedom could make one happy is just another irrelevant myth that circulates in the globalized world, which in reality, both the rich and poor millennials have rejected. At the same time, for their parents' and grandparents' generation being rich meant a lot.

In the pre-industrial world, one should be either be a part of the feudal oligarchy or be a part of the serfs. In the industrial world, the division of the bourgeoisie class and proletarian class were evidently pursuing middle class values and both the classes were influenced by the ideology of "divine providence". The bourgeoisie and prole-tariat were mostly the liberated serfs who, in the Marxian sense, upheld middleclass (burghers) values. But the division got widened when those who could control the wealth in the industrial revolution become greedy and extra manipulative capitalist bourgeoisies, those who got marginalized due to the severe mechanization became the poor proletariats. In the globalized and financialized world order such divisions have become irrelevant. Now the mechanization is at the zenith one noticeable fact is the origination of *plutocrats and precariats.*

In twenty-first century, the ideology of aggressive individualism and the use of the automatized machines are intrinsically connected. The ideology of aggressive individualism works as the super structure of all other ideological systems, including traditional religions. The ideological based political systems, religions, human rights organizations, other such charitable associations, etc. are dependent hugely on the wealth of the plutocrats. As a mission the plutocratic systems wants everything accessible to everyone and wants to take everyone to freedom and independence at the shortest possible time, with the least efforts where mechanization become mostly by AI run systems. It is presumed that only with a systemic change across the board, we can achieve total freedom for everyone to live in the world, or to create an open society. Which enables everyone to improve each's individual choices passionately.

The world of artificial intelligence is driven by a kind of scientific rationalism. The structure of scientific philosophy that we follow, since nineteenth century, after Kant and Hegel, is meant to create theories that are proven by scientifically veri-fied knowledge sources. This period is known as the age of reason and also the era of enlightenment. I call philosophy since this period of time as scientific philos-ophy, because the philosophy, after Hegel, from the eighteenth century followed only scientifically proven knowledge sources as valid. And, the philosophers archived all other sources of knowledge and also shelved the conceptions of virtue ethics based on transcendental ethics, and declined any prudent conception on metaphysics. The scientific systems were built on the method of objective analysis only. This method had created a passion for materialism or turned everything suitable for objective analysis, including human personalities. Material acquisitions should be the way to find happiness that would be the foundational thought that also should continue to shape up all the narratives in the postmodern globalized world order. As a rule, the scientific knowledge had negated all other kinds of knowledge, notably common-sense knowledge or traditional knowledge or spiritual knowledge or knowledge acquired from instincts, or taught by the forefathers. As a rule, the validity of all knowledge should be scientifically verified and should thoroughly be established through discourses in the public and scholarly domains. Now, materialism and objectification do work as the superstructure of all our thoughts.

The social consciousness that is centered on the narratives relating to the social order of today, is based on the rich versus poor narrative—like in the earlier periods. Even though the postmodern world order found newer definitions to explain life and the value systems, still our presumptions about the social order is ancient. It is presumed that the rich should be happy with their wealth, and the poor should also be equally having the right to be happy, but their lack the opportunities to have more things should have made them very miserable. So, the only solution is to making things in abundance and selling them at cheap prices to everyone. Now both rich and poor can get whatever things they want. That may be the reason why Hillary and Joe are equally unhappy and equally discontented with the very act of living their lives. Having a lot of material wealth means nothing, to the globalized world in terms of happiness from possessions. Contrarily, in the industry 1.0 and industry 2.0 periods the disparity between rich and poor were wide, and the poor had no opportunity to have some necessary possessions. Those who were poor challenged the rich and then various kinds of revolutions happened as a result. In those times, there was a class of people that had everything and another class who had nothing. In the millennials case, both have everything but have nothing to hold on, because both are controlled by the deep structures of the alt-reality world order. Both rich and poor are unable to understand the real reason for their sufferings. Their lives can be compared to those who fallen inside a matrix, repeatedly searching, or those who live inside a cave thinking that the world inside is real and true. (Republic: 514a–520a).[1]

The matrix of postmodernism, in the era of globalism is a cruel reality of today. It rubbishes all core values that defined our lives for millenniums. We, like the people in the cave example of Plato, live in deep ignorance, thinking that the alt-reality that we experience is true and organic. Maybe the only way to get out of this matrix is to get out of the AI controlled systems, but it is difficult because the world systems since industrial world are built on scientific reasoning, which follow the reasoning of progressive judgments. And it is based on the either/or binary logical structure. For getting out of such a system we need to pursue regressive methods. We need a new

---

[1] Plato (2007), p. 234.

logical method that may help us to negate using the neither/nor premise to analyze the world order of today comprehensively and organically, taking all aspects about human life in the world into account.[2]

Joe can eat the same kind of readymade packaged food, same as anyone else of his age, delivered at the doorstep, and he can, watch any kind of entertainment programs, available on the Internet; and can be accessible, almost freely, using a networking device. If freedom is defined as the liberty of having sex, he can get a girl delivered at home for a one-night lovemaking without any sort of commitment or responsibility that comes up with a regular marriage. If he is completely broke, he can ask for a social security support or can depend on a charity run eatery, like soup kitchen, etc. around his neighborhood. The rest of the freedoms that the democratic society would offer may not evoke any sort of interest in him. He never votes, he never travel abroad, he never will get married or will have any serious relationship with anyone. If Joe is an American he can apply for food stamp as social security assistance, if he is Japanese or Spanish or French he can get social security as monthly allowance money in cash. In Switzerland, he can expect to get $ 1700/month. But, if he is an Indian he can get BPL rations (Below Poverty Line) as food support. Such schemes are there, available depending on the economic and political situation of a particular country. Joe can create a kind of safety net around him with or without being a part of the community. He lives in that net and die within it. When "creative work" is removed from the living world, it brings in a kind of creepy dullness and an excruciating lethargy to human life. Why is creative work important? What it does on the life of a human being? The simple answer to these questions is that it can make living a life worthwhile, and an individual can improve his/her self-worth.

In the case of millennial millionaire like Hillary, the same agonizing creepy dullness sets in; despite being a superrich plutocrat, albeit she can get everything that money could buy. But unlike Joe, she has a family (patch work family). She is a plutocrat by virtue of being born to a global investor as her parent. She went to a school meant only for plutocrats' children. Much of the students' parents were living away and the teachers were very professional as they strictly followed the rules and manuals, given to them that made them behave like teaching machines. As a rule, they should behave legally and politically correct always, when dealing with the plutocrat's children. They all honored her "freedom and freewill" and followed strict political correctness in their jobs. She went to the same company owned school and university where she was taught to follow the kind of values that made her to appreciate her elitist and superior status. It is very simple and naïve. She was taught how to behave politically correct in all aspects of life: How not to offend someone, etc. Notably that is the postmodern narrative about freedom, freewill, and the rights of those who are important to be followed. Those instructions also include supporting the rights of the disadvantaged, the women, the poor, the LGBTQ community, the refugees, etc. that normally come into discussion in the mainstream and social media; but at the same time, she should reject and oppose Nazism, fascism, nationalism, colonialism and religious views, as bigotry.

---

[2]Varghese (2020), p. 9.

As her mother left her, after divorcing her father, to another country with a new husband, her father had made a patchwork family with a woman who had two sons. They were all apparently kind to her. They often met at parties and other such special social occasions and had partied and enjoyed time together. She sometimes talked to her biological mother over phone. But, those interactions ended, without much intimate conversations, or emotional exchanges. Though Hillary had the best chefs in the world, who cook for her, the best foods, she often would eat food delivered to her home from various fast food delivery services. She found the foods prepared by the expert chefs were very delicate, blank and tasteless, and soon enough it made her hungry again, as that it makes her only to eat some salty sugary fluffy fast food again. She is so used to the fast food that she got used to eat at her school and college cafeterias. She mostly spends time by playing games on her computer, smart phone, or the virtual reality consoles that are handy for her; or watching animation movies on those devices; or watching some kinds of porn movies. She hardly travels, never votes, nor has any experience of being touched by a man after the starting of her menses cycle. She is scared of all men including her father who would take only about money and some other silly things, such as the advantages of being rich. For her, he is a constant bore. And also, for her, all men are like beasts with some kind of brute power, waiting to unleash onto her. So, with all men she used to take a preemptive defensive attitude. Lack of human interaction and fear of being profiled, in some manner, in an all-permissive world order is a problem for all millennials to confront in a progressively technologizing and globalizing world order. Therefore, a deep adherence on to political correctness and to a protective notion to "freewill and freedom" act as a defensive cover for all her interactions with "the others" in and around her living world.

Much of the young students of today are either like Joe or Hillary. They are dull and living in a world of their own, where they try their best to protect "freewill and freedom" with a kind of blunt faith. They don't move much, they don't play much together; they just follow what the outside world notably the media narratives tell them to do. And they neither use their legs nor use their hands much. Lack of mobility of the body creates various health issues and most of them are obese. Most of the millennials are bored and therefore dull, inactive and disinterested with life. To avoid the boring situation, they enter into the world of entertainment, especially computer games where one can reset continuously and be a master of his/her fate. The contours of creative work are unknown to them, much less about the hand-brain faculty that helped to create the civilization as we experience today. The gaming logic of reset somehow runs behind all our viewpoints and attitudes.

A kind of monotonous process on growth and progress acts as a metanarrative in to the millennial globalized world order. The continuation of that monotonic process which is based only on the growth of everything including human mind–consciousness—with the acquisition of material wealth and prosperity thence. It is expected to be in a phase of constant progress without any regress. For which we need to adopt a logical method that is suitable for progressive judgments only, where any sort of regresses is condemned. About this monotonic process or the ideology of ever-increasing growth, Russian philosopher and social theorist Alexander Dugin describes "The monotonic process is the idea of constant growth, constant accumulation, development and steady progress. This was the myth of the Nineteenth century. Life, in contrast, is connected to the eternal return".[3] He writes that if we need to reject this idea of monotonic process of growth which is unscientific and inhuman: "the monotonic process in all its forms, that is, evolution, growth, modernization, progress, development, and all that which seemed scientific, in the Nineteenth century but was exposed as unscientific, in the twentieth century."[4] The millennials are to live in a mythical world of such a monotonic process of life where ideas of economic development reign as the guiding idea. The monotonic process acting together with the technological system is what created plutonomy that controls and maintains all human activities of today. The millennials are the innocent victims of such a monotonic process focused on ever increasing growth and prosperity not on human well-being and human flourishing. The very idea of progress and prosperity is retroactive and self-destructive. The progress always faced with regress. It never should be a monotonic process of progress alone. The surge of plutonomy with such vehement destruction of wealth is a good example to cite that monotonous process of progress needs to find a way for self-regress, lest we may face the likelihoods of our unexpected destructions.

References

Dugin, A.: The Fourth Political Theory. Arktos Media, UK (2012)
Plato: The Republic. In: Lee, D. (Trans. and ed.). Penguin Books, London (first pub. 1955), reprint (2007)
Varghese, M.: Nāgārjuna and the Art of Negation. Sanctum Books, New Delhi (2020)

---

[3]Dugin (2012), p. 64.
[4]Ibid, p. 65.

Chapter 9
Plutonomy: The New Financialized World Order

The term plutonomy was introduced by John Malcolm Forbes Ludlow, in the nineteenth century, which meant the science of production and distribution of wealth, but in the twenty-first century it appeared in an internal report of the Citibank, in the journal *Citigroup*, in the USA in the year 2006. This internally circulated report was meant to serve as a document for their future investments and banking activities.[1] This vision document essentially narrates that in the twenty-first century world situation, where a small percentage of the world population, the plutonomy (around 10% or less) would control the major portion of the world wealth, and they would become economically significant. Since "the rest" would use only a negligible portion of the wealth to live on, they would become economically irrelevant and be insignificant. Under plutonomy "the rest" can only act as "the other," to the economic activities of the plutonomic world order, though they are economically irrelevant. This report told an alarming statistic about the precarious economic condition of "the rest" that had emerged, around the world, generated out of unemployment.

Companies began economic restructuring by reducing human workers that become an activity being followed as the method of economic reform everywhere. This activity of denigrating workers' rights on a justifiable share of the created wealth began to result in huge wealth accumulations. Some thinkers feel that even less than 1% has the controlling power over the wealth of "the rest", 99%; and they would be marginalized with the dynamic and active negations of "the other", who are deemed as the irrelevant, insignificant, and inept. Though the wealth is created only to benefit "the other" who are poor, illiterate, backward, etc. Nonetheless, the wealth division or distribution happens at a frighteningly low proportion in the contemporary world, which is unprecedented in the human history. Now the plutocrats are estimated to be less than 1% and "the rest" is more than 99%. The group of "the rest" is soon becoming insignificant and losing all the control over wealth and life. This document was written on the context of the emerging world order in the twenty-first century globalized world, where the economy at large would move in to the control of the

---

[1] Kapur et al. (2015).

© The Author(s), under exclusive license to Springer Nature Singapore Pte Ltd. 2021
M. Varghese, *A Brief History of Creative Work and Plutonomy*,
https://doi.org/10.1007/978-981-15-9263-8_9

super-rich plutocrats, in the system of plutonomy, that will only support the financial industry by doing investment business and the trading of financial products.

9.1   The Plutonomy Charter

9.1.1   The Relevant Points

- The World is dividing into two blocs—the Plutonomy and the rest. The U.S., U.K., and Canada are the key Plutonomies—economies powered by the wealthy. Continental Europe (ex-Italy) and Japan are in the egalitarian bloc.
- Equity risk premium embedded in "global imbalances" are unwarranted. In plutonomies the rich absorb a disproportionate chunk of the economy and have a massive impact on reported aggregate numbers like savings rates, current account deficits, consumption levels, etc. This imbalance in inequality expresses itself in the standard scary "global imbalances". We worry less.
- There is no "average consumer" in a Plutonomy. Consensus analyses focusing on the "average" consumer are flawed from the start. The Plutonomy Stock Basket outperformed MSCI AC World by 6.8% per year since 1985. Does even better if equities beat housing. Select names: Julius Baer, Bulgari, Richemont, Kuoni, and Toll Brothers.[2]

The Greek word plutonomy means the norm of the rich; in other words, a rich oligarchy would rule everything. There is an unexpressed sub text to this strident declaration of the activities of the plutonomy, and that is to declare a new class under which the entire world affairs would be controlled. But in actuality, it comes out of fear and deep ignorance. When we read closely this whole document, it is clear that the investment banks and the financial industry are scared of normal human nature of investing their money in various businesses that would make the world markets to be faced with further turmoil by falling into the cycles of boom and bust, as being happened with many big corporations in the later part of twentieth century. In order to avoid such difficulties, it is presumed that using the base of a few entities in a few countries that could control and manage the whole investment activities in all important sectors. The progress of financial industry, as a major player in shaping world socio political affairs of today has a strong foundation in shaping this kind of draconian perspective. The plutonomy of today is brazenly making "the rest" as "the other", or "the irrelevant" that should be negated, annulled or controlled brazenly by whichever way possible. The 1% plutonomy now has created a new entity of precariats (part-time workers) as "the other", the working class; and as a result, wealth distribution through work is not happening at all. Now that controlling spirit can be seen in the doings of the plutonomy. In other words, the foundational concept of capitalism on "the divine providence" had gone mad. It is impossible to bring in

---

[2] Ibid.

a synthetic unity between the plutonomy and "the rest"—the precarity. Precarity is defined as a situation of insecure employment and insecure income, not helping one to subsist: a situation, the plutonomy should *worry less*, or might disregard completely.

The report was meant to instruct the executives, giving investment directives, for mobilizing resources for future business activities from the plutonomy. When this document was prepared, the plutocrats, under plutonomy, were assumed to be less than 10% of the population in the rich developed countries, that were economically significant, and to be approached for all kind of financial investment activities. One scary aspect of this report is that for the sake of plutonomy the rights of the non-plutonomy ("the rest") would be ignored; which is more than 90% and owning only a miniscule potion of the total national wealth. It also implied that the wealth movement in the future would go into the direct control of the plutonomy that would become influential in all aspects of human "life", the nation-states may have only a limited say over the national wealth. The plutonomy then would negate all the influence and relevance of the "the rest", and also would be able to negate authority of the nation states. The two-value binary logical system could help the plutonomy to negate the opposing value, "the rest", the non-plutonomy, constantly as being stated in Hegelian dialectics, as double negation.[3] The Hegelian philosophy and dialectics help them to generate the "act of Negation", on to "the rest" to create a good situation by selecting the plutonomy as the only choice. Hegel proposed that the perfect spirit of God would negate all worldly imperfections (negatives), that could constantly be negated. He transposed the absolute spirit of God as the absolute spirit of the nation state that would negate all imperfections with an act of "legislative and legal" system that should control all. But that divine godly perfect spirit is now centered on the freewill of plutonomy.[4]

In the globalized postmodern conception of the Hegelian "act of negation" is that Plutonomy represents the perfect sprit and "the rest" represents all the imperfections as they are not required for the financial industry to function smoothly. As the structure of binary logic implies, the spirit of Goodness (God) should negate the bad spirits (devil); the truth negates all untruths; likewise, the plutocrats negate the non-plutocrats and could control them by constantly negating the rights of the new working class, the precariats as the opposite to constantly be negated; like God constantly negates devil to protect the world from evil.

The underpinning prime narrative, in this plutonomy "charter", is to avoid the risk that may emerge in a future economic crisis situation, where normal investors do investments in accordance with certain naïve sentiments. As far as the investment activities are concerned "the rest" of the people would behave erratically, so by

---

[3] Hegel wrote in *Philosophy of the Right*: "The efficient or motive principle, which is not merely the analysis but the production of the several elements of the universal, I call dialectic. Dialectic is not that process in which an object or proposition, presented to feeling or the direct consciousness is analyzed entangled taken hither and thither, until at last its contrary is derived.... But the higher dialectic of conception does not merely apprehend any phase as a limit and opposite, but produces out of this negative a positive content and result." Hegel, G.W.F.: Philosophy of Right, pp. 36–37. Prometheus Books, New York.

[4] Varghese (2020), p. 101.

making their relevance, less important, in any such activities would avoid future economic crashes to a large extent, but would not dared to annihilate them completely. They want "the rest" to exist in subhuman conditions. The perfection provided by the use of artificial intelligence can help the plutonomy to keep up the control mechanism permanently on "the rest". When we scrutinize the world situation of today, we can understand this fact clearly. Now AI controlled investment operations are successfully cushioning economic crashes, but unemployment, economic disparity, economic insecurity, etc. are on the rise, nobody could suggest a solution to mitigate it properly. When the human involvement with work has declined, justifiable wealth distribution suffered drastically.

9.2   The New Dialectic of Plutonomy Versus Precarity

As Karl Marx alluded human "work" would evolve as the synthetic unity in the dialectics between bourgeoisie versus proletarian when the proletariat participate in the dialectical process. If the proletariat is silent then the bourgeoisie would constantly negate the proletariat, using another aspect of Hegelian dialectics, where like the absolute power of God negates devil constantly, bourgeoisies constantly negates the proletariats making them insignificant. Nonetheless, at the time of Marx, proletarians have a control on work even though machines were used in production. But the dialectics between the plutonomy and "the rest", plutonomy wins like the absolute God, because of the use of Artificial intelligence, as AI would control both the plutonomy and "the rest", benefiting only the plutonomy to amass astronomical sums of wealth. Algorithmically programmed machines would do all kinds of business activities without any active creative human interventions. The best ethical activity that these plutocrats do is sending money to charities, like what billionaire plutocrats do through their foundations for "the rest" to have free access to money. Giving free money may make the life of the receiver with a source for minimum sustenance, but eventually making him duller and bored, and would eventually force him to live a life engrossed in the total fear of economic deprivation. When economic insecurity happens, one definitely would lose the control over one's life. Most of those would, just stop doing any kind of creative work, and be enslaved by the plutonomy permanently as a networked system of algorithmic programs could establish control mechanisms that could breed fear. The free money given are meant to mitigate revolts and resentments from the precariats, but when the precariats learn to live their precarious lives, the evolving control system try to manage them by taking away their basic rights as human beings.

The widely held understanding about the existence of plutonomy is that it is a classic case of anomalies, in wealth distribution especially at the time of bourgeois capitalism after the industrial revolutions. And the nation states should be careful in controlling the superrich, and should tax the rich plutocrats more and more, so that the wealth distribution would be equitable and be used for/by everyone. The classical leftist Marxian idea of bourgeoisie versus proletarian is the basis of this understanding. But in the nineteenth century situation where the bourgeoisie would negate the economic rights of the proletarian, but at the same time, the bourgeoisie class were dependent on the "work" of the proletariat, so the revolting proletarians could redefine the bourgeois controlled "world order". The ideology of anarchism originated out of this quest for disruption. But today Plutonomy can ignore anarchism or scare away, any anarchic movement clandestinely, with the ghost of money. The abundant money that plutonomy hold is unimaginably high and for them such scare from the nation-state would be easily mitigatable issues.

In the case of twenty-first century plutonomy, a class struggle is nearly impossible and therefore redundant. Today the plutonomy can thrive on technologies supported by Artificial intelligence, where it doesn't need the supports of the common workers (proletarians) as almost all works can be mechanized that would minimally use human workers. We now have precariats (part-time workers) replacing the proletarian. The hard "work" of proletariat was necessary for the industrial houses to function properly in the earlier industrialization periods; whereas precariats (part-timers) are not attached to any of the business houses directly because they are being hired through a—labor—dispatch company, or through human trafficking agencies. The direct wealth distribution through labor is at its bare minimum today. The labor dispatch companies would take a better part of the workers' compensations. According to Guy Standing: "One understands the reluctance of Marxists to dispense with the dichotomy of capital and labor, though while they dismiss ideas of a new class they often talk of 'middle class,' a most un-Marxian concept. But their desire to compress the precariat into old notions of 'the working class' or 'the proletariat' distracts us from developing an appropriate vocabulary and set of images to guide twenty-first century analysis."[5] The semantics of the term precariat is introduced to address this issue better. The continued growth of middle class is important for creating a balanced society with values that could continue for the existence of life wholesomely. But with the spread of plutonomy, the middle class that represented the bourgeoisie is now getting insignificant and finding it difficult to discern. The middle class through hard work and perseverance could become a part of the bourgeoisie culture. On the other hand, the exponential growth of AI is the reason why such a class is now getting obliterated, and being pushed to a pathetic situation that a miniscule population of plutocrats could replace the hope and aspirations and the economic freedoms of billions of middle-class people. Maybe one of the failures of communism is that they failed to appreciate fully the structure of middle-class society and its importance in protecting traditional values for the human civilization to have formed after millions of years of evolution.

---

[5]Standing (2014), p. 31.

References

Kapur, A., et al.: Plutonomy: Buying Luxury, Explaining Global Imbalances. https://delong.typ
    epad.com/plutonomy-1.pdf. Retrieved on 16 Sept 2015
Standing, G.: A Precariat Charter. Bloomsbury, London (2014)
Varghese, M.: Nāgārjuna and the Art of Negation. Sanctum Books, New Delhi (2020)

Chapter 10
The Salient Features of Plutonomy

In the emerging world order under plutonomy, we may have to use a different method of analysis to understand it clearly. The structure of plutonomy is different from the class order of the pre-globalization periods. We can see that in the emerging class order is unimaginably different from what the Marxian class division would explain. Because it is different from the bourgeoisie versus proletariat interpretations, the modern plutonomy created a different class of wealth control masters and also a different class of workers into its complicated and complex system. According to Guy Standing: "Starting at the top of the income spectrum, the elite or plutocracy consists of a tiny number of individuals who really 'super citizens'; they reside in several countries and escape the obligations of citizenship everywhere while helping to limit the rights of citizens almost everywhere. They are not the 1% depicted by the Occupy movement. They are far fewer than that, and exercise more power than most people appreciate."[1] He argued further on how the old system is syncretic in evolving the new system, "……Each epoch and productive system spawn its class system. As argued in *The Precariat*, globalization, starting in the 1980s, has generated a class structure, superimposed on earlier structures, comprising an elite, a salariat, proficians, an old 'core' working class (proletariat), a precariat, the unemployed and a lumpen-precariat (or under class)[2] I borrow this class divisions to explain the emerging dialectics between plutonomy and precarity; specifically, part-time workers (precariats) and superrich class (plutocrats).

In other words, the "super citizens" who control the wealth through their money (invested on various businesses) are much less than one percent. But the plutocrats could rival the majority of workers that would be precariats (part-time workers) who get to do a major share of works but never get any controls on the activity of wealth creation, and who could demand any kind of rights or privileges, as they could do in earlier times. The rest of the groups in the hierarchy are just a part of the emerging and viciously actualizing plutonomy to keep the wealth creation less wide-ranging but

---

[1]Standing (2014), p. 13.
[2]Ibid, p. 13.

© The Author(s), under exclusive license to Springer Nature Singapore Pte Ltd. 2021
M. Varghese, *A Brief History of Creative Work and Plutonomy*,
https://doi.org/10.1007/978-981-15-9263-8_10

more protective for benefiting only the plutocrats, or the "super citizens". However, the precariats have no authority over the created wealth because they are being hired for executing a particular work and are fired soon after the accomplishment of the job. And no sureties whatsoever are there that they would be hired again. The constant feeling of being discluded would worry a precariat as s/he can only live in the fringes of an organically evolving society; a truly marginalized community with no economic or emotional security at all. And both plutocrats and precariats live practically in the alt-reality world like Hillary and Joe.

After the globalization started in the 1980s, there began a big shift in the dynamics of the work culture on the basis of the control mechanism—from top to bottom—began to vary differently. It is much different from what is being described in the classical Marxian interpretations. The new system is based on the superstructure of plutonomy, where a plutocracy works under the directions of the *plutocrats,* and thus a mechanism for wealth control began. The plutocrats are on the top under which a set of *salariat* (or salaried employees): starting from the CEOs to the junior level executives who notably control the technologized systems and make it functional. Then the system is supported by a group of professionals known as *proficians,* who could work only on contract basis, who would assist the production system giving professional advices, helping the plutonomy to get access to the state of art technologies. They act as consultants, advisors, commissioners, etc. for the business entities that they are hired to represent. This group, the professional consultants, control substantial amount of wealth in the modern businesses that they are used for outsourcing the production work and also for advising the company on various new aspects of production methods and systems. That could ensure low-cost production. These three groups comprise of what the classical Marxism defined as the bourgeoisie. This is the pivot of plutocracy that governs the globalized world order. They can easily implement the ideals of plutonomy, meaning moving the wealth control into the hands of a few entities.

The erstwhile core group of workers, who were known as the proletariat, can be now divided into three groups: The *core working class* (old proletariat). Then the huge number of *precariats* (part-time workers) who may be now around 70% of the total work force; wherein this group includes domestic part-time workers, transnational workers, etc. and also the unemployed who may be living on some sort of charities, social security assistance, etc., and also including with this group are the disinterested workers, the unemployed persons who depend on others, such as parents, family, friends, etc.; and also the working poor, and most importantly the underemployed. And then the third group of *lumpen-precariat* who do all kinds of underclass jobs, such as cleaners, janitors, etc. The old core group—*proletariat*—who used to be the main production workers, now, are insignificant and very miniscule in size. The authority over "work" by the skilled workers who could give creative input to production activities is now challenged by AI systems. A company today need not depend on the creative work input from the skilled work force. The AI systems are so precise on its ability to create and design on the basis of the accumulated data, which now could generate self-design and control the machines by itself. The application of it is employed to control production and to manage distribution networks with minimum human inputs.

The majority of production and services, workers of today, can be defined by the new term, *precariats*. Those who never get any access to steady employment nor proper living wages. Since the manufacturing is fully automatized, and the automatons that could depict human labor are widely prevalent, human labor has nothing significant there to contribute. The new term emerged in the twenty-first century can explain the plight of people like Joe: the meaning of *precariat* is the one, who has to live a life in a precarious situation, that mostly his rights and privileges as a human being are determined on how important he is in making the technological systems functional. The work contribution, he can exercise is that of a watchman. With the effective incursions of artificial intelligence into our times, part-time workers have to compete with the AI. And in reality, when they have to compete with the AI, they would definitely fail.

Nonetheless, this situation was subtly defined by Karl Marx in his communist manifesto: "If one's skill in a job is not allowed to be not appreciated in various modes of production his life would go through precarious situation."[3] When Marx wrote about this, there was a move to start an uncontrolled mechanization that could destroy the workers' rights in the early part of the nineteenth century. He understood that appreciation of human skills in executing a job has more to do with one's life than the economic benefits one may get as payments or other monetary emoluments. A worker may not get to enjoy the creativity involved in doing a job, when the total work system functions on the technologized mechanical systems. Marx, as a thinker who studied classical Greek philosophy, should have understood, philosophically, how creativity can shape up the human personality, and that he was hugely worried about the aspect of work satisfaction, as the world of industrialization and mechanization would systematically deny, the worker, to be creative in executing jobs. In his work on the materialism of Epicurus, the Epicurean doctrine on *eudaimonia* is based on hedonistic pleasures where executing any kind of work creatively should provide a flourish of happiness. He may have understood that If such pleasures are denied, a worker may suffer uncontrollably. However, in comparison to the time of Marx, where machines were largely under the control of humans, but that scenario has now drastically been changed to machines that control humans in almost all aspects of *work* and *life*. The process of mechanization of creativity started since industrialization in all aspects of human life.

However, the policy makers and thinkers of today resolutely consider this situation as a simple instance of the classical rich verses the poor issue, and if we find a more advanced way to distribute wealth to the poor, we may be able to solve the issue of wealth distribution perfectly well. A kind of charitable sympathetic outlook is being meted out towards the poor, as it is the duty of the elite society to protect the poor through charity and social welfare support projects. The systems under plutonomy fear, the poor, the most, because humans have a natural inclination towards justice, goodness, truth, harmony, etc., for the deprived should be controlled through charity.

---

[3]Communist Manifesto (2016).

The entities that follow plutonomy fear the disadvantaged the most, that the poor would wake up one day when they realize the reasons for their poverty, then the poor would revolt against the plutonomy who game them nefariously, like the proletarians revolted against the bourgeoisie at the time of communist revolutions around the world during nineteenth and twentieth centuries. Most of the research and studies onto this is, just, giving some information about the gaming theories of the rich (plutonomy) such as the conspiracy theory, etc. but not on how humans may exist by developing human faculties, doing creative works. We must understand that the origin of plutonomic system is founded on the fear factor of impending economic crashes. So, they created the system to follow one technocratic control mechanism. And now they are disseminating that fear in to the deeper layers of the social fabric through media or through manipulated information, by buying up the entire information spectrum.

The conspiracy theory generally says that an authoritarian oligarchy, in order to fulfill their self-interest, conspires, at will, to control everything, where their motives are only to maximize the self-interest through control and manipulation. To explain it better, we may have to take the view that the millennial class structure is a natural formation, not created by any one controlling entity, but made it possible by the opportune use of artificially created intelligence by declining the natural human abilities harnessed through creative work. The entire world after the industrial revolution believe in the monotonous process and expect that humans can win death or could live longer than 120 years by the resolute and regimented use of science and technology. And we presume that purposeful use of AI is the answer to all our problems.

The new class structure introduced by Guy Standing expresses a self-sustaining power and vitality in plutonomy, where the hierarchical system works smoothly as the AI energizes the hierarchy to move forward without the support of any creative work inputs from the workers. The devastation, of life situation for normal workers, is an unintended consequence of that mission of self-interest maximization of conquering death, diseases, and other such human weaknesses. Along with the conception of the monotonous process, capitalism and the conception of self-interest maximizations helped humans to reach the prosperity that we experience today. The ethical doctrine of self-interest founded on "divine providence" of the Stoic philosophy was one of the motivating ideologies that enthused Adam Smith when he wrote the *Wealth of the Nations*.[4]

The system of plutonomy is the sum vector of several self-interests of many entities such as, for governments more control and taxes, for businesses against loses, for banks for new borrowers, for investment banks for new investment opportunities, for hedge funds for riskier ventures, for entrepreneurs more funds for startups, etc. They all can find due advantages in installing algorithmically controlled AI systems everywhere. As a result, normal human life may end up without finding any kind of fulfillment or contentment as we can slave only to the machines. The self-generated precarious situations all around make suicides, depression, violent behavior etc., as

---

[4]Varghese (2009), p. 237.

the new normal. It is now understood that stopping technologization of everything is nearly impossible. Mostly economic thinkers deeply believe that *creative work* has no major role in human life, it was only a small phase of the monotonous human progress A good number of discerning thinkers today have understood that there is something that goes wrong with the way we think about the creation of wealth and money on the basis of "self-interest maximizations". When the plutocrats grow abundantly by amassing wealth, the precariats also grow by not possessing any kind of wealth, because wealth and money have fallen into the black hole of financialization run by the plutonomy. According to Alexander Dugin the world systems of today have started to assume a kind of financial centric autonomy because of various factors relating to human activities have fallen under plutonomy: "The main challenge is how to organize the post-modern and finance-centric economy around continuing growth, overcoming the widening critical gap between the real economy and the financial sector whose logic and self-interest become more and more autonomous."[5] Now we read financial news that has no connection to production and consumption, that everything is centered on the trade of financial products. A new kind of victimhood would arise where the perpetrators and victims could share that same space. When the financial products can't find markets, that might turn in as valueless paper (digital data) assets.

How self-interest maximization creates the autonomous phase and how would it actually be reflected to the lives of millions? A document published by Oxfam at the Davos forum in Jan 2016 says that 62 individuals own as much wealth as half of the population in the world, i.e. 3,500,000,000 (3.5 billion) individuals.[6] This means each individual rich person's wealth has grown bigger than the national GDPs of many countries. But those kinds of amassed wealth have only dead value, as there are less and less chance for investing it somewhere, or chance for using it to help one's life. The monetary wealth amassed by the plutocrats cannot be used in any other manner. If they give it on charity or as free money, which would collapse the value of money because of oversupply of money against goods. There are no new investment opportunities as all avenues of investment are having dried up, because almost all available wealth is already been financially securitized into some kind of private financial control. In fact, if the plutocrats want to distribute a part of their wealth, they should create more opportunities for the humans to do creative work, then the wealth used would find some value, because earned money and the opportunities to earn more money would help one to spend money confidently for living life, but when that happens, the financial industry would lose its ability to resource wealth: plutonomy may fail with their huge monetized assets.

But, all works are set to be done by using and applying artificial intelligence; the created wealth would be unused and destroyed as it may turn in to dead wealth. There is no job growth and a very negligible amount of money is distributed through that way. All works are done either by AI systems or by precariats (part-time workers).

---

[5]Dugin (2012), p. 77.

[6]https://www.oxfam.org/en/pressroom/pressreleases/2016-01-18/62-people-own-same-half-world-reveals-oxfam-davos-report.

The system of AI has taken over the creativity aspect of work. "Creative work" is the key aspect for happiness in life. Plutonomy would morbid all creative instincts from human life, and could create only plutocrats who would destroy *work and life* of "the rest".

The influence of AI can be explained with the method of the "act of negation", an aspect of Hegelian dialectics. The AI can function as a superstructure that controls everything relating to work making precariats and plutocrats irrelevant even with their active involvement; in which case plutocrats' wealth has only destructive and pseudo value. Scientific rationalism could function only as the foundation of these two-value predications. Act of negation is the result of the application of the two-value logical system. The wealth of plutocrats would negate the wealth of "the rest", with the synthetic power of the Artificial intelligence, where huge wealth accumulation happens for the plutocrats; simultaneously, wealth exploitation from "the rest" materializes. But unused wealth of the plutocrats would make it as the dead wealth. Now artificial intelligence works like the absolute spirit (God), in Hegelian philosophy.[7] The lethargy and indifference in living a life is there, because both plutocrats and "the rest" are made irrelevant by the unseen synthetic power of the artificial intelligence, and that is going to be the absolute power to which everyone needs to submit fully. People are not dared to speak out against it. However, some may criticize about the superrich plutocrats as the postmodern version of the feudal oligarchy or the erstwhile bourgeoisie. But in those times "creative work" played the role of bringing up some sort of synthetic unity.

Life in plutonomy is a curious thing. See the life styles of these two millennials—Joe and Hillary—are same though they are from exactly opposite social and economic background. I think that even with all the differences both are living lonely lives: eating same kind of foods though bought from two different fast-food outlets. They are sleeping on similar kind of beds; playing the same kind of games on the Internet; listening to same kind of music; watching same kind of videos. And both have no interest for any sort of social and community life, as in all probability both would stay single, that they never going to commit into any marriage or any kind of relationship, because both are afraid that they may lose their "freewill and freedom" on such lifelong commitments. Equally both have no idea on what are the do-ables and the non-do-ables in life. And both never have learned anything about the importance of maintaining a spiritual life. Both live in the world of innumerable propaganda narratives. The media is the prime source of education, information, knowledge source, where each hears only the narrative that suits their chosen comfort zones and feelings. The mass media discharges various kinds of fears and cautions to control people by injecting more fear into their thoughts. Actually, both live in some kind of unknown fear and anxiety. Fear creates ignorance; ignorance creates suffering; and suffering forces people to end their lives without any cognizable reason as can be seen in the burgeoning suicide cases of today. Wealth distributions through work and good life have some unknown innate organic spiritual aspects that are yet to be defined in the postmodern context. Notably in the postmodern globalized world the

---

[7]Varghese (2020), p. 110.

faith in protecting "freewill and freedom" is similar to that of a crusader on "Cross and Holy Trinity": only death can detract them such a resolute faith. The purpose this book is to investigate that crucial aspect. Why is human creative work important in defining our lives? What is there in the conception of *work and life*?

References

Communist Manifesto: The original text at: https://www.marxists.org/archive/marx/works/1848/communist-manifesto/ch01.htm#007//. Retrieved on 17 July 2016

Dugin, A.: The Fourth Political Theory. Arktos Media, UK (2012)

Standing, G.: A Precariat Charter. Bloomsbury, London (2014)

Varghese, M.: A Dialectical Analysis of the Conception of 'Self Interest Maximization' and Economic Freedom. In: Green, R.S., Mun, C. (eds.). Blue Pine, Honolulu (2009)

Varghese, M.: Nāgārjuna and the Art of Negation. Sanctum Books, New Delhi (2020)

Chapter 11
The Marxian Discourse on Capitalism: Bourgeoisie Versus Proletarian Narrative

Karl Marx's discourse on the bourgeoisie-controlling proletarian's life is arguably a persuasive thought on capitalism since the time of industry-1.0. This Marxian doctrine had analyzed capitalism that is hugely influenced by Protestant Christian religiosity, especially the conception of the "providence of God". Honesty and hard work of an individual worker should be rewarded, and the truthful would be paid well beyond everything else that the faithful only could do the God's work. One should be praised for spreading the knowledge of the all protecting God, and one also be provided with equal opportunities, as for generating the community of a vibrant middle class (the burghers). Thereby the master–slave narrative of the pre-industrial world could be annulled. And everyone in the community should be given equal opportunities for getting good education and job. They followed the Biblical dictum: "If anyone wants to be first, he must be the last of all and the servant of all." [Mark 9.35] and such a person would be resolutely following the ideals of the "providence of God", as the way of living life. Based on these ideals of the "providence of God" figured variously, in the interpretations of protestant Christianity by John Calvin, that made industrial capitalism to find its religious roots. That again made the method of capitalism to be followed with a kind of religiosity for the hardworking ordinary people. The ideals of capitalism with the deep trust in the "providence of God" changed the history of Europe in the modern period, but not in the postmodern period, where such lofty ideas are deemed as reactionary and bigoted.

In Europe, at the time of the first industrial revolution (industry-1.0), wealth creation was the central concept for all economic activities, because it was presumed that the created wealth would be distributed by providing work to a large section of people, and the owner was also a part of the working class. They would then be forming the middle class that could grow, very well, by the knowledge learned from work. Some may become rich through acquisitions of knowledge and hard work. The presumptive belief behind this attitude was that the leaders of the society help everyone to use one's God given gifts to help them grow naturally. Providence of God (nature) should be understood as the natural ability of humans to learn more about one's living world. The owner of an enterprise is also the servant of God who

© The Author(s), under exclusive license to Springer Nature Singapore Pte Ltd. 2021
M. Varghese, *A Brief History of Creative Work and Plutonomy*, https://doi.org/10.1007/978-981-15-9263-8_11

received that providence as his ability to create and manage wealth. Since providence of God is the conduit that really functions in this case. The worker and owner should act for benefiting each other. Notably, the owner should protect the honesty of those who depend on him and helping him. The early capitalists were church going pious Christians. An egalitarian system might be formed under the strict regime based on the "providence of God": Providence in the form of work skills; providence in the form of creating wealth and managing it, etc. The middle class (burghers), then, formed a steady social base of producers and consumers; and therefore, they were respected highly by the society. This should have resulted in the formation of the new wealthy class—the bourgeoisie.

Unlike the earlier wealthy class—the feudal oligarchy, the new bourgeoisie class comprised of those who are educated, skilled, and understood science and technology, could reach to the status of middle class and by better education and hard work could reach to the top, partaking the status of the owner class. On the other hand, those who were uneducated, unskilled, and never understood science and technology should have been marginalized. The plight of those low skilled poor working under-class workers were a concern for the newly industrializing society, where their income was insufficient even to meet the basic needs. The mass of unskilled labor became a kind of social burden in the industrial world; whereas, skilled workers were a part of the newly emerging middle class. Soon, the underclass become an object of scorn and contempt, and their labors turned in to be exploited easily, as they had no bargain power as being not accepted as a part of the industrial economy. They then formed as an insignificant working class that they could not better their lives through hard work, as the "providence of God" concept taught them, by religious discourses, that they would be protected by the emerging world order. But they had been progressively excluded, because they had no way to use their God given skills. And the society ruthlessly exploited their backwardness and poverty, by objectifying them as losers, with a subtext narrative that poverty is sin, and sinners should be punished. Marx carefully defined them as the proletariat—the underclass workers replacing the serfs of the preindustrial world order. He defined them as the new underclass of capitalism in the historical progress of class antagonism.

The industrialization had generated a new set of owners to the property and wealth or the newly rich middle class (burghers) who improved their lives further through hard work and education. Marx had observed them as the newly evolved master class of the industrialization, noticeably replacing the feudal system, and he introduced a new term to name them, the bourgeoisie. The new class were not just the middle class (burghers) but also had members from the feudal class who were educated. A majority of the newly formed middle class were from the former serf class who were underclass in the middle age Europe. Various socio-religious changes since fourteenth century, such as the Christian humanist movement, European enlightenment, industrialization, etc. had changed the fate of those underclass serfs that they could gain a lot of political and economic power through education and right attitudes; whereas the uneducated and unskilled workers turned in as the new underclass.

During the industrialization period, the Christian thoughts on "freedom and freewill", founded on the conception of the "providence of God", began to flourish everywhere. There existed an unseen misery in the society due to inequitable distribution of wealth to the less skilled workers and also there existed, a huge exploitation of their work by the bourgeoisie class. As being an insignificant and unorganized majority, the proletarians' effort had not at all been well regarded. In the capitalist system, originally founded on high spiritual values, started to configure the most immoral and reprehensible definition on "freewill and freedom", by the new class of wealth controllers, the bourgeoisie could reap all the goodness that were originally founded on values that could help to form an equitable organic society. The interpretations and narrations began to flourish favoring the formation of bourgeois culture; the motivational catch phrases like the "sky as the limit", or "one must seek happiness at any cost as life happens only once"; therefore, there is nothing wrong in pursuing once greed as the root of one's self interest.

On the other hand, the poor working class had to live in limitless poverty in some part of the industrialized world. They lived on the edge. And their plight was hugely ignored by all, as the wealth of the bourgeois thrived. Industrialization, colonialism, finding of Americas, etc. had increased the power of the bourgeoisie. And Protestant Christianity and its religiosity, which is liberal and conservative at the same time, had helped the subjugation by the bourgeoisie over the working class (proletariat). The helpless unorganized workers were exploited using various means by the bourgeoisie for satiating their greed for profit. Marx writes: "The bourgeoisie, wherever it has got the upper hand, has put an end to all feudal, patriarchal, idyllic relations. It has pitilessly torn asunder the motley feudal ties that bound man to his "natural superiors," and has left remaining no other nexus between man and man than naked self-interest, then callous "cash payment." ... It has resolved personal worth into exchange value, and in place of the numberless and indefeasible charted freedom—Free Trade. In one word, for exploitation, veiled by religious and political illusions, naked, shameless, direct, brutal exploitation."[1] The feudal oligarchic system had exercised a kind of idyllic patronizing kind of relationships over the serfs and the rest of the society that existed for many centuries in the western Europe during the entire middle ages. There should have been a natural organic relationship existed between different communities in such a society which was based on serving the feudal oligarchy, and the feudal system gave a space for serfs to survive by serving their interests. The process of industrialization and the accent on progress, development, freedom, growth, modernization, and spiritual sanctions had created a monotonic process.[2] This monotonic process should have thwarted the man-to-man relationship existed between serfs and the feudal oligarchy. The bourgeoisie who followed the path of "self-interest maximization" with a motto of "sky is the limit" and a double down accent on to find "freewill and freedom" had continuously followed that monotonic process with strong commitments. This monotonic process that had worked with Protestant religiosity, created a new value system that was founded on money which began to be applied in for each and every aspect of human relationships. As a subtext such religiosity was serving the interests of the bourgeoisie considered poverty as

---

[1] Communist Manifesto (2016).
[2] Dugin (2012), p. 66.

"sin" and the poor should be undergoing some kind of divine retribution, of being cursed by God.

The growth of the industrial world was engineered by the growth of the capitalistic system where the bourgeoisie began to control all aspects of life using systematized scientific economic management method. The speed of capitalism in the reindustrialization—industry-2.0—period that had exploited resources exponentially could make a kind of enviable material progress in the twentieth century for the capitalist industrialized western world. The ideological systems, like capitalism and communism that found its progress in the post war period, had focused on aggressively applying scientific systems founded on scientific rationalism drawn from the dialectical methods introduced by Hegel. Hegel's spiritual version of the "providence of God" helped the capitalists to thrive with Christian religiosity and piety. For Hegel the Christians, who are blessed with the Christian way of living in the new era, would be discharging their spiritual duties, and capitalism is the best way for that. However, the materialist interpretation of the same doctrine by Karl Marx had acted as a resistance mechanism against the ruthless methods of capitalism using spiritualism as the cover. But, with the failure of communism, the exploitation of the marginalized under the sway of capitalism thrived. Nonetheless, with the twenty-first century globalization and with the opportunities for trans-national economic activities, the capitalism now turned into plutonomy with a huge global reach where wealth confiscation happens with bare minimum distribution making the dialectics between bourgeoisie versus proletariat redundant and obsolete. Under plutonomy, the distribution of the huge wealth of the plutocrats is not happening at all. However, they are not worried about it at all, but for distributing their unused wealth everywhere, now they are influencing political decisions by creating plutocracy—of lobbyists, consultants and special interest groups; and by applying AI systems everywhere, they are also trying to establish technocratic controls systems for instilling fear.

Almost all the major economic and intellectual activities were focused on the concern of the western world, since eighteenth century, while the concerns and problems of the other parts of the world were not particularly been discussed in the academic or public discourses. Because of which, the doctrine of diffusionism is being followed everywhere today: "The Western culture tries to imbue other non-western cultures. The world systems, today, follow the sociopolitical culture of the west."[3] The Western view on everything began to thrive and prosper around the whole world. The societies in China, India, Levant, etc. began to follow the western views. The methods of huge exploitation of wealth become a new normal that everyone needs to follow everywhere. The weaponized financial arm of the postmodern capitalism, nowadays, tries to exploit more wealth from every other part of the world to help to run their financial industry successfully. When that financial industry set to thrive, all fairness in the wealth distribution would get constrained and restricted, because it should focus only on wealth creation and wealth confiscation from "the other".

---

[3] Barkan (1992), p. 39.

Marx knew about this coercing power of the bourgeoisie that, in pursuit of wealth, they might lose all moral and ethical and religious inclinations. And they would use all available methods in order to suppress the bargain power of the proletariat and common folks, who resolutely follow all aspects of moral, ethical and religious teachings and traditions. The bourgeoisie used this weakness as a chance to exploit the hard work of the proletariat, because for bourgeoisie, the prime aim of all social relations is of finding economic benefits only. That is why Marx thought true democracy will ensue naturally when the proletariat get their due share of economic independence. Knowing the intellectual vulnerability and emotional susceptibility of the working class, Marx told the European communists to stay with the proletariat and work towards their ultimate empowerment.[4] During twentieth century, the major communist countries like China and the Soviet Union (Russia) formed communist bloc of countries and aggressively attacked the bourgeois values of capitalism, and also used an authoritative and centrally controlled administrative system, by the communist oligarchy, to the distribution of wealth for benefiting the common-man worker. They called their system as the people's republic and argued that it is the system with true democratic values where the workers' rights are being duly protected and given high value recognition for the labor of the working class, who formed the majority.

The communist system truly believed that only a proletariat-controlled system could effectively fight the greed of the bourgeois values of the industrial capitalists. The bourgeoisies' greed, for more, have promoted an utter disregard for human values especially the importance of *creative work* in human life. Marx fervently discussed thoroughly this aspect of life in the communist manifesto drafted in association with Frederic Engels for the communist activists in Europe and published it as the main manifesto document for the communist movements since 1848. However, Communism is only a kind of divergent view of the capitalism's founding principles based on the protestant Christian doctrines on "providence of God", just replacing it with "providence of nature" and with the aggressive materialistic interpretation of Hegelian dialectics, where the Hegelian doctrine on the progress of objective spirit is replaced by dialectical materialism, meaning the objective spirit can be discerned by a dialectical process of the historical control of the material wealth of nations that, according the Aristotle should be used for benefiting everyone in a nation state. As for Marx and the communists that control was syphoned away by the crocked acts and fake religiosity of the bourgeoisie in capitalism.

Communism, as a sociopolitical and economic system, has suffered huge setbacks in recent times due to its aggressive stand against capitalism and bourgeois middle class values. In fact, in the era of globalizations the class difference between bourgeoisie and proletariat has turned out to be very thin. It was not as strong as in the former feudal versus serfs or bourgeoisie versus proletariat discourse. During industry-3.0, it was only education and acquirement of skills in knowing and working with high technology in applying it in the industrial work that mattered much. However, it created space for a new dialectical relationship to take shape; and now the influence of Protestant Christian doctrines on capitalism is less influential in the

---

[4]Ibid.

western civilizations. In our times, the ideologically founded systems like communism and capitalism are irrelevant. But the flair of such ideologies is still alive, and plutonomy uses the ideals of communism and capitalism expeditiously nowadays. And now the new dialectic is between plutocrats and precariats, where the synthetic power of AI makes sure that the precariats never could find their due share from the society.

References

Barkan, E.: The Retreat of Scientific Racism. Cambridge University Press, New York (1992)
Communist Manifesto: The original text at: https://www.marxists.org/archive/marx/works/1848/communist-manifesto/ch01.htm#007/. Retrieved on 17 July 2016
Dugin, A.: The Fourth Political Theory. Arktos Media, UK (2012)

Chapter 12
Capitalism and the Religiosity of Protestantism

Karl Marx found that the puritanical authority of the bourgeoisie, had drawn from two imposing authoritative western intellectual sources. They were the John Calvin's interpretation of Protestant Christian religiosity founded on the conception of "providence of God", and on the Hegelian dialectics. The founding thought that inspired John Calvin was the stoic conception of the "Providence of Nature" that he reinterpreted basing on the Christian doctrines. The nature which is a creation of God provides everyone with everything, and humans have an authority over it as being the chosen creation of God. The other influential principle for the bourgeoisie is the Hegelian interpretation of Aristotelian philosophy, where the absolute of God's will (thought), is revered. The spiritual authority drawn from the Calvin's and the Hegelian views founded the core values for the Protestant Christianity that had gone deeply into the making of the bourgeoisie, giving them an undue spiritual authority on wealth of the entire world. In the modern scientific world order, the inception of the "providence of nature" is being interpreted as "wealth", which needs to be exploited using techno-scientific knowledge that wealth in any form should be exploited to benefit everyone, so the society need not wait for God's providence.

Colonialism, since seventeenth century was a by-product of this imposing authoritarian thought. The controlling authority over wealth is always been supported by a metanarrative of charity and "divine providence". The so-called Christian values became the universal values in the era of colonialism: the purity of "the right", who should be the true followers of God in human form—Jesus Christ—would make right decisions based on the providence and equality that is enshrined in the protestant Christian religious values. The modern worldviews were hugely influenced by the Christian virtues, the white racial purity, and the white superiority. The idea of providence as a way to redeem the world from the eternal sin of poverty had given a kind of moral and spiritual superiority to the followers of Protestant Christianity. The definition that poverty is sin, and the way to solve it is only by economic freedom, and a true Christian who chose to follow the "right path" taught by Jesus Christ would help redeem all from the sin of poverty for living a virtuous life. The book, *Philosophy of Right* by Hegel discusses this authority on controlling the wealth by a

© The Author(s), under exclusive license to Springer Nature Singapore Pte Ltd. 2021
M. Varghese, *A Brief History of Creative Work and Plutonomy*,
https://doi.org/10.1007/978-981-15-9263-8_12

true Christian who would work tirelessly towards achieving the aim of creating the "kingdom of God" on earth, through economic prosperity, and dividing the wealth justifiably to everyone concerned. He also alluded that the Germanic tribe are true inheritors of that divine authority as they are inherently brave, intelligent, and rational to adopt to the scientific ways of thinking and living.

Therefore, the view of "the right" was considered as the spiritual authority of the God fearing, Bible reading, church going, hardworking Christian, and their unstinted deep faith in the teachings of Jesus Christ. And the spiritual authority of the Bible should be what might control his life and actions. The supremacy of capitalistic value was the supreme spiritual virtue for this brand of Christianity, especially its spirit of creating the "Kingdom of God" on earth for everyone by creating and distributing wealth. A true capitalist should provide and respect the honest work of any other "worker" with a view on equanimity of humanity and on basic human rights to coexist. His life should epitomize how the Christian notion of "freewill and freedom" to love all human beings and the humanity. Marx was skeptical about the honesty and authenticity of such kind of religiosity in the modern industrialized world, where bourgeoisie vision of self-interest maximization was the only motivating factor, and the bourgeoisie would use all coercing methods, to exploit the ignorance of the common worker, about the advent of the kingdom of God. The establishment of the "kingdom of God" should be the essential purpose of human life according to the Judeo-Christian religious beliefs. The Christian notion of freewill should be adopted by Martin Luther from the philosophical view of Saint Augustine that soul of a person should have the freedom to choose all that could help him to realize God. In that effort the soul of man should be absolutely free. Modern capitalism selectively used that freewill and freedom in matters relating to wealth for benefiting the bourgeois class.

Marx was seriously doubtful about, in accepting these obscure religious values in wealth management by the modern bourgeoisies, who thrive mostly on seizing and amazing lots of wealth by any means possible. He wrote about the bourgeoisie control on Christian religion and how they use the so-called human values to increase their power in every aspect of human life. About this intermixing of Lutheran Christian values with the scientific rationalism of Hegel, Marx wrote: "When the ancient world was in its last throes, the ancient religions were overcome by Christianity. When Christian ideas succumbed in the eighteenth century to rationalist ideas, feudal society fought its death battle with the then revolutionary bourgeoisie. The ideas of religious liberty and freedom of conscience merely gave expression to the sway of free competition within the domain of knowledge."[1] The Protestant Christian religion after Hegel followed his idea of –scientific— "reasoning" for realizing the spiritual nature of God, which gave the bourgeoisie a kind of divine endorsement to accumulate wealth. The bourgeoisie weaponized the benign ethical values of Protestant Christianity notably its application of scientific reasoning, to exploit the hard work of the common workers, Hegelian thoughts on human reasoning as the path towards God had stroked the fears of common man who used to follow faith as a way to God.

---

[1]Communist Manifesto (2016).

The capitalist bourgeoisie thrived by using the religiosity of the ignorant common man for own benefits. But the irreligious plutocrats live in a different world order, where the common men are not ignorant religionists, yet they could use human ignorance on ethical values, democracy, social equality, freedom, etc. only to thrive on amazing more wealth, by creating the draconian system of naïve narratives.

The main argument of the post Hegelian protestant movement was that God's existence and presence is experiential for everyone and one must strive to realize that omnipresence as God; and scientific rationalism must be the way to realize the absolute spirit of God. A true Christian should strive to conserve and preserve those God given values of providence, right thoughts, reasoning and wisdom. This view on religiosity out rightly turned against the adherence to convictions, beliefs, and traditions promoted by the Holy Roman Catholic church. But Hegel proposed that the absolute spirit of God could be realized through the faculty of reasoning that could make substantial changes in a person's life as intelligence should control reasoning. The one who could use reasoning would understand how the true essence of the natural world was created by God with his infinite wisdom. Education invoking the faculty of reasoning could help humans to know the secrets behind all the natural laws, which ultimately would reveal the pneumatic spirit of Jesus Christ. This is the religious framework for applying scientific reasoning in the modern world. The Protestant movement challenged the authority of the Roman Catholic Church, which had supposedly subjugated the rights of common-men under the feudal oligarchic control. In the middle ages, Catholicism was the religion of the common folks as well as the feudal lords and was the only unifying factor, but faith in God as trinity was the main framework that controlled everyone's religiosity in Christianity. In the dialectic between faith and reason, in the modern world—reason—won.

The philosophical works of Hegel who promoted Protestant values added a new intellectual fervor and strength to the Protestant movement and capitalism in the industrialized world. The freed serfs, or the common man, of the feudal society who could use reasoning found a new energy to fight against the feudal oligarchic power structures and the authority of the ruling classes. The Hegelian narratives on Christianity and reasoning were the forerunner of capitalism, where education played the role of the liberating spirit, and considered it as the right path possible for one who might accept the way of Protestant Christianity. Based on Hegelian philosophy, one needs to be educated in scientific reasoning for to be an active member of the society. The objective absolutistic spirit of Christ is the nature of the "world spirit" which is the essential spirit of rationalism. The nation state should depict the exact nature of the kingdom of God on earth. And according to Hegel, German nation state was the model for everyone else to be followed as it adopted the Christian values as the guiding doctrinal thought.

The modern-day capitalism with its roots in Protestant Christianity is viewed by Mark C. Taylor as the main reason for the spread of capitalism and free market economy like a religion. He observed, "Capitalism would not have developed as it did without the literacy and numeracy cultivated by Protestantism. … While Catholicism is organized around rituals and sacraments, Protestantism centers on the Word in scriptures and sermon. During the Middle Ages, literacy was confined almost exclusively to the clergy and the Bible was in Latin... Breaking the church's monopoly on literacy had important consequences that extended far beyond religious life. People who knew how to read were able to make the transition from agrarian to mercantile society and later to industrialism much more easily... By encouraging literacy and numeracy, Protestantism helped to create the educated workforce that early capitalism needed."[2] The educated work force had hugely supported industrialization and the kind of urban life style that followed thereafter. Protestant Christianity played a significant role in popularizing education, and the educated class of common men could have aspired for a higher social status; whereas, the uneducated middle class could only get a pitiable lifestyle much worse than that of the erstwhile serfs. The society was naturally divided into two, on the basis of education: those who could be educated and be a part of the industrialized world would get more, because of their knowledge, which was necessary for to be a part of the bourgeoisie class. But the uneducated could only get less, because their labor was available in plenty, because of their naivety and ignorance due to their adherence to the traditional religiosity based on faith. The change from agrarian economy to the industrial economy was quick and fast with the circulation of gold backed paper money in the same period. Transactable paper currency had revolutionized the distribution of wealth into the different layers of the society.

The wealth distribution in the society was exclusively done in the form of distributed money and that money helped circulation of the wealth, where the society and economy had grown in tandem. The power of money in matters relating to economy had increased steadily; and the leading spiritual thought of guidance was the Christian idea of providence and charity. The newly liberated men through education could do everything to replicate the act of God, helping everyone by providing an honest living. People, directly in European countries, were attracted to this attitude of Christianity originally introduced by the followers of Martin Luther who interpreted the "providence of God" in a language understandable to the common men who had no freedom in the erstwhile feudalism-controlled systems under the sway of the faith-based religiosity of Catholicism of the Holy Roman Empire. Those who attained freedom through education have themselves called as the dwellers of the "city of God" or the civilized ones. This concept originally being vivaciously narrated in the philosophical works of Saint Augustine who proposed, the love and compassion of God should adorn perpetually in the "city of God" and be followed by all true Christians. Contexually, Martin Luther was an Augustinian monk.

But in the industrial world, the interpretation of the "city of God" was taken over by the educated and rich western men, whose acts, would be there to help the uneducated and poor. They also went into an effort to propagate the Western civilized thoughts to the uncivilized savages, who live in the non-western non-Christian cultures like Persia, India, China, and countries in Africa. Colonialism thrived because of this patronizing attitude of the so-called Western civilized men. Karl Marx rejected this kind of division of humanity as civilized and uncivilized. He called the educated and

---

[2]Taylor (2014), pp. 58–61.

rich as the dwellers of a fictitious city of God where the sole aim is to confiscate and hoard wealth. He called them the bourgeoisie; and the ignorant poor common man who never could be a part of that city, as the proletariat. But the dwellers of the "city of God"—bourgeoisie—are not spiritually inclined to following the ideology of "divine providence" that was the rule in the city, but used it as a way to propitiate their middle-class values of greed and passion for getting more.

The Catholics soon introduced the mission of spreading literacy and numeracy as a part of their mission and introduced it through the mission-work of the Jesuits, Franciscans, etc. to introduce scientific reasoning as the new way of thinking. Through colonization these ideas soon spread into other continents, regions, and countries. The enthusiasm of the common men into the so-called Protestant values put pressures on others to follow the ways and views of that religion. That began to set a kind of intellectual revolution during industrialization. The influence of Protestantism towards a new world order is explained by Scottish philosopher Thomas Carlyle as: "If Luther has not stuck to his guns at the Diet of Worms, where he stood before the Holy Roman emperor and refused to recant ('Here I stand'), there would have been no French Revolution and no American: the principle that inspired those cataclysmic events would have been killed in the womb."[3] Holy Roman empire was the pan European political entity that was controlled by the dictates of Roman Catholic Church in the Middle Ages. Almost all the thinkers of the West in the modern period were inspired by this act of Martin Luther.[4] Philosopher Hegel's workers are all inspired by the spirit of Protestant religious beliefs conserved by Luther and his followers. Hegel also believed and propagated the view that the followers of Protestant Christian religiosity as the real men who would love "freedom" and could rationally understand the word of God and would restructure his/her worldly life in line with ideals of "divine providence" and charity. Protestant Christian religion has given its followers a kind of individualistic freedom to connect directly with God and to self-identify and negate all the evils in the world. At the time of colonialism this spirit of the righteousness of Christianity had invigorated the western colonists as the civilized high culture and the rest of the world in Asia, Africa, the Americas as the savages, whose beliefs were much lesser than that of the White race. Colonization had thieved because of this hubristic vigor and enthusiasm of the Western white men.

Hegel's reverence to Protestant Christianity can be seen in his proclamation: "The German Spirit the spirit of the new World. Its aim is the realization of absolute truth as the unlimited self-determination of Freedom-that Freedom, which has its own absolute form itself as its purport. The destiny of the German people is, to be the bearers of the Christian principle."[5] Hegel was very proud of the racial superiority of the Teutonic tribe of the Nordic region, which we could see in his seminal work

---

[3] Ibid, p. 41.

[4] The Holy Roman Empire included the territories of present-day Germany, Switzerland, Liechtenstein, Luxembourg, Czech Republic, Slovenia, Austria, Croatia, Belgium, and the Netherlands as well as large parts of modern Poland, France and Italy.

https://www.britannica.com/place/Holy-Roman-Empire. Retrieved on 15/07/2020.

[5] Hegel (1956), p. 341.

The Philosophy of Right (1821). Hegel devised his idea of scientific rationalism as the conduit on the individual freedom to choose and follow the protestant Christian ideals. The ideals of Christianity should be the guiding spirit and the righteous way. The pneumatic spirit of Christ, God in human form as the only absolute for which all our actions would converge. He wrote: "What is rational is real; and what is real is rational."[6]The loving, protecting, providential spirit of Christ is the nature of that ultimate reality which one can realize using reasoning.

For achieving the scientific rational mind, we should follow the real spirit of Christianity, which would be deduced into the higher scientific dialectic. By following such a dialectic, we could find, how God created the world by scientifically analyzing empirical evidences, and also could establish rationally the creative spirit of God that is uniformly acting on everything and everywhere. The unity spirit of God is embedded in each of the entities created though a rational process that is discernable to human intelligence: only humans could do that. But at the same time, to establish it comprehensively, Hegel knew very well that knowing about the color "black" is necessary for understanding about the color "white", similarly for discerning, "devil" for "God", "bad" for "good", "antithesis" for "thesis", and so on. But in normal life, we might not find pure black or a recognizable devil everywhere; we could only find "shades of gray" in the place of pure "black", and shade of ignorance and of evil in the place of devil. But we could arrive at the pure black for knowing about, its antithesis, pure white by negating everything that is not black; or it does by bringing the amount of whiteness into zero from gray. By knowing what is black helps us to know white. This method of using negation for the removal of ignorance through refined thought and that is the method employed in the Hegelian scientific rationalism, ultimately to find the creative spirit of God.

As for Hegel, the double negation should methodically be done and should not be based on personal feelings, impressions, belief, convictions, etc. that might shadow and deter our mind. Hegel might have thought that finding a singular universal theory about God could be achieved through scientific reasoning which is extant in the doctrine of Protestant Christianity; he declined all other religious and traditional views as primitive denigrating to the natural human freedom to know the reality, the spirit of Jesus Christ, God incarnated into the world. Hegelian philosophy of "right" finds a synthetic unity with the absolute "right" negating all wrong views where "pneumatic spirit of Christ" is the only help. In that way, he brought down the realm of new world order to the religious spirit of Protestantism with a scientific turn. Hegel reinterpreted Aristotelian idea of reason to know the true being of the entities and the unity that stimulates all entities.

Hegel using his philosophical doctrines negated the traditional views of Catholicism, Buddhism, Vedic religions (Hinduism), Islam and all other religious views to publish his views on the Protestant Christian conception of the (pneumatic) spirit of Christ, as the true being of the unity, that is also objectively discernable. He viewed all other religions were following traditional dogmatic beliefs based on faith and convictions, not on reasoning and critical scientific evaluations. He argued that the

---

[6]ibid, p. xxvii.

Pneumatic spirit of Christ is the foundation of the absolute truth (God in human form) that is objectively understandable; and also argued that scientific methods should be the way to reach that absolute truth in the form of concepts and theories. He concluded that pure reason is equal to God, or the ways of reason could reach us to the perfect thought of God, the ultimate reality. He invoked the view of Aristotle on reasoning to prove his point. As for Aristotle the ability to use reasoning is the nature of God in man, or the true being of soul that strive for its eternal unity. Hegel might have, also, thought that the proof for God could be discerned by rationally analyzing the objects created by God, and the method, to be adopted, is scientific analyses and theoretical judgments. We can see that kind of religiosity in matters relating to science and technology, and the world systems created out of it. Theoretical judgments are the foundations of everything in the world since nineteenth century following the Hegelian exhortations on scientific reasoning.

Therefore, with the advent of capitalism, the narratives of a new human personality have emerged, the protestant Christian persona, who chose to follow the path of reasoning that could lead one to the absolute knowledge about God and the conception of "providence". This is the idea on which Calvin founded the principle doctrine of capitalism. Calvin adopted this idea of providence from the works of stoic philosophers like Seneca. Stoicism promoted self-sacrifice as a spiritual method to redeem one from suffering. This new personality would be working towards the benefit of the whole world, and he should help to fight the sin of poverty: one should generate wealth and distribute it by offering "work" with a living wage, and by offering charity to "the rest", and thereby everyone should be benefited from the created wealth. The modern capitalist plutocrat who conserve the values of Protestant movement is expected to do the work of God on earth for creating, protecting and distributing wealth to benefit the world. But as an unintended consequence or accidental aftermath, while adopting extreme reasoning in matters relating to wealth, the capitalist could feel that he could replace God—the absolute spirit—through his immense control on wealth. Today, many plutocrats have self-defined themselves as God or doing God like acts, because of their ability to use the invisible "hand of money" in manipulating all sociopolitical decisions.

The direct access to wealth, from the colonies including America, made this nineteenth century bourgeoisie capitalist personalities' presence evermore invincible and powerful. They began to amass wealth, claiming that the created wealth would be used for uplifting the humanity from poverty, illiteracy and backwardness. Mark C. Taylor argues that the protestant Christian movement initiated by Calvin is the true guiding spirit of the capitalist bourgeoisie: "For some of the Calvin's radical followers, the Reformation, like the act of creation, was not a once-and-for all event but is an ongoing dynamic process. The restlessness, which is both creative and destructive is not merely spiritual but extends to social, political, and economic relations as well. What Hegel eventually labels "the restlessness of the negative", a secularized version of divine activity, which Marx reinterpreted as the ceaseless circulation and expansion of capital. The negativity inherent in Protestantism's perpetual Reformation unexpectedly reappears in the relentless planned obsolescence of modern capitalism."[7] The religiosity of Protestantism centered on providence and charity once again reinforced the propagation of capitalism with a human face into the poor underdeveloped countries during industry-3.0. But in actuality the injection of capital made a kind of resistance as that money has nothing more to securitize, and the income from money is negligible. The methods of injecting capital into the so called under developed areas to make it as exploitable wealth is a method continuously followed by plutonomy today, wherein unusable money could find value and could control national wealth of the poorer countries. That has done under the guise of development and progress under plutonomy, but huge wealth confiscation of the poor is done to wasting it in the form of financial products with no practical use. It is similar to the housing properties brought by the plutocrats in many big cities, as a destination for their investments, are used by none but decaying as time goes by.

The capitalist personality who adopted protestant Christian religion, should uphold the middle-class values, he should follow the ideals of the true path of Christianity taught by the Holy Bible, he should also believe in the values of freedom, freewill together with the virtues of Goodness and truth. Therefore, one must also be educated in understanding the scientific rationalism, and should believe in the Calvin's notion on the omnipresence of the "divine providence" as a way of life. The idea of divine providence, of heaven on earth, shattered the static hierarchical universe of the Middle Ages.[8] This spirit of Calvin's conception of Protestant Christian values had negated all other socio-religious views and values of all other religions and cultures as the dialectically opposing knowledge. The total negation of all other religious views including Catholic and Orthodox Christian views on wealth management made capitalism a property of those who followed the ideals of Protestant religion. All capitalist economic activities were guided by the super structure of Calvinistic "divine providence". For, the Hegelian dialectics had developed a procedure in that regard, which acts as the socially accepted norm even today: The West against "the others". If "the others" won't accept the views of the West, they would be opposed aggressively, either through war or through propaganda narratives. Because the West represent the ideals of the "Kingdom of God", they have the divine authority to discharge "divine providence" that would help "the others" The nature of "right " divine providence and the affairs of the world as the dialectics of "good" against "bad" of the binary two-value logical interpretation on everything enabled the capitalists to grab any sort of wealth anywhere in the world by using force or other coercing means. Capitalism spread unopposed through the parochial teaching of Calvinism and Hegelian didactics, especially using the dialectical procedure of double negation.

But curiously, this view of Calvinism inspired another thinker, the father of modern economics, Adam Smith: "The bridge between Calvinism and market capitalism is Adam Smith, who, in effect, divinizes the machinations of the free market by

---

[7]Taylor (2014), p. 54.
[8]Ibid.

effectively appropriating Calvin's doctrine of providence."[9] According to Adam Smith the new capitalist man founded his values on the "divine providence" values of Christianity, that a true Christian should naturally share his wealth with all others as a part of the religious life's duty. So, a true capitalist would employ people in his industrial enterprises, businesses and farms, for sharing the wealth he created, to all others, by providing them with work that should generate, distribute and give a sense of living with the divine providence to everyone around. He is only doing his divine duty after amazing sufficient wealth. Providing a way to live a life for himself and the others around by creating and distributing wealth. But ironically for the middle-class people (bourgeoisie) to be fully functional, in a competitive world, the exploitation of the workers (proletariat) was an absolute necessity, especially when he had to face competition from everywhere. The proletariat should work and should also act as consumers of the producers' products.

Marx foresighted that the danger of monetary profit, and the unhindered availability of printed money could make the bourgeoisie with a lethal power to control the fate of the unskilled workers, and the future of humanity. The unlimited authority on matters relating to wealth and money by the modern plutocrats should be having several inherent dangers. This is the source of tyranny in capitalism, as Karl Popper noted: " a paradox that can be expressed by saying that unlimited freedom leads to its opposite, since without its protection and restriction by law, freedom must lead to a tyranny of the weak by the strong."[10] What we are seeing today is an expression of that freedom of "divine providence" without any religiosity originally enshrined in Protestantism, has turned capitalism into a tyrannical system. The superrich of today are atheist with uncontrolled thirst for grabbing money, and are ethically puerile, living in the world of pure ignorance. The philosophical thoughts of today based neither on reasoning nor on faith, but on ignorance ridden narratives that works for enhancing the self-interest maximization as the sole aim of life. So those narratives selectively use faith and reasoning in order to satisfy the technocratic systems that are being developed for replacing the absolute spirit—God—and the divine providence.

References

Communist Manifesto: The original text at: https://www.marxists.org/archive/marx/works/1848/communist-manifesto/ch01.htm#007/. Retrieved on 17 July 2016
Hegel, G.W.F.: The Philosophy of History. Dover Publications Inc., New York (1956)
Popper, K.: The Open Society and its Enemies, vol. 2. Routeldge, London (1945)
Taylor, M.C.: Speed Limits. Yale University Press, New Heaven (2014)

---

[9]Ibid.
[10]Popper (1945), p. 48.

Chapter 13
Creative Work Versus Artificial Intelligence

Creative work and the appreciation of it in the postindustrial societies became very minimal and given way for mechanization for higher production and efficient distribution. This aspect began to infringe into the natural functioning of *hand-brain faculty* that made the human societies for structuring a social fabric that had sustained our civilization. The industrial economic system was built on that structure; but we give least credence to those in the emerging world order. When creative work was appreciated, workers skills at all levels were necessary, but today those skills are the source for AI systems as the digitally exploitable data.

Differing from the ancient societies, in the middle ages, feudalism thrived, with the serfs as the underclass, and in the industrialized world, the two new classes had emerged, bourgeoisie and proletariat by the way of opportunities and chances. As for two siblings from the same family, one could be a bourgeoisie and the other be a proletariat. Such a prospect might not be the case under feudalism in the preindustrial world where people's destinies were determined by birth and association. Access to education with the adoptability to scientific rationalism, and an audacity to accept the new ways of living and thinking were the key principle to be accepted into the bourgeoisie—middle class; and the inabilities to do so were the factor that determined the fate of a proletariat—under class. In the feudal oligarchical system birth into aristocracy or nobility was the way to be a part of the system.

The communists were seriously concerned about the flow of wealth and capital into the hands of a few private individuals and the coercing power of capitalism empowered by the Christian idea of "divine providence". The freedom to connect with God directly meant that one should view the world as a place where one could serve the God's intentions. Therein, the capitalists had created a metanarrative that in order to protect wealth scientifically and keeping the social harmony, the educated people should have first access to wealth and should protect it to benefit everyone. The concept of divine providence and the narratives on wealth management, which had been adopted as the essence of western industrial values and they were reverently been adopted subsequently into the religiosity of Islam, Buddhism, Hinduism, etc. John Calvin defined poverty as sin and a true Christian's duty is alleviating the poor by

© The Author(s), under exclusive license to Springer Nature Singapore Pte Ltd. 2021
M. Varghese, *A Brief History of Creative Work and Plutonomy*,
https://doi.org/10.1007/978-981-15-9263-8_13

providing them work, so that both, rich and poor, could participate in the God's work of creating wealth that could benefit everyone. The prospect of redefining one's life through work is very difficult in plutonomy. The scientific reasoning that helped one to redefine one's own life is nearly impossible as the creativity in jobs are increasingly taken over by AI. And therein the concept of the Providence of God ruling over our thoughts as a metanarrative in "work" related activities also become obsolete, much less, the understanding of providence as doing creative work by appreciating the hand-brain faculty.

The authority and power, that were a part of the newly emerged master class, the bourgeoisies, in the industrial period, had made them invincible, because of the spiritual authority that they imbibed from Calvinistic Protestant Christian religiosity. The bourgeois capitalists had made their mission of appropriating and controlling as much wealth as possible with a kind of spiritual permissiveness received from the heavens. The metanarrative of religiosity of Calvinism had made the capitalists feel that they were not like "the others", but they were the chosen ones as they had chosen to follow the ideals of Protestant Christianity. As per Hegelian doctrines, Protestant Christianity is the most revealed religion and that it had the power to uplift "the others" from the sin of poverty. The western capitalists were educated and civilized, so they needed to control all the wealth. On the other hand, "the others" who won't follow it were either ignorant or illiterate savages, so their wealth needed to be controlled from being destroyed it in any manner by their ignorant behaviors. That was the fundamental thought that powered the capitalists' thoughts with a kind of "missionary seal" attitude on wealth creation and control. The true capitalists considered that creating and controlling wealth as the mission of their life. To accomplish that benign mission of life, they should have to stretch to any extent and even to face the most unchristian act: the fall. For Christians "the fall" is sacrilege equal to destruction or death of the soul. During colonial times, so many heinous crimes were committed in several of their colonies around world on the basis of such a supremist thought on controlling the wealth of "the others". But Christians somehow tried to avoid the evil of "the fall", through repentance, the most revered Christian spiritual act. But the postmodern narrative on "fall" is considered as something implicitly good, so one can avoid doing any penance. According to Taylor: "For faithful Christians, the fall is fortunate because God always brings good out of evil; for the faithful economist, greed is good because the omniscient, omnipotent, and omnipresent market always creates profit out of self-interest."[1] Here the interpretation of fall is little different from the Christian teachings. The fall due to life's trials and tribulations are good because God gives opportunity to a faithful to redeem from such falls.

The concept of "self-interest maximization" might be the most applied economic *techne* in all of the industrialization periods. If one has the passion to maximize his self-interest, he could resurrect from "the fall". Spiritual "fall" should be avoided as it pushes man into "sin" or evil, but fall due to problems of life where one can find an opportunity to understand God and resurrect from such trials and tribulations.

---

[1] Taylor (2014), p. 56.

Likewise, greed could help one to earn more and find more opportunities everywhere. Apparently, self-interest maximization is bad; and by acting on it with greed one can earn economic propriety. Since the evil aspects connected with self-interest maximization ought to be permitted. Why? Because it could save "the others" from the *sin of poverty*. And if evil is committed to saving the others from the sin of poverty, then the ever-compassionate God would show the ways to resurrect. As the Christians are the chosen ones; God never would stand on their way that they are allowed to use any means to accumulate wealth as they are performing the act of working together with "divine providence" for perpetuating it. Communism promoted violence based on this conception of "the fall". Violence is evil but if it is done to help "the others"— proletarian—from the *sin of poverty*, then it can be justified.

To the new postmodern capitalists' definition on fall and greed and an incessant urge for fulfilling this mission of creating wealth through maximization of self-interest made the plutocrats more powerful as that they could influence the decision-making process of the respective local governments using coercions of various kinds including violence. In the postmodern world order, the plutocrats are mostly irreligious and they do charity to accentuate greed and emphasize their passion for self-interest maximization, in order to act like gods. This is contrary to the case of the capitalist bourgeoisies who did penance for their sins, by helping "the others" with some acts of providence and charity. Marx understood that the conservative spiritual values of the bourgeoisie are a cover that should be shattered and removed first. He made a counter narrative using Hegelian dialectics. The irreligious communist manifesto for explaining on the real situation that has inspired and encouraged millions of thinkers all over the world, and it is used as a source text to fight against the vilification by the bourgeoisie over the proletariat. The vilifications of the capitalist bourgeois over proletarians were so brute and vicious and were done by stroking human passion, jalousie, envy etc. in the pretense of Protestant spirituality. Marx categorically asserted that both bourgeoisie and proletariat were from the common men, freed from the serf class and their ilk, who were subjected to the feudal subjugation in the preindustrial period Europe. Thereby he revealed the face of the bourgeoisie. But unfortunately, in plutonomy the chances for applying Hegelian dialectic on synthetic unity is impossible, because that unity happened through human "work" is now taken over by AI, so another Hegelian dialectic of negation of the negative—double negation become possible, by negating the workers' rights to *work and life*. That is the reason why the new working class could only do part-time jobs, or to do precariat works.

The picture of the middle classes is such that those, who were liberated after Protestantism of Luther and Calvin, and who had discarded their traditional religious views, and who also had adopted the new religiosity of capitalism supported by Hegelian notion of rationalism, absolutism, scientific determinism, etc. The capitalists are those who could work towards maximizing the self-interest using greed could have all the powers equal to that of the mythological demigods. On the other hand, the same freed middle-class people or erstwhile serf class, who were marginalized, who couldn't understand the nuances of those capitalists' values, who could not get educated in the methods of science, rationalism, etc. had to live at the mercy and control of the bourgeoisie class. And they were deeply religious expecting that the magical wand of God's providence that could protect them from the fall of the excessive greed of the bourgeoisie. In distress, the poor class always wait for a messiah, who would libertate them. Now plutonomy is trying to do the role of the savior.

The labor of the proletariat class was a necessary factor for the industrialized world and for strengthening the power of bourgeoisie by operating various machines. The skilled workers could get more and even would transform to bourgeoisie class, but the unskilled could get only little and would remain as the underclass workers: the proletariats. But Marx found that the power of bourgeoisie centered on material production and consumerism where the work of proletariat was essential but could replaceable easily. He also suggested that the synthetic alternative for the anomaly in the production process was the absolutism of the "work" of the proletariat, instead of the greed of the bourgeoisie. Marx replaced the Hegelian concept of self-perfecting absolutistic spirit, using double negation, with the incessant growth of creative "work" of the working class. Marx should have believed in the idea of the "providence of nature" and the brotherhood of humanity in protecting and dividing the wealth in a justifiable way. Providence of nature is the foundational principles in the philosophy of the Epicureans and Stoicism in the Ancient times. Contextually, Marx was a scholar of Epicurean materialism.

Therefore, in the globalized world for the dialectic of plutocrat versus precariat: neither the aspect of creative "work" nor the purchase power of precariat is a significant factor. It is in the dominion of "Artificial intelligence" that acts as the absolute. It is like the Hegelian conception of the dominion of the absolute sprit of God. The power of Artificial Intelligence is now developing into the dominion of technological singularity and technocracy. We all have to submit to the dictums of a networked system of technology, where nobody acts as the supreme controller. The precarity that is being developed in the recent times is much beyond what Marx has envisioned in his writings.

Reference

Taylor, M.C.: Speed Limits. Yale University Press, New Heaven (2014)

Chapter 14
Tyranny of Plutonomy: How Capitalism Redefined

Financial Industry and the Invincibly of AI have created a kind of tyrannical situation in the human society with the emergence of the new kind of "dominion of plutonomy" and the situation of a never-ending greed for profits and gains by the plutocrats.[1] The justification that the western capitalists held is the unique spiritual authority they hold on to the wealth everywhere. In the twenty-first century under plutonomy too, they continue it vehemently. In the world of globalization, their capital initiated a kind of worldwide spread of digital technology, with the mathematical function of algorithms using big data. Without any kind of moral foresightedness or apprehension, they invest money anywhere and everywhere, in order to circulate their unused bogus money into areas where exploitation of wealth has not happened yet. They narrated it as a revolution that gave an impetus for the educated working class to maximize their self-interest and assume prominence, especially in the world of technology using self-programming computer automation systems.

In the postmodern globalized world, financial industry become prominent that it displaced the economy that has been dependent on production and consumption. And since wealth distribution through human work is hardly happening, the AI could enhance the flow of wealth into the control of a miniscule few, who only could further their investment activities using those fake money. The financial industry is now very active. Now, a large part of the trade of the financial products are done by algorithmic driven AI systems, which essentially could self-program according to the needs of the situation, especially against all kinds of market crashes. Using huge amount of data, this industry could make decisions automatically, on the way, it is programmed to perform. Those self-programming systems can bankrupt any entity that receives investors' money. Now, that the contribution from the non-plutonomy population into the world economic system is minimal, the system only can inflate the wealth of the plutocrats; the working class is now precariats (part-time contract workers) who have no creative role to play, unlike in capitalism, on helping the

---

[1] The Hegelian notion on the dominion of objectivity as foundation of spiritual life may transform to dominion of plutonomy. See, Varghese (2020), p. 164.

© The Author(s), under exclusive license to Springer Nature Singapore Pte Ltd. 2021
M. Varghese, *A Brief History of Creative Work and Plutonomy*,
https://doi.org/10.1007/978-981-15-9263-8_14

system to function properly. Because the difference between these two classes is very vast, it never will be able to complement each other. The underclass represented by precariats has no role in the globalized society and the global community largely ignores them. It becomes complicated and complex as the times progresses. This aspect alone would make plutonomy irrelevant in future. The world systems under plutonomy is a difficult phenomenon to comprehending easily, as for a world that is deteriorating from the fundamental principles of human life; one of those principles that could save us from total destruction is *creative work* with the due appreciation of the *hand-brain faculty*.

Under the structure of plutonomy, we would try to comprehend the former bourgeoisie class that it has now become entities such as *plutocrats*, *salariat* and *proficians*, but unlike the bourgeoisie class, none of these entities has any direct responsibility to the enterprises they manage. They do it to benefit the investors whose money would run the enterprises they manage. Similarly, the erstwhile *proletariat* has now become *precariat*, (the majority: part-time workers); a few old proletariat (the workers who enjoy some privileges and rights) who now can work mainly for government run enterprises; and the rest, *lumpen- precariat* (the workers that does menial works) who are now becoming a dominant group. The new wealth distribution system that started to evolve in the advent of plutonomy, is with the wealthy plutocrats who make less than 1% or may be even less than 0.01% are holding more wealth than "the other", 99%. The plutocrats are mainly comprised of investors, shareholders, technocrats, financiers, etc., who may not be actively engaged with the business they invested into, yet at times may act only as a face of an enterprise, and act as facilitators. They hold two kind of wealth, one is their personal worth, and the other is the worth of their invested wealth in other enterprises and charities. Their main concern is only to maximize the benefit each of them gets from their investments. This is against the classical principle of owning a business with a number of stakeholders who would invest their skills, money and time; and also, would actively participate in creating new wealth. Unlike today, those stakeholders used to take the responsibilities together with the ownership. But in the case of plutonomy that ownership and responsibility are being evolved into a base minimum, or nil. The investor mercilessly could leave the company s/he invested into, with his money, setting up the company into bankruptcy. The irony is that this happens without the active knowledge of the plutocrat investor. For him the AI controlled system did it, after carefully assessing the relevant data. But, today they just focus on creating policy decisions and manipulating public opinion to protect their investments. They create charities, fund political parties, fund media, keep the intelligentsia under control, etc. to enable them to harness public opinion in their favor. Production is by outsourced entities, operation is by the salaried workers, implementation is by consultants, entire administration is by AI systems. The whole operation is highly cost-effective employing a very few workers.

The second and third groups are two sides of the same coin. *Salariat*. These people receive a salary as compensation to the services rendered; they comprise the CEOs and all executive staff that help to run the business, and who work to perform the assigned responsibilities on the basis of contractual obligations. These *Salariat* are mostly hired on contract, for executing specific tasks on a specified time period. Similarly, the third group is a class by itself, growing exponentially in OECD countries: the *proficians*, who are independent professionals, mostly consultants, and those who sub contract works for a certain enterprise, and execute a particular contracted task on its behalf. They are now forming own companies and providing consultancy globally. But their responsibilities are limited to the point of the executions of the contractual obligations. These three groups replace the erstwhile bourgeoisie that has been referred in the *Communist Manifesto* of Karl Marx. In the industrial period, bourgeoisie had to protect the stakeholder's interests with the company. From the re-industrialization, industry-2.0 period, to the globalized period (industry 3.0) the responsibility factor has shifted from the stakeholder's responsibility to the shareholder's reasonability. It is only to protect the value of the invested money. But, now the responsibilities of the stakeholders are reduced substantially, and it is now reaching almost to zero. These three entities, *plutocrats*, *salariat*, and *proficians*, are the curious part of the financial industry that normally function on behalf of the shareholders only. The shareholders' interest is now acting as a superstructure of a business enterprise with least organizational or management responsibilities relating to stakeholders' interests.

Financial industry with the support of AI can control everything. A curious aspect of this system under plutonomy is that there are many companies that go out of business, yet the *plutocrats, proficians, or salart* would stay on without losing much in their personal assets, if they own enough invested financialized assets to back them up, they could stay afloat. Nobody takes any responsibility for bankruptcies, and filing for bankruptcy is considered as an art of the deal, in solving redundancies. When the company makes profits, the plutocratic system takes their self-interest as the company's interest; when it loses to enthuse the investors, the self-interest become each one's personal interest. Since business enterprises are run on the support of financial industry, they are being controlled on the agenda of "self-interest maximization" of those who involved in providing finances. All those three entities of plutonomy: *plutocrats, salariats,* and *proficians* do not hold any personal interest other than protecting their own monetary interests with the company. These entities of the plutonomic system can change their investment portfolios to any other company that offers them more profits. The *salariat* would leave as soon as their contractual period is finished; the *proficians* are not a part of any company they work for, as they only give professional advice. *Salariat* works as the external face of company that coordinates everything including public relations. At the same time, the internal activities of the company are done on consultation with the *proficians*. As a result, the company can be run without any production activities or even marketing activities. All can be outsourced and the financial industry controls everything for maximizing the investor's self-interest, with a fully functional AI system watching over everything. The *proficians* make sure that the company spends less on production, marketing etc. and they receive a hefty consultancy fee. All these three entities are on a kind of "pack and fly away" mode. Their responsibilities are that limited with regard to the businesses they have invested in, as they are mostly concerned only about the worth of their investments. They should not have any major worry that the investments are managed by AI controlled systems which could make up any untoward challenges; that may be the reason why wealth rapidly moving into the hands of a very few entities who do nothing like the millennial plutocrat investor, Hillary.

Similarly, precariat (part-time workers) replaces the proletariat of nineteenth and twentieth centuries. Unlike proletariat, the precariat has absolutely no stake in the business. They are being used as hirelings with no responsibility beyond executing a given specific assignment or task. The second group who was the old "core" working class (*proletariat*) is becoming insignificant in an alarming rate, and together with them the labor unions, too, have become powerless and have only a very limited role to play. And then the third group, the *lumpen -precariat*, or the underclass, who work mostly on calls, who may get jobs on hourly basis, or on daily basis, or at maximum on monthly basis as they do unskilled works, their lifestyle is worse than anyone could imagine as financial security for them is a very distant dream. Their number is on a constant rise. The irony is that they never meet any human person of authority directly, as they do their job on calls basis only. Finally, the unemployed and disinterested workers are there, in large numbers, including huge number of unemployed youngsters in their 20 s and 30 s. Since the reindustrialization period from 1960 to our times, the economic system only looked at monetary profits, where the bargaining powers of the workers are substantially reduced, because of the rapid mechanization, and what affected was the natural propensity to bargain and gain more through protests, strikes etc. Those acquired rights for negotiations of the workers, under capitalism, are almost now disappearing. The *lumpen-precariats* are like the daily wage workers in the agricultural sector, but they were all attached to the landlord's family as Marx alluded "feudal ties that bound man to his "natural superiors"".[2]

Humans can append machines to enhance the ability of hands, but machines should not append humans for making it work. It will lead to a stage machines would append each other and destroy human life. In a world of humans appreciating machines, the workers and their labor would become cheap and valueless. Humans working at a particular work spot have to compete with the mechanized high precision AI systems, outsourced works, expatriate workers, and with other such tricks used for enhancing the profits of the plutonomy. This is partly working because of the failure of the so-called communist bloc countries where the system was meant only for supporting the proletariat, where they least cared the skilled middle-class workers, a claim that nationalists and fascists made in the turn of twentieth century.

Now, the plutonomic system replaces communism and capitalism making the working class insignificant. And this system warrants all citizens of a nation-state to protect the interests of the plutocrats, not the precariats. Plutonomy is now supported by the elites, intellectuals, academia, and the political class with the same communists' zeal of dedication for protecting the proletariat. The plutocrats and the oligarchy of politicians with their "self-interest" would act as the deep state in the democratic capitalistic countries like the USA, Britain and Western Europe where plutonomy is

---

[2]Communist Manifesto (2016).

very active. The democratic system of today functions on such a conundrum of deep oligarchical interests controlling everything as the interests of the rich investor nefariously influences political decisions. The technological unemployment energizes this system of oligarchy and making a few foolishly rich billionaires, but turning their worth and the idea of wealth meaningless. Now we live in the tyranny of plutonomy, where the plutocrats now help to create what should be known as plutocracy. Now it is almost accepted that world wealth should be with the plutonomy and "the rest" must live on UBA (universal basic income).

References

Communist Manifesto: The original text at: https://www.marxists.org/archive/marx/works/1848/communist-manifesto/ch01.htm#007/. Retrieved on 17 July 2016

Varghese, M.: Nāgārjuna and the Art of Negation. Sanctum Books, New Delhi (2020)

Chapter 15
Advent of Plutonomy in Japan

Japan is a country that valued creative work and appreciated the hand-brain faculty very highly since ancient times. However, the "power of money" over "power of creative work" should have begun in Japan after the World War-II. After Ikeda Hayato's economic reform and revitalization era of Japanese economy, Japan Jumped from a traditional agriculture economy to a leading industrial economic powerhouse. At that time, Japan used integrated co-operative method of economic management for overall development. Integrated co-operative methods means, the company that produces goods, the banks that finances, the employees that work, and the government that make policy decisions would work as a unit in harmony, with the sole aim of achieving prosperity for an organically functioning society. But, for making the system purely functional the "hard work" and dedicated commitment of the workers had acted as the prime source of strength. The company worked in the spirit of bushido—samurai—values. The system works on the commitment and dedication to one's duties for benefiting the family and community; wherein, everyone's work was important and should function as a unit in harmony. The executives and management would work together with the workers for providing decent living wages to all those who are involved. The central bank of Japan and the government agencies work as the nodal point, where the companies used the state of art technology to produce goods at comparative prices, for bringing prosperity to the country and its people who worked to create those products.[1] The central banks would provide sufficient funds that be returned as assets in the form of foreign currencies, precious metals, and other such kind of wealth that could be used for international trade; especially, to the purchase of raw materials and other resources from the international market.[2] The commitment and dedication enshrined in the Bushido teachings to one's duties was the source of strength for the modern Japanese capitalist after the war. But similar to the Western counterparts, a tectonic change happened in matters relating to moral and ethical perspectives, when plutonomy's ideology got integrated into Japanese

---

[1] Thomas (2016), p. 211.

[2] https://en.wikipedia.org/wiki/Japanese_economic_miracle.

© The Author(s), under exclusive license to Springer Nature Singapore Pte Ltd. 2021
M. Varghese, *A Brief History of Creative Work and Plutonomy*,
https://doi.org/10.1007/978-981-15-9263-8_15

system as the controllers of wealth, and later got integrated itself with the global plutonomy. Plutonomy has denigrated the labor of the workers through mechanization. Machines that are meant for helping men, are now appending humans. The process of mechanization today eats away jobs because plutocrats can neglect the rights of workers.

The second group of the plutonomy—*salariat*—is notable here to mention. Since the 1960s, during the reindustrialization—industry-2.0—of Japan, the life of salariat (*salariman*) was an indicator to show how the common men had enthused to be a part of the exponential growth phase of Japan. A paradigm shift in the work culture of Japan had taken place in this reindustrialization period, same as being happened around the western world. This was the post war generation of the baby boomers: The newly emerging workforce that powered the post-World War-II industrial economy. We can review the life and times of Noriyasu, who might represent several thousand *salariman* of the Baby Boomer generation, meaning the children who were born after the Word War-II, into the post war industrial world order. Noriyasu was a normal hard-working Japanese *salariman* (salariat) of this generation who held the hopes and aspirations of that period. He, like many others in Tokyo came to the city from an interior village, of traditional farmers in the northern Japan, migrated into Tokyo for being a part of the newly reindustrializing Japan. Back home, the farming community followed a tradition of contiguity of doing some work, where everyone could work without retirement, which was the norm of "work" for Noriyasu. The traditional family system ensured work security until one's health would permit. But the life in the city in 1980s and later made him to live in a world that did provide him any continuity for doing any work as he had to retire prematurely. The contiguity factor relating to work has disappeared at the time of industry-3.0. The work culture that has changed between industry-2.0, and industry-3.0, is difficult to discern, but it certainly destroyed the harmony that existed in the time of co-operative capitalism, where everyone could work till their retirement with a good pension.

However, his wife Yuriko represented another aspect of the baby boomers, she was from the city bred or citified kind of the baby boomer. Her father was a writer and thinker, who travelled widely in to various parts of the world, and also was very close to various leftist movements in the 1960s and 70 s in Europe and Asia. He was a typical left leaning intellectual of the 1960s in Japan; also, a typical *profician* (professional) of the time of co-operative capitalism, who earned a living from his acquired professional academic and intellectual skills. Historically, a skilled professional could earn a lot of money, even though the job would provide any sort of guarantee at all.

Surprisingly, Noriyasu got a job to work in an American company where he had to practice a new work culture that followed the new postmodern western management system, which was completely new to him, but agreeable for him. Except him, all the main employees were either America returned Japanese or white Americans. He felt the pinch of alienation from the beginning. Noriyasu became a member of the new class of the postmodern community of workers in the globalization period—industry-3.0. Under plutonomy, the Salariat will be rewarded hugely if they perform very well and if the company would do well. In that case even an ordinary salariman can climb up to be proficians, such as consultants, etc. The ladder of progress is simple with right amount of hard work and luck, a salariat also can easily be a plutocrat. This was nearly impossible under the feudal oligarchic system of the rural Japan where one can expect limited growth within one's limits only. But if things work otherwise, a salariat might have to face a hopeless life with no future whatsoever. Most of the plutocrats of today were either salariat or proficians in the 1980s and 1990s. The postmodern entrepreneurship largely depends on how one can get an access to the investment system of the financial industry. And if one could be a part of that, one also be a part of the exclusive club of the elitist plutocrats. The coursing power of plutonomy is so strong that it could change the fate of a person. But if things are not favorable, the reverse coursing power is also equally strong and destructive.

Noriyasu's life in the city was different and was not very good. He felt total alienations and lonesomeness. The security, he found himself that of being a part of the Japanese feudal system with own farmland together with a supporting extended family, and many healthy relationships around, would no longer be a reality in his city life. He left with a lonely life situation of owning all responsibilities by himself which was a new experience for him. He should be responsible for everything. The life of the baby boomer generation in Japan was work, more work, and more work for to be called a successful person. He worked hard and harder to be a successful Japanese for to get the goodies of the new life in the Tokyo city that was emerging as a postmodern high-tech international metropolis. Though from the farm, he might not get enough money, the life was easy and trouble free there, because of being a part of a well-supported family and friends. Contextually, the job and life with the cosmopolitan family of a well-educated wife was an experience that he earlier dreamt of and craved for, from his school days. Like all aspirational young men of his time, he was a very ambitious man who kept an air of elitism and snobbishness from his early school days. He dreamt that with proper education he could reach to all the greater heights. But, in actuality, now he experiences a kind of alienation and loneliness.

Japan is not a protestant Christian country but it greatly accepted, the Christian values as modern values into its sociopolitical and economic systems. A significant change happened in the postmodern globalized socioeconomic order of Japan which was the amalgamation of Western capitalism with the ancient Japanese Samurai (bushido) values. Hegelian dialectics is the foundation of the work by Adam Smith's work, *The Wealth of Nations*, which propelled the modern capitalism, and the counter thesis on capitalism by Karl Marx, *The Communist Manifesto*. These two works represent the two sides of the same coin, that were trying to interpret the "divine providence" discoursed in Protestant religion, and how wealth should be disseminated to benefit the people. Both capitalism and communism were talking about how the new middle class, derived from the freed serfs of the erstwhile feudal era that transformed and divided as the rich middle class, the bourgeoisie; and the underclass workers, the proletariat since the time of industrial revolution. In the case of Japan, instead of the Christian notion of divine providence, the aspects of Samurai values got amalgamated into capitalism since the first phase of industrialization. The Christian capitalist was a charity loving, honest and religious personality who would take care of the interests of the workers (proletarian) as the sworn religious duty. In the same manner, Samurais were keen on protecting the interests of the disadvantaged. The communists and Marx found the bourgeoisie capitalist as a coward who satisfies only own greed by breeding more greed and pushes the innocence of proletarian into complete submission. The capitalists make the proletariat to feel that the poor life situation that they experience is due to the curse of God. In another way of viewing this issue, in the case of Japan, the Samurai values amalgamated with the capitalist and communist values distinctively unified into one-fold.

The former serfs were the foundation for both the classes: Marxism proposed a classless society. But capitalism supported the private control of capital and the rich class by following Christian values of providence and charity that would benefit the whole society. In both cases, the works of the working class were well appreciated. Work was the synthetic unity, that enabled the distribution of wealth effectively. In Japan, it was the Samurai (*bushi-do*) values, with its duty-bound dedication supplanted the Protestant values of "divine providence" and the common folks' commitment and trust to the tradition. In the case of Japan, both the bourgeoisie and proletariat were highly committed to doing efficient work, especially "creative work". In fact, instead of conflicts, there emerged a synergy of the two, equally benefiting each other. But, in the Western countries the conflict between the two increased where new systems emerged to offset the bargaining powers of the workers. The origin of the shareholders' and investors' control on economy that started from this urge to offset the control of workers on business decisions. In the bourgeoisie system where stakeholders' control made the economic system to find a natural balance, but today the plutonomy tries to grab any kind of wealth into its control only for distributing it, to the shareholders, bankers, financiers, etc., much less to those who engage in production, labor, service, etc. But, today the sway of plutonomy is borderless and boundless and it guzzles wealth everywhere into its draconian control and spit it out into a sewer for permanently destroying it.

Reference

Thomas, V.: The World Transformed 1945 to the Present. Oxford University Press, New York (2016)

Chapter 16
How Plutonomy Thrive

There is an effective dialectics emerging between the economy of stakeholder versus economy of shareholder in the period of industry-3.0, upsetting the values and conflicts that sustained capitalism. The capitalist system came under severe competition in production—industry-2.0—period, roughly starting from 1960 to 1980s. This is the reason for starting the era of globalization aiming at creating a unified global market. With the commencement of the third industrial revolution, in the era of globalization since 1980 onwards, there started a new production and marketing method that had set to dominate all the world systems. During industry-3.0, technologization and digitalization of systems began to flourish creating new "work" opportunities. During this period, a few developed Western countries identified financing and investment as an industry, that the kind of profit financing could bring from China by financing all production activities there, and marketing the cheaply produced goods globally at a very competitive price is huge and astronomical. Financial industry benefited substantially from this kind of unusual production and marketing activities. When financialization happened, the lesser-developed countries became the manufacturing centers and they craved for investor's money in order to develop their economies, where they competed with each other, producing products cheaply and giving tax rebates to the investors—manufactures. The financial industry put a huge financial net around the world, for financializing the entire global economic system. With the easy availability of investable money, production in many countries thrived, and as a fall out, there generated a sizable market with an increasing size of middle-class population as active consumers especially in China, India, etc. At the same time, the middle class in the western countries began to disseminate, as domestic industries moved out of the respective countries to the so-called low-cost manufacturing centers making a sizable population to live in precarity and the major work force as the precariats—part-time workers, or people who can exist only on charity and handouts. As easily tradable financial products kept the financial market healthy and vibrant for the investors, and plutonomy thrived as a global phenomenon.

The third industrial revolution (industry-3.0), in the era of globalization, had created a complicated situation in the world of business and economics, where

© The Author(s), under exclusive license to Springer Nature Singapore Pte Ltd. 2021
M. Varghese, *A Brief History of Creative Work and Plutonomy*,
https://doi.org/10.1007/978-981-15-9263-8_16

intense competition at the global level became a complex and unexpected reality. And as an after effect, the organization structures of the companies had regularly and continuously been changed. The main source of funding came from investors both individuals as well as institutions. The oligarchy of investors got an invincible power and control over the world economy during the industry-3.0 period. Intellectually, the invincibility of the power of finance in all those operations is a curious discussion point, but it remains in that world of thinkers. The shifting of manufacturing from the developed western countries began to experience a huge shrinkage in their middle-class population and their purchasing power due to lack of dependable jobs. The deficiency of dependable works strained the wealth distribution in a justifiable way into different levels of the society. And this shrinkage in distribution of wealth becomes more complex, making a few as the hoarders of dead money, and a large majority having no access to wealth. The economic system during industry-3.0 turned in like a cruel joke that can be discerned with the statistics that worried philosophers like, Alain Badiou, who wrote that just 264 people possess as much wealth, inheritance and income, as the 7 billion others, the rest of the world population should understand that something is seriously wrong with the way we view the affairs of the world.[1] The economic independence of 7 billion people is being destroyed by a few plutocrats, who hoard all the wealth or wasting it by hording it, and not using it. According to Aristotle, economic independence is the string that wove the unity that sustains a nation. It connects the individual with family, family with community, community to form a nation state.

16.1   Noriyasu's Trauma: Life in Precarity

The strength of Western civilizations after the Protestant reformation was based on the purchase power of the middle-class families, which had declined steadily making people to experience a kind of postmodern poverty and that destroyed the traditional family system. The financial industry with the newer methods of investment improved their manufacturing activates in the newly emerging countries. And, in order to resist intense competition, the companies were forced to do cost cutting activities by reducing the workforce and by installing more cost-effective mechanization using AI systems. Banks would give easy financial options for installing AI systems. The markets began to be flooded with cheap products destroying domestic manufacturing and marketing sectors. The financial industry always looked for more opportunities with quick investments on project that could give them quick monetary returns that made them ever stronger. The process of technologization happened in two fronts. One, by shifting almost all the manufacturing works abroad to low-cost labor countries, or technologizing with high tech manufacturing of domestic industries. The second, by making the service jobs with automatized machines such as ATMs, dispensing venders, AI managed retail sales systems, call centers, robotics,

---

[1] Badiou (2019), p. 9.

etc. The wealth began to accumulate into the hands of a few who have no idea, how to use the stockpiled wealth in the form of fixed assets and financial products, such as bonds, CDS, CDO, SPV, etc. There created a conundrum of easy interest free money, of easily available tech systems, and of easily available manufactured products from low cost countries like China. Human involvement with work has dropped like a huge fall. The present Chinese monopoly in manufacturing industry should be studied in retrospective of the rise of plutonomy.

And people like Noriyasu began to lose their jobs as a part of cost cutting activates from every side. The pressure from the capital market is a kind of stress that a company never could ignore or endure. In most cases they experienced the pulling back of invested money from the company by investors that scared its executives and board members about losing of their cozy jobs. The worry here is multiple that the entire investment system is run by AI controlled automatons that only can analyze big data and make decisions based on some models imbibed in to computer programs. Any company can go bankrupt at any moment of time. So, cutting workers is the best way to show a profit on the yearly balance sheet and the financial statements in order to keep the shareholders happy; and the excess compensations received by the executives are there to purchase the shares of the company they work for, in order to keep the share value going high. The perpetual activity of share "buyback" helped companies to stay alive in the alt reality world of share—investment—markets.

The synergy that existed between stakeholders' interests with the shareholders' capital in a manufacturing industry become redundant. It is only working to protect the shareholders' interest. Almost all profit-making businesses are brought up or amalgamated into single units to avoid competition, so that the investors' interest could be duly protected. In the globalized world, both the stakeholders and the shareholders came under the vicious control of the automaton or robotics run financial industry. We have no clear idea on how it works, but certainly sure that it does not work for the sake of stakeholders like, workers, customers, depending small industries, commercial banks, etc. The bourgeoisie of the industrialization period become one aspect of the financial industry and his personal worth began to spike up or dried out. Anyhow, bourgeoisie is irrelevant under plutonomy. On the other hand, the proletariat lost all control on work related activities with the advent of technological unemployment. The invincibility of the shareholders' capital and the availability of easy interest free money began to dominate everything that is there with some economic value. The share market has changed its functioning model in the globalization period, instead of being a place for investing one's own extra wealth in profitable companies for receiving a deserving dividend as being done during the re-industrialization—industry-2.0, period, by the general public; now it is a place for gambling. The financial industry acts like, the gambling centers following various gaming theories. With the progress of day trading, short-term trading, bond markets, and the market for other kinds of financial products such as treasury bonds CDS, CDO, currency trade, gold bond trade, etc. A new kind of market in financial assets began to dominate business as cheap—interest free—money began to circulate everywhere. And with all these, a new kind of casino capitalism began to emerge everywhere. Following some kind of ethical values in trading of such products are forgiven, due to the influence of survival instincts. Now the financial market is following the rules of gambling casinos brazenly. According to Mark C. Taylor: "We have already discovered that Las Vegas and Wall Street have a strangely symbiotic relationship. For investors as for gamblers, the name of the game is how to beat the house. What is less often recognized is that Vegas also has a close relationship to both information theory which has shaped financial markets for more than half a century, and wearable computers which were the precursors of displays like Google Glass."[2] Now the plutocrats use various tools to access and confiscate wealth almost anywhere in the world. It is because of the application of gaming logic, and the use of advanced algorithmically controlled information technological systems, and above all with the easy availability of interest free money, they can penetrate into any wealth that can be financially appropriated. Such gaming logic is fed into computers that act as automatons when investment decisions are made. Algorithmically managed digitally controlled programmatically self-governing systems, with easily available interest free money following gaming logic, could make any human involvement with business activities meaningless including that of the plutocrats.

The issues relating to the distribution of wealth through work is acting only as hot taking points for politicians and armchair intellectuals. They discuss it at different discussion forums without getting in any kind of tangible outcomes, where they argue passionately about the widening gap between rich and poor, with a presumptive view that the rich can enjoy their money at the expense of the poor. Such old narratives are irrelevant today. It is clear that nobody could visualize the seriousness of this issue comprehensively. The public opinion on this issue is managed and controlled by the entertainment and infotainment industry. The business enterprises are forced to cut operational costs whichever way possible, so as to keep up the demands of the financial industry. Mostly the plutocrat's money controls the entertainment industry and the propaganda news media for propagating emotionally tight content favorably. Notably, the use of algorithmically controlled AI systems, in making managerial decisions, have created situations that can make somebody immensely rich without one's direct knowledge, or can make one poor absolutely, when the automaton that read the data, configures the entire system, based on standards created by the system analysts. In the recent past, we could see some of the plutocrats who had such authoritative controlling power, found their wealth wiped away hugely if the investors withdrew their investments, because of the decision by the automaton that run the systems. Out of fear, they invest a lot of unused money to run shadow governments; with their immense financial power, they could control, globally, all the socio-political decisions of national governments. Most of the companies are owned by gaming enthusiasts, who may play a game with the wealth that matters the whole world. Based on the logic of having a dilatable instrument in a game, and normally one of those instruments is the employees of a company; such enterprises could use minimum labor force and, in most cases, they use contract workers by using services of work contractors, and dispatch companies. Those workers can be removed soon

[2]Taylor (2014), p. 224.

enough. The employees demand could trouble the profitability of a company in every aspect, in comparison with the AI run machines. One of the fearsome situations is that every digital game of today has reset buttons, which can be set—*on* and *off*. If the plutonomy decides when their games are going haywire, they can use several reset buttons that may create unconscionable difficulties to normal human life.

Noriyasu, after losing his job, found that he is moving, into a kind of deep loneliness, leading him in to a kind of self-petrification and deep depression. All those identities that he found, comforting and supporting, had fallen deep into a kind of terrifying experience, which he never experienced earlier in his life. The feeling of being an achiever and a successful person, in the face of his family and friends, is now turned out to be a source for more and more alienations, petrification, and never-ending troubles in multitudes. Moreover, naturally his friends in the company and elsewhere become unfriendly and hostile. They stopped talking to him, and were even unavailable on his calls or knowingly avoided him. Now it becomes an undeclared social rule that nobody wants to deal with unsuccessful failed individuals. This may be because of the fear that one could be the next one, or may not want anyone to encroach into their comfort zones, in which, one is habitually coached into feeling a kind of safety. There is an increase in the number of suicides in Japan under plutonomy. The mass media under report or suppress such news fearing of the typical copycat actions that may repeat in other places. The spiritual training that was given as a part of religious practices, did meant to create an internal strength to an individual person to face all difficult life situations. In the postmodern scientific world order, that aspect is forgiven and being considered as an area for the psycho-analysts to deal with. Life in the postmodern Godless world is difficult to define, and the meaning of life is left undefined, where the future scares, the present troubles, and the past remained unexplained. Roman philosopher Cicero says, "the greater number of authorities have affirmed that existence of the gods; it is the most likely conclusion, and one to which we are all led by the guidance of the nature."[3] Our beliefs in gods are there, because the nature guides us to such entities; and thinkers established the existence of gods from the inherent nature of humans. Now such beliefs are relegated as the beliefs of the ancients. However, pop-stars, celebrities, gurus, soothsays, rulers, fakers, etc., have taken over that vacated space, and have assumed the status of gods and angels for themselves, not just ordinary mortal beings. They are to replace the classical conception of gods in heaven as in the case of ancient philosophy. Contextually, aggressive individualism is a byproduct of such a godless thought, and it acts as a cover for one's true self, and it is the view that controls human life in our times. Here, plutonomy tries to assert itself as the superstructure by spreading money everywhere to adduce such weaknesses of the humans.

In the ancient world God acted as a solace for the bereaved. In situations, when facing with discomfort and meaninglessness in life, one could seek refuge in God or in the spiritual teachings given by great thinkers like Buddha, Socrates, Christ, etc. or follow the teachings in texts like Bible, Gita, Koran or follow traditional religiosity based on Dharma as being observed in Hinduism of India. Yet, in a scientifically

---

[3]Cicero (2008), p. 1.

organized world order and world systems such religious beliefs are deemed as mere unscientific and puerile or the practices of the ancient aboriginal world order; and therefore, those beliefs should be discarded. But the conception of God, as the perfect representation of something existing out there that lingers in the mind of all humans. Therefore, even in postmodern times we look for such entities in our immediate proximity by theorizing scientific truths as absolutes and also look for a political system that could replace the perfection of the heavens. In the postmodern world order where traditional gods are being replaced by, movie stars, sports personalities, politicians, etc., and they are being worshiped and their actions are emulated, copied and followed like that of the gods and demigods. We also try to emulate the heroic image of a living person in the society is a popular myth that goes around, in the world today, with the pop—popular—culture. In fact, the godless, religion-less world of today, is attempting to find a new world order. At the same time, blunt beliefs in traditional Gods also are on the rise leading to fanaticism and religious bigotry, which must be seen as a failure of the evolving systems.

The expected behavior of a modern man is that he should be rational and should always follow the scientific sources to deal with everything in the world. He should be a follower of the "cult of reason" who should be willing to sacrifice all freedoms in order to protect the scientific systems. Therefore, the postmodern religiosity is scientism, where epistemology has taken the place of philosophy. Which means no metaphysical doctrines or ethical paradigms are essentially being followed when using Aristotelian logic (*prior Analytica*), and epistemology (*posterior Analytica*) and epistemology matures into scientism founded on crude rationalism by relegating ethics and metaphysics. Which means any conception of God is discarded and all conceptions of ethical behavior beyond the domain of national laws and social narratives.

But in actuality humans are driven by emotions and feelings, which the views of scientific rationalism never have taken seriously. It is considered as something that the modern men should avoid when dealing with life, or only to be accepted as the belief systems of the other subaltern communities. The Godless world only creates demigods who are all fake representations of some idea of perfection. Such cultism is on the rise everywhere. A good example is Hitler who demanded God like respect and veneration from the people who belonged to the "third Reich". The cultism may give temporary solace to those who follow the living human demigods. But when they lose the attachment to the cult followers they may experience a kind spiritual "fall", which would be fatal. Hitler suicided, and his followers devastated and fragmented. Noriyasu experienced that kind of spiritual fall when his belief in the industrialized world order had taken a serious setback. A precarious life of a precariat blooms large under these circumstances.

Though a compassionate and well-educated woman, with a clear deeper understanding about the order of life in the twentieth century, Noriyasu's wife, Yuriko also became depressed as she had to present him to others as a jobless incompetent man in a world that revere only winners and achievers. The un-heroic image of her husband deeply troubled her. When others present the achievements of their spouses, where she had to talk about a depressed housebound husband, staying put at home, struggling; obviously, she began to ignore about his presence and stopped normal communications with him. As for her he did not exist. He tried to find new jobs, but except part-time jobs, which were so denigrating for a highly educated person like him, he couldn't find any other work. Most of those part-time jobs were nothing more than operating various kinds of AI machines. He fell into—a forlorn—precarious life style: nothing promising to look forward than finding emptiness everywhere.

Why is part-time work so pitiful? Because: there could be no creative satisfaction drawn from such part-time gig jobs, that should be the answer. The living world becomes so shallow and meaningless for people like Noriyasu. He was taught that following the Western way of scientific rationalism is the only way for finding solutions for everything, but now that view is not helping him anymore. The religiosity of scientism failed him. The scientific rationalism that hugely conditioned human life since the nineteenth century is now "technological rationalism" that powers AI, and we should note that the "cult of reason" of the nineteenth century is now the "cult of technology". Thinking using a rational framework for systematically arriving at theoretical conclusions is the method of science. But today, the human involvement in that thinking process is hugely denigrated. The machines are designed to perform the systematic reasoning and to form independent thoughts; those thought would drive technology. The scientific method is now advanced into the methods of following machines powered by technology, which can function accurately than the humans. In short, natural human reasoning is now displaced techno scientific reasoning of the artificial intelligence systems that follows everyone everywhere like a phantom, collecting data, for self-programming for dominating natural human abilities. Under these circumstances human life suffers hugely as it loses all opportunities to use intelligence, by activating the hand-brain faculty.

Noriyasu pushed himself to get adjusted to the new situations, but no real positive results were forthcoming. He couldn't find a new matching job similar to the one that he did before. He could only find jobs that are beneath his qualifications and dignity. He only helped making a machine to do its programmed work, but nothing new to be learned by just making a machine working. All jobs are same that is of making a machine to work. He has no role to play there. He is just a replaceable interface like a smart phone App. He lived with a presumptuous thought that there is something big waiting to happen in the future. But the news about job situations in general, in other OECD countries, were more depressing, especially on hearing about the spread of technological unemployment everywhere had depressed him furthermore. Reasoning is considered as the regal power of spirit for a human being. The classical philosophers equate it to the nature of *soul and God*, but they also have considered that the other aspects of human personality such as emotions are equally impotent. The natural reasoning is now taken over by scientific reasoning and now it is taken over by the "cult of technoscience" where emotions are antithetical. Humans have only mechanical value: so long as one can make a machine work, he is useful; or else he is equal to trash. But for whom those machines work is an irrelevant question now. The cult of plutonomy thrives unabatedly under the emerging new world order of systems; unlike the old-world order there is no conception of the divine providence that somehow would have protected the social fabric intact.

At the end of reindustrialization period—industry-2.0—and in the beginning of globalization—industry-3.0—technological unemployment has become a part of human life mostly due to the positioning of the plutonomy and their wealth control methods. Though Noriyasu had many chances to work in factories or restaurants for getting some money, as did by his friends from his native village. He felt those are not going to help him much. In the world order known to him, "work" was considered as a source for getting some satisfaction and sense of accomplishments together with money. The Eastern philosophy and culture venerate creative work as a way for liberation (salvation). In Asian societies such a concept about "work" was duly emphasized and revered. In the Indian idea of Karma or the Chinese idea of Dao, creative work has a unique meaning, it is a way to get happiness and good life. Asians considered that doing "work" at every stage of human life is the mark of good living. In the new world order, the link between *work and life* is now disseminating badly.

"No work is equal to no life" was the norm of life for the Daoist philosophy. The baby boomer generation of Japan has to face severe life situations that unsettled their traditional beliefs and convictions. The work culture today is largely controlled as a way to amass wealth for benefiting the plutonomy. The modern conception of racism can be explained, that those who have control over wealth are the superior race; in the plutonomy, plutocrats are the superior race, but "the rest" of the others, the inferior race with no access to wealth are in the majority—the precariats. The precariats like Joe and Noriyasu are easily be forgotten by everybody and could only live in the fringes of the society as insignificant entitles. They are today's serf class. As a foundation of all these developments that implies no way of returning for them, we in fact madly follow an updated version of European universalism, with aggressive individualism that is trending since nineteenth century. According to Alexander Dugin: "But in essence, we simply dealing with an updated version and continuation of a Western universalism that has been passed down from the Roman Empire, Medieval Christianity, modernity in terms of Enlightenment and colonization up to the present-day phenomena of postmodernism and ultra-individualism."[4] The plutonomy of today is a revised and efficient version of feudalism without any sort of morality and ethics but with a kind of ultra-individualism that alienates everyone from "the others". The individualism that deems "the others" as hell is trending up everywhere. So, to save oneself from hell, an individual is required to objectify everything else dispassionately and coldly.

---

[4]Dugin (2012), p. 74.

References

1. Badiou, A.: Trump. Polity Press, Cambridge (2019)
2. Cicero, M.T.: On the Nature of the Gods. In: Brooks, F. (Trans. and ed.). Dodo Press, London, 45 BC (2008)
3. Dugin, A.: The Fourth Political Theory. Arktos Media, UK (2012)
4. Taylor, M.C.: Speed Limits. Yale University Press, New Heaven (2014)

Chapter 17
European Universalism: Exceptionalism and Racism in Plutonomy

European universalism and white racism condition the perspectives of the globalized world in the twenty-first century. We are now conditioned to view the entire world through a Eurocentric prism, which is the preamble to all our understandings. And even when we reject racism, we implicitly accept the racial segregation as a scientific truth that can be substantiated with the nineteenth century work the *Origins of Species* by Charles Darwin. The Darwinian ideas about the origin of species later imbibed into explaining the evolution of human culture on the basis of a new narrative on anthropology where the scientific minded Western population especially the north European tribes assumed prominence as the superior race. "The modern meaning of race originated in eighteenth-century zoology, and was later being applied to humans by Johann Friedrich Blumenbach, who formulated a terminology of physical anthropo-categories: black, brown, yellow, red and white."[1] The hierarchy of race using cultural Darwinism became the focal point of understanding the world since the nineteenth century, when science and technology began to shape up the human rational thought. Human nature that was defined on the basis of rationalism transformed into scientific rational thoughts and the cultural anthropology on the basis of the Darwinian evolution had become a benchmark: The white Europeans and "the others" who would be less advanced in comparison.

Following these perspectives, the eugenic society of Britain conducted research in line with Darwinism, where they preemptively evolved a theory that the Nordic white race is the superior race that can naturally think rationally and understand the natural laws using all scientific paradigms. The fact that made the race theory so compelling was due to the observable differences in human physical appearances. Moreover, the Judeo-Christian kind of Protestantism and an emphasis on God as the absolute of everything had played a significant role in the conception of the modern nation state. And it played a significant role in helping Nordic white man to form fictitious notion of the superior race. According to Elazar Barkan, "Physical

---

[1]Barkan (1992), p. 15.

© The Author(s), under exclusive license to Springer Nature Singapore Pte Ltd. 2021
M. Varghese, *A Brief History of Creative Work and Plutonomy*,
https://doi.org/10.1007/978-981-15-9263-8_17

differences were correlated with cultural and social studies through biological justification... Political domination buttressed by biological rationalization proliferated
during the second half of nineteenth century- one result of the growing reputation of
the Origins of Species. The theory of evolution inherently illuminates changes."[2] The
race theorists cleverly used the Darwinian theory on evolution of species, revealed in
his work the *Origin of Species*, that they curiously intermixed various other historical
developments applicable to the situations in the nineteenth century. Notably, during
the industrialization of the western world, it has given a feeling that the Nordic white
people are a class of its own kind who are the suitable people for meeting all the
requirements of the industrial world. They particularly stressed upon the idea that
the classical Greek conception of using reason is an original mark of the so-called
Nordic Aryan Race: the people who are inherently brave, naturally rational and also
who are the only intelligent achievers, according to Hegel and neo-Hegelians.

The Eugenic society of Britain placed substantial role in creating the superior
white race myth into a believable one. Again, the Eugenic society in order to bring
uniformity has proposed the creation of a new racially similar tribe, for the British
people by creating an artificial tribe of British Whites: the English, and the Scottish,
and the Irish and the Welsh into one tribe: the British (tribe).[3] The hubris attitude
of the British after exhortation of their brand of nationalism is the reason for later
events in the twentieth century. The British imperialism is founded on the thoughts
of the Eugenic society of Britain, and they considered themselves as the best among
the best having some divine authority over all other races. The national socialism
of NAZI Germany created a counter narrative by introducing third Reich with the
racial superiority feeling of the Nordic Aryans against the Anglo-French concept of
racial superiority, which played huge role in the making of the World War-II. Various
academic disciples began to creep up, for booting up this notion of superiority, by
advancing studies on subjects such as cultural anthropology, sociology, etc. for to
explain deliberately the life style and attitude of this newly emerged nationalist tribes
in Europe.

By moving fast forward into the postmodern globalized world, we can see that
a differently enabled notion of superiority of a new tribe emerged with the advent
of plutonomy. According to Alexander Dugin, the postmodern world order is conditioned by a kind of monotonous process: "History is considered to be a univocal
and monotone process of technological and social progress, the path of the growing
liberation of individuals from all kinds of collective identities."[4] The use of money as
the super-structure of all human activities has started since this technological monotone process took the control of everything. The examples of such a monotonous
process is the example of the German third Reich or the British imperialists that
had thus evolved in the last century in the same way as the tribe of the plutocrats
under plutonomy today. If the British imperialists or the NAZIs were evolved on a
conception of the racial superiority, the new tribe is formed on controlling the entire

[2]Ibid., p. 16.
[3]Ibid., p. 49.
[4]Dugin (2012), p. 74.

wealth using financial control. Plutonomy has that vicious power and are the post-modern tribe of financiers and investors, who could control almost all-conceivable wealth in the world. This tribe tries to attach and securitize all kinds of wealth using all kinds of nefarious and crooked activities. Contrary to the methods of bourgeoisie business practices, where they found "peace in the society" was an important aspect for establishing their businesses, but the plutonomy takes war as an opportunity to spread their unused money into the killing fields for finding value by circulation in funding the wars. War would open up the most profitable investment opportunities as the post war reconstruction could help them to use up their unspent money for new reconstruction activates. War for the plutonomy is now like, discovering a new country, in the sixteenth century by the European White explores. Since sixteenth century, discovering new continents and countries, was the method followed by the colonialists to get an access to the wealth and resources of "the other" countries. The exploitable "other" is what is again being followed in the plutonomy too, but who are "the others".

Looking back at the history of European universalism originated from the narrative understandings and conceptions of the superiority of the white race and the inferiority of "the others". But now that understanding has gone through years of transformation into the world of postmodern narratives giving new meanings, and the plutonomy of today uses all new methods of creating narratives and propagating it selectively to advance their investment opportunities everywhere smoothly. Mass media is a great means to advance such kinds of narratives. Now the tribe of plutocrats is not just the Whites only club but anyone can join in it, if someone can show substantial control on wealth and skill: like the Saudi Arabian princes, or the Indian merchants, or the Chinese neo-rich, or the Russian oligarchs, or Japanese technocrats, etc.

However, during the second half of nineteenth century most of the world was under European domination, especially of the U.K: in North America, South Asia, Africa, and Australia; whereas for France: in North Africa, some parts of North America, and some other regions around the world; and for Spain: in South America, and parts of North and central America, etc. Apart from that, there were a few colonies were there, for the Netherlands, Italy, Belgium, etc. According to Ashley Montagu race was a concept invented by the ruling class at that period of time.[5] Yet the racial theory hasn't got its highest pitch until Count Gobineau the "father of racist ideology mixed aristocratic pessimism, romanticism, theology together with biology, all of which become a part of the shared European value system based on racial discrimination. Gobineau's views on race were a culmination of pre-Darwinian ideas: a description of permanent type aimed at a moral genealogy."[6] The European Christians got a clumsy yet a convincing reason, to authenticate their brutal subjugation of the people in the colonies. They considered themselves as carriers of the Christian idea of "providence of God", and are helping the uncivilized natives into the path of scientific reasoning and the civilized ways of living. The colonialists essentially used the perspective of Gobineau, directly like the third-Reich and the British Eugenics, who brutally

---

[5] Montagu (1974), pp. 38, 39.
[6] Barkan (1992), p. 16.

controlled the world using such convenient narratives. Now in a different milieu, Plutonomy too thrive on such narratives.

The conservative values that were protected and upheld after the protestant reformation movement by Martin Luther had become the motivating fundamental force for the newly reformed and civilized Christians. The Protestant Christian religious fundamentalism created a value system that soon got universalized for everyone to follow especially after the World War-II. This has again intermixed with the European enlightenment values to make an indomitable discourse on European universalism that is suitable for the world order since seventeenth century. Later the issue of racism inadvertently linked to the universal economic development through globalization. Japan though a country of the so-called Yellow race, became a part of the Western white world order, because of their adoptability to the Western technoscience, and to the capitalist economic model, but China didn't. People like Noriyasu who born in the period of re-industrialization (industry-2.0) were very proud of the economic super power status of Japan. But like many others, he could not understand the postmodern globalized version of that superiority conscious. Today most of the populations in the developed countries are like "the others" who are the postmodern version of savages in the colonial era.

Hegelianism was fundamentally religious; communism was irreligious; third-Reich (NAZI), and Fascists were irreligious but also racists. But the Anglo-American liberalism is tactically religious but equally racist like the third Reich and Fascists. But all these western ideologies since nineteenth century rejected the culture and life styles of people in the areas of Mesopotamia, Africa, India, China, South America and all other regions that followed ancient cultures and religiosities. They were all "the others": the non-white, non-western cultures, who should be taught the Western values and technoscience. The north European paganism is obsolete completely. The world community implicitly began to believe that the real progress of humanity has started with the European enlightenment movement after the popular introduction of scientific methods. But during the early years of twentieth century the development in science came to an end, yet the attitude on the dependability of science has continued, which again been transformed into a kind of slavish dependence on techno scientific systems. And it is now followed by an arrogant contempt for the past and "the other" cultures, a vulgar materialist interpretation of spiritual life and culture, a focus exclusively upon economic factors, and an exaggerated attitude towards removing social differences through economic progress have become the new normal for the hugely technologically flourishing world order in the modern times. According to Alexander Dugin: "The very ideology of progress is racist in its structure. The assertion that the present is better and more fulfilling than the past, and continued assurances that the future will be even better than the present are discriminations against the past and the present, as well as the humiliation of all those who lived in the past, an insult to the honour and dignity of our ancestors and those of others and a violation of the rights of the dead. In many cultures, the dead play an important sociological role... In Chinese civilization which was built upon the cult of the dead and upon their reverence alongside the living.... The ideology progress represents the moral genocide of past generations."[7]

The people of the post-World War-II baby boomer generation were educated with a notion of the superiority of the white race and with all the good aspects of European universalism that had been founded on their authority over using scientific knowledge efficiently. This reverence become a kind of faithful submission to the views of the West. And the Protestant Christian democratic values founded on the ideals of "divine providence" and determinism of the white race to transform all aspects of life into the strict narratives of technoscience influenced the world and it took a new turn in the post war re-industrialization period. Even though significant changes happened in the globalized world, there exists an unquestioned submission to this technology minded western values that made the use of Artificial Intelligence plausible, acceptable and credible. Noted social philosopher, Immanuel Wallerstein, wrote about the European universalism and how it influenced the world in the post war period: "But after 1945, this world-system came under heavy attack from within. It was partially dismantled first by the national liberation movements and then by the world revolution of 1968. It has also suffered from a structural undermining of its ability to continue the endless accumulation of capital that is its raison d'etre. And, this means that we are called on not merely to replace this dying world-system with one that is significantly better but to consider how we can reconstruct our structures of knowledge in ways that permit us to be non-orientalists."[8] The ideological inquisition of the Western view made both communism and capitalism as world views. But, the failed Western systems—both communism and capitalism, now try to latch on to a new narrative for finding new acceptability through the implementation of technological systems even though it can create only trivial results. The struggle of the Western societies, to constantly redefine their limitations using the facade of science and technology by any means, is the method followed in the world order of today. The constant emphasis on the non-orientalist status of the white race's worldview substantially influenced the non-whites, as "the others" group. "The others" is a fluid group that, now, is all those who won't follow the economic and worldviews of the Anglo-Americans are deemed as "the others". However, according to Alexander Dugin: "Globalization is thus nothing more than a globally deployed model of Western European, or, rather, Anglo-Saxon ethnocentrism, which is the purest manifestation of racist ideology."[9] At times the group of "the others" include and disclude whites and non-whites. The poor Anglo-Saxon white Americans, the rednecks, can be included into "the others", whereas a wealthy Saudi Arabian prince, Nigerian oil oligarch automatically be a part of "the neo-Whites". The twenty-first century race issue are there because of the continued persistence on following European universalism and the contours of Eurocentrism.

The hegemonic attitude of the Westerns started to create suitable narratives and that had inimically supported the wellbeing of the new class, the plutocrats into the

---

[7]Dugin (2012), p. 45.
[8]Wallerstein (2006), p. 48.
[9]Dugin (2012), p. 45.

globalized world order. Still, fear is a dominant emotion today. Fear normally originated out of "ignorance and speculative views" and ignorance should have originated out of the lack of ability to think using proper "reasoning". The irrational distribution of wealth happens through a system that is founded on the emotion of "fear". The postmodern narrative on fear conditions our thoughts. In the pre-industrialized world order "faith" was the emotion that was discarded by reason; now in our times "fear" is the emotion that displaces "reason". The destructive power of plutonomy is so strong today with worldwide surveillance system emerging to control natural human freedom to think and reason naturally. Plutonomy is thriving with AI as its auxiliary power penetrating into all kinds of human activities, and the major workforce is emerging to be the part-time workers who are the helpers of those machines. The lack of "creative work" opportunities would reduce the natural human ability to think innately and act properly. The precariats are increasing exponentially as the AI machines running on big data would replace "creative works" and creative thinking.

Since 1960s to our times, the numbers of people who choose to join the group of *salariat* have increased hugely around the world because of the job security it offers. The work force then divided in to two major groups, for manufacturing and for services. People in the developed countries preferred service jobs with a comfortable salary supported by good pension systems. This system was being followed in most of the developed OECD countries that ensured economic security. Due to globalization, the erstwhile manufacturing business community shrunk; the power of money began to dominate all aspects of businesses; chances for making money has increased when trading of financial products happened in the globalization period. Investing in the financial products like shares etc. becomes a part of life in plutonomy. Most of the businesses that could use the new financial market sources could make a lot of money that could again be re-invested in investment companies who would ensure security and high returns. The number of plutocrats is less in number, but hold astronomical sums in the case of wealth holdings; similarly, the number of erstwhile proletariats who elevated to the level of plutocrats also has increased. The corruption and plutonomy thrived around the world, as plutocrat's money can buy anything and everything around the world. Plutonomy now has become transnational and race blind. But, at the same time, due to the pressures from the financialized world systems, it become inevitable for the financial industry to create new markets and newer manufacturing methods. Creative work, work satisfaction, communities of workers' unions, etc. are replaced by the quantity of money and the happiness and satisfaction that money could buy or money could provide. All the human issues except that regarding money have relevance only as talking points. The problem of technological unemployment started to creep in aggressively everywhere. Out sourcing of jobs and the using of robotics etc. are to be taken as the reason for technological unemployment. With technological unemployment, the new underclass employees have increased that they could assist machines for the benefit of the plutonomy only. The herd of precariats, who have no economic freedom have increased everywhere. Precarity—lack of employment and income—became a fact of life. These external changes have glossed over the relationship between *work and life* that used to have a unique spiritual meaning in "the others"—the non-western cultures' traditional ways of living.

Noriyasu was a *salariat* who experienced the value of work as a way to self-educate and self-learn, not just a means for getting money. When the neo-bourgeoisie become a plutocrat, the less than 1%, "the others": the more than 99%, soon become the underclass with no relevance at all. A new dialectics is now being developing between the hubris of the White race and the sophrosyne of "the others". This kind of naïve reaction from the affected 99% making the use of Artificial intelligence possible, in which case plutocrats are emerging as a synthetic monster with uncontrollable power of destruction on the human species. Plutonomy of today has the coercing power of European universalism, exceptionalism, and the metanarrative of white racism. And it is now becoming transnational and colorblind. They are the most significant force that can influence any kind of sociopolitical decisions in any part of the world. Above all European universalism is acting as the superstructure perpetuating aggressive individualism.

References

Barkan, E.: The Retreat of Scientific Racism. Cambridge University Press, New York (1992)
Dugin, A.: The Fourth Political Theory. Arktos Media, UK (2012)
Montagu, A.: The Play of Race. Oxford University Press, New York (first pub. 1942) (1974)
Wallerstein, I.: European Universalism. New Press, New York (2006)

Chapter 18
The Era of Maniacal Depression and Suicides

How can we analyze the trauma of Noriyasu? On an average estimate, there are almost 40,000 people that suicide every year in Japan. That means in a day around 100 individuals end their lives in suicides. Studies say majority of them have gone through some kinds of existential traumas similar to Noriyasu. This is not particular only to Japan: it is everywhere. The number of people who lost all interests in living a life is, on the increase in the globalized world. The common men of today are being subjected to some kind of fear leading to maniacal depressions and traumas, and at worst cases they end their lives willingly. This may be the case of day-to-day trauma of many in the world. To address this psychological decline, the modern psycho-analysts, can immediately suggest any perfect sure shot solutions. The dispensation of antidepressant medication, and other psychotropic drugs by psychotherapists and doctors is a major problem in the world today. Drug over dose fatalities, according to American CDC report is 70,237, in 2017.[1] We may have to understand this problem of depression as a problem of the newly emerging globalized world; if we want to find any solutions, this situation would escalate into a major crisis in future. However, the Western thinkers of today who are the thought leaders can suggest only some clichéd solutions, same as those might be given by the modern psychoanalysts, lest such analysts should come out of the box and think more creatively we will find no tangible solutions at all. As a habit in the world today, everyone waits for ready-made solutions that should come from the Western world, for to be followed unquestion-ably. The whole world is waiting for sure shot scientifically acceptable—western psychoanalysts' verified—solutions to the problems such as maniacal depression, suicides, etc.

On the basis of psychological sciences, there are innumerable solutions, but none could solve such problems well. For, most of them are found through questionable academic research and psychiatric clinical studies. However, in general those studies try to address those problems with naïve reasoning for solutions, knowing fully well

---

[1] https://www.cdc.gov/nchs/products/databriefs/db356.htm#:~:text=In%202018%2C%20there%20were%2067%2C367,than%20in%202,017%20 (21.7). Retrieved on 14 June, 2020.

© The Author(s), under exclusive license to Springer Nature Singapore Pte Ltd. 2021
M. Varghese, *A Brief History of Creative Work and Plutonomy*,
https://doi.org/10.1007/978-981-15-9263-8_18

that human mind never could be objectified for any thorough analytical research procedures. The mind, as its innate nature, structures thoughts incessantly, which is a difficult problem to be addressed for humanity. Most of those contemporary social philosophers and researchers can give only figurative suggestions not any concrete ones. Those are mostly meant for systemic changes: some decline capitalism; some decline socialism; some uphold more democracy and freedom; some propose more interventions to change the systems of other people and cultures; at best most of the modern academia call for getting more scientific rational studies for finding more clarity on this. However, none thinks about the internalized solutions, for protecting the inner life of people like Noriyasu to be healthy and strong, where modern techno-science has no idea on the validity of upholding the inner life of a person as a valid method for solving problems.

Now we have done everything except looking at the "inner life" of people like Noriyasu. Modern philosophers considered talking about the "inner life" as unscientific, therefore unacceptable and archaic, especially after Hegel and Marx. Since the advent of Capitalism and Communism, the health of economic prosperity has as the most important aspect that would provide immediate sure shot solutions for all the human problems. The prosperity would reflect in the life of everyone, providing permanent happiness; nobody ever thought differently after the first industrial revolution. The externalized solutions that we can find are suggesting only for making more drastic systemic changes for more reflections, more researches, more data analyses, etc. But I think the changes that should have happened would come forth only by providing more opportunities for doing "creative work", because human thinking would be natural when one engages in creative work for generating better health for our inner lives. Body and mind work in tandem as a unit, when activating the *hand-brain faculty* to its fullest potential. According to Aristotle it is *techne*, one learns the principles by the art of creation, which helps one to invoke *eudaimonia* naturally; *techne* is similar to *episteme* (knowledge) that one discerns by rational analytical methods, but *techne* could be realized only through *creative works.*

According to some contemporary neuro-biologists, creative work is the most necessary factor, for generating a robust consciousness (an ego-tunnel) for protecting the *inner self*. The *ego tunnel* is what is responsible for generating an active conscious space that acts in the most necessary aspect for living a good life. This conscious space is what protects a person's life at every stage, from childhood to old age. Creation of such a conscious space is possible, only, by engaging in some kind of creative work or by partaking a creative work of being a beneficiary. In which case, we can find that human work is not just a way to earn money but to earn creative knowledge in the form of work experiences. Money can buy food, clothing and housing, beyond which, it can buy only illusions and fantasies; whereas, according to classical philosophers and thinkers, creativity in work provides knowledge and a feeling of freedom, a well lived life experience. According to Aristotelian philosophy, finding *eudaimonia*—good flourishing happy spirit—as the purpose for one to live a life in the world, and he considered *arete*—excellence in virtuous action is the way to realize perpetual happiness in life in the world. The latest studies on consciousness and its relation with human body and the neural circuits shows that creative work plays an all-important function in making a meaningful and enjoyable life, which means that creative work helps one to internally activate the instincts of satisfaction.

Now we can figure out why Noriyasu suicided? We can see plenty of people in the world facing such traumatic situations of depression, fear, self-petrification, suicide tendencies, etc. Noriyasu's death is just a case point not an exception. He had sufficient wealth and means to survive but no means to find internal spiritual happiness—*eudaimonia*. When creative work was denied, the creation of the conscious space (ego-tunnel) and the maintenance of it never would happen naturally. And normal life become dull and uninteresting. The story of Noriyasu is the typical case for understanding the situation of some people who belong to the baby-boomer generation. They were lured into city lives, but with the risk of losing everything, after losing their jobs. Though many of them lose everything with the losing of jobs, a good number of them could survive on charities of various kinds; but would never get an opportunity, to engage in any kind of creative works again. The scientific rationalism that fired the world systems since eighteenth century could only provide a kind of protection of "life" in the world by suggesting some externalized solutions such as freedom from poverty, political freedom, religious freedom, etc. but not the freedom from fear and worries or maintaining the freedom of our inner lives. The inadvertent attachments to those kinds of thoughts have created only more sufferings. Humans are naturally destined to find solutions for being protected their internal and external life by finding internalized solutions. Today the internal life of an individual is denigrated to the bottom level by injecting fear and scare using various control systems. After, with the advent of externalized scientific solutions as the main method for understanding and explaining "life", the human society beginning to imitate "the others" or negates "the others" for living through their lives. In the postmodern globalized world, the importance of creative work was progressively declined by making natural day to day life a much-tormented experience.

Chapter 19
The Emergence of a New Class System

Let us walk through the story of Noriyasu to see how the new class hierarchy in plutonomy formed with plutocrats at its top. In the new system instead of the oligarchies of bourgeoisies or feudal lords, on top, a new oligarchic control system emerged that made human work completely valueless, superfluous and unessential. For the artificial intelligence (AI) supported systems should keep the synthetic unity by making creative work less valuable and plutonomy more resourceful. As Noriyasu comes from a village in the north Japan of traditional farmer's background, where the age-old tradition of rice cultivation had been followed with its boring repetitive phases that went on, for year after year, and day after day, as a way of life; nonetheless, almost everyone followed them with reverence and dedication as a living tradition. There prevailed a kind of routine governed existence. But, since 1960s for the newly emerged re-industrializing new world order gave increased opportunities everywhere, especially for the young Japanese of the post war period. The opening up of new opportunities, since 1960s, especially in the big cities made young man like Noriyasu, to follow the trail of many like him, in pursuit of the dream of prosperity and plenty, with a convenient way to escape from the boring repetitive phases of the village life. As a result of this, urban sprawl had emerged making the Tokyo city of today itself with 36 million people, a population equal to that of Canada.

And personally, for Noriyasu the huge success of 1964 Tokyo Olympics was a spark that ignited in his soul and was waiting to flare up into a full-blown dream; and it pushed himself to pursue a new life in Tokyo. After completing his school studies, he did higher studies at a university in Tokyo, from where he got graduated with a degree in Business management, for to get a dream job in the emerging vibrant industrial world. The paradigm shift that happened with work in the case of Noriyasu was that he had been habituated with a life style, where earning profit was not the only purpose of work, but work was a way of life. But now that has changed into work for pursuing only some monetary gains. He should live a life where everything is being decided by the power of money. So, he couldn't find any kind of happiness from doing his work, which was stressful, repetitive, and undignified.

© The Author(s), under exclusive license to Springer Nature Singapore Pte Ltd. 2021
M. Varghese, *A Brief History of Creative Work and Plutonomy*,
https://doi.org/10.1007/978-981-15-9263-8_19

Almost everything in his college life was highly exciting for him. Most of his teachers were from the Western countries like America, Britain, Canada, Germany and France, who are all trained in teaching modern civil humanistic values. He enjoyed his city life with an exhilarating feeling of joy and happiness with great delights. He was attracted to various activities at the University and was a part of many student activities, including student politics. An unexpressed air of neo-racism, elitism, was a part of life in the re-industrialization period since 1960s. Those acquired values were not original to Japanese culture, but mostly originated out of being an individual who happened to have born in a highly industrialized advanced country.

As a feature of this period most of those who moved in to the cities could get better life, and could work towards for being a part of the emerging industrial culture. Noriyasu met his future wife, in the 1970s in one of his activities connected with a leftist student movement in Japan, that had followed by the leftist ideologies of the 60s and 70s. His heroes, like many of his generation were Che-Guevara, Fidel Castro, Mao etc. Noriyasu felt that he was a rebel with a purpose. The Zengakuren student movement in Japan followed 1968 student movements in Western Europe that was against the moral decline and corruption in the society that went against the stated purpose of the republican values and the system of government that was founded on the principles of equality and freedom for everyone. He found friends that shared with him such opinions and viewpoints, who also share the dream of a better future in the line of a society of the liberal socialist democratic system. His future wife was one of them. Later they got married. And he then got a great job in an American company. Noriyasu became a *salariat* (salariman). The company did well, but for more profit and for new investment, the company reformed its economic activities and as a part of the company's restructuring activities, they downsized the work force; wherein Noriyasu lost his happy job.

The pursuit for profit and other development oriented activates of the company had reflected adversely upon the life of Noriyasu. How can we relate these aspects with the internalized structure of Noriyasu's life? How can it be reflected with the help of latest neurological studies? How the deterioration of the consciousness—the ego tunnel, happened in him? The complicated situation upset his psychic life. The idea of "ego tunnel" is also known as "personal self-model" that is meant to express the conscious space that one develops by living his life.[1] In the case of Noriyasu, the entire life experiences with his life should have formed an individual specific neural structure much different from that of the friends and family of his native village. Unlike to the folks back home, he could live a life by fulfilling his dreams, imaginations and fantasies; this is a typical situation for some people of the baby boomer generation whose life progressed into the globalized world of chasing one dream after the other. But the *personal self-model* or *ego tunnel* that he created is being destroyed systematically by making his generation of baby boomers as insignificant and redundant after taking away the possibility for doing any *creative works*.

The highly qualified and smarter workers who formed a part of the bourgeoisie class could get direct access to some fixed asset after the 1960s, like houses, land,

---

[1] Metzinger (2009), p. 26.

etc., but Noriyasu gets only a yearly salary instead of any such assets. He belongs to a different variety of workers, the *salaryman* (salariat), much different from the proletarian of the industrial period, who used to work on day-to-day basis but he works on long contracts for a salary. The proletarians had no dreams but to live for the day and struggle with his fate eternally: live not knowing nothing about their rights and freedoms of being human beings. The salariat are from educated proletariat and are in the middle: if things work well they can also be the super-rich, plutocrats, but if things go bad they can be in the underclass of today the lumpen class who may live on charity. Noriyasu's situation is almost similar to that of a lumpen precariat. The bourgeoisies' amassed wealth should have made him feel secured and could have a feeling that his legacy would survive through the "self-interest maximization" activities only. Self-interest maximization was the main aim of the bourgeoisie life. But the bourgeoises in general used cleverly the creative work of the workers by buying them with money. Noriyasu was brought up and lived in an era where youngsters like him were inventers and extraordinary achievers that were a feature of Japanese social life in the post war period especially since 1960s. The baby boomer generation marveled the world with their trend setting innovations.

But in the globalized world of the postmodern period, those things have been challenged and changed by artificial intelligence (AI) replacing human creative work absolutely. Plutonomy replaced the capitalist bourgeoisie's hold on wealth as investor's money securitized the wealth of the world progressively. Artificial intelligence now works on self-analysis using huge amount of sourced data, on human behavior normally from the activities and behaviors of individual persons, by using various data accessing methods. The making of artificially created systems would destroy opportunities for work and the importance of the working class redundant. Similarly, the bourgeoisie class becomes redundant like the feudal class of the pre-industrial world. And since the importance of human work become insignificant, communism also had to face a huge challenge of finding some respectability.

The leftist movements in the 1960s and 1970s should have redefined the world in those times and should have removed poverty by finding much effective methods for wealth distribution. But a different occurrence happened in the later phase of industrialization, industry-3.0. The intellectuals of the leftist movement began to join the world of financial industry, with a motivational thought that making finance available easily for investment should be the best way to bring prosperity to everyone and that we can create an open society that works for all. The works of Karl Popper, on an open society motivated this attitude of the intellectual class. Those educated entrepreneurs then turned in as the professional consultants, the *proficians*: those who would provide freelance expertise consultancy services on contract. The world of such freelancers is a feature in all of the twenty-first century world economic systems working only for money. They are everywhere, working to financialize any kind of property with commercial value anywhere and everywhere in the world. Financializing wealth is the economic model that is being followed almost everywhere.

The erstwhile bourgeoisie of the earlier industrial periods has almost been disappeared and now being replaced with a new generation of wealth controllers under plutonomy, but nobody can identify them as a distinct recognizable group as like the bourgeoisie of the industry-1.0. As being discussed earlier, one of such controllers is *proficians*: the professional consultants who would amass a huge chunk of money, but with no responsibility with the company or its activities beyond the accomplishment of their assigned jobs. Most of the outsourcing of works to cheaper manufacturing centers are done with the active support of the proficians, that they co-ordinate various manufacturing and service activities for their clients, who again market the manufactured things using a similar mechanism of high-tech streamlined system for maximizing efficiency and profits. Their commitment to a job is entirely professional and ends upon the accomplishment of a given particular job. The proficians could be lobbyists for various special interest groups, working with various other kinds of consultants who just should activate good situations for high profits on any venture, and also be acting as consultants who would manipulate public opinions, by influencing the media for creating suitable narratives for propagating certain chosen viewpoints, etc. They make any opinion workable by using all available means including sensational events that could make public opinion in their favor. And they use the magical power of money as the tool to make things workable anywhere. Their coercing power is unimaginable. A chunk of profits from outsourcing of manufacturing activities, in fact goes to proficians as consultation fees. They also execute all kinds of contract jobs mostly outsourced to countries like China, etc. But at the same time, they have no responsibility beyond the job that they are entrusted to do by the CEOs of the companies. This group mostly amasses as much wealth as possible and turns it into financial or real estate assets of various kinds around the world. As and when a work is accomplished, they become insignificant and redundant for the company.

Since the company used Chinese marketing facilities as per the advice of some consultancy firm, Noriyasu lost his job. Though he travelled a long way, from the feudal Japanese work culture to the life of a salariman (salariat) of the industry-3.0. He expected to have protected by the same work cultural practices of the traditional Japanese society, but not been in the emerged highly financialized situation. But when he was required to leave the job with immediate effect he couldn't understand the gravity and reality of the situation of the industrial world, industry-3.0. Why? In our times, the difference between a CEO and an ordinary executive is assessed with one's ability in creating profits. Noriyasu couldn't understand on how can he be useful in creating more profits for the company. He lost his job, because he was not profitable anymore, in comparison, to a worker from another outsourced location. He thought it is temporary or maybe he could find another job with much better future prospects. To be out of active life in his late forties is something he never imagined, or ever prepared to confront with. He, in fact, wanted to have children for extending his family. He had hoped for a promotion and a hike in salary. But, instead he was asked to leave with immediate effect that was more than a shocker for him. He knew from his earlier life in the village that there is no retirement for anyone in his traditional extended family. His grandparents and parents never had to retire. They could continue working, up until their death. If there were some problems, they all shared them together willingly or unwillingly. But the family always stayed together supporting each other. Struggling to stay together with any difference was the kind of family and community life he used to. On the other hand, he had experienced a kind of scorn and rejection from everywhere of being unemployed and unwanted. Nobody has complained or criticized, but has ignored or rejected him. Though he could find some part time jobs that would earn only a little money, he found them less rewarding and largely boring, and hugely beneath his education and dignity. Or, he slipped from a *salariat* to a *precariat* and then to *lumpen precariat*. But he needn't have to choose something unpleasant like that of working as a part-time worker for money alone as his wife had enough properties to provide him the basic supports. The spiritual growth that should have happened progressively hasn't happened in the case of Noriyasu.

Working for monetary reasons was not a concern for him. But, he had lost his identity as an educated and well-trained business specialist, and the natural ability to progress in life doing some creative works, whereby, his conscious space (ego tunnel) begun to collapse and lost his personality that should have structured through creative work as his personal self-model. Yet, the trauma of Noriyasu is difficult for anyone to understand properly. If not for money why should he be so worried about being unemployed or underemployed. It should have been a blessing in disguise that a lot of free time and sufficient money should have acted as a boon for him to do whatever he had dreamt of doing. But in reality, he felt it as if he was facing a dull and meaningless life that didn't provide him any happiness from doing a creative work. Because of which he experienced a sudden lurking of sadness and a kind of self-alienation and self-petrification constantly. It was like people who are sitting in a cave looking at the moving shadows as in the Plato's example of cavemen's existence; or like those who watch a shadow puppet show where the meaning of the shadow play is so obscure and so absurd.

In the changing world of high pitch financialization, the plutocrats have piled up a lot of dead wealth but the common belief on the rich is that they are lucky and can do anything with lots of money. We have no idea what money could do for our lives, and also have no idea how to conduct a life when we have lots of money, but when we have too little or no money, we still have no idea how to live a normal life. It is difficult for the plutonomic world order to understand, money is one factor of life that can provide you a good life. We must note that the modern and postmodern world systems, are developed on Hegelian or Marxian philosophy, on the basis of binary logical propositions, that allow only to make either/or propositions; it is difficult for finding any suitable solutions from within the confines of those closed binaries. The nature of those binary systems is such that it fervently rejects the opposite only for choosing a single selected option. The plutocrat always argue that his wealth is feeding millions of poor in the developing world, by providing them with the outsourced jobs; and for the workers who lost their jobs after the shifting of domestic manufacturing jobs, the plutocrats would argue that the domestic population can find more time to spend for themselves and enjoy life with less work. They create and propagate a kind of self-nourishing narrative by using binary logical interpretations. But philosophically by using binary (two value) logic everywhere we forget to give a perspective about the totality of the phenomenal world. For, we may view human life on earth in the perspective of the national economy and high GDP, PPP, etc. On the contrary, even though the national economies are working well, that would work poorly for the majority, because of poor wealth distribution through jobs, which is a big reality today. Unfortunately, the intellectuals too are caught up between two opposing arguments, trying to prove an argument on the basis of their preferred choice.

The national GDP will be very high even if there are huge disparities in wealth distribution. The two-value logical system will not allow us to find a third perspective in all such situations. In the dialectics of plutocrats against precariats, we need a new perspective where man should live and prosper by doing creative works, not just making the mammoth of unused wealth.

Reference

Metzinger, T.: Ego Tunnel. Basic Books, New York (2009)

Chapter 20
The Plutonomic World Systems and Marxian Thoughts on Work

Karl Marx in his *Communist Manifesto* wrote about the thought-history on the class theory of work; starting from classical periods in antiquity to the modern industrial period, before introducing the concept of bourgeoisie and proletariat as the class antagonism of the industrial world. Marx was a philosopher who thoroughly studied about the socio-economic systems of Europe, and how the Hegelian method of dialectics could be developed to address the problems of wealth distribution. He evolved his method by applying Hegelian dialectics on the basis, of the historical developments of wealth distribution from the classical periods to the modern times. The class antagonism as the foundation of the material based dialectical process which is meant to find a synthetic unity that should emerge as "work", in order to distribute wealth in accordance with the needs of an individual and society. The pivot of this dialectics is founded on the conception of the "providence of nature", not the "providence of God" as found in Hegelian dialectics. But he found that the newly emerging and expanding bourgeoisie class mercilessly would negate the right of the ordinary workers—proletariat and their right to live using the double negation method of the Hegelian dialectic, i.e. bourgeoisie constantly negating the rights of the proletariat.

The injustice that happened on all aspects relating to the distribution of wealth between the two classes after the industrial revolution worried a lot of intellectuals. They realized that the spirit of European enlightenment movement had eroded, the issue of the unequal distribution of wealth with another class replaces the feudal oligarchy. As modern capitalism originated out of the religious commitment and the charitable attitude of the Protestant Movement, especially on the conception of "divine providence", which was inspired after the influential teaching of Martin Luther, John Calvin and others, where a capitalist should act as an agent of the "providential" aspect of God in providing some means, to survive, for the poor and needy. The feudalism in Europe was endorsed by the support of the holy Roman Empire largely ignored the rights of the serf class. A capitalist is predisposed to give honest works and honest wages to the workers as his God given divine duty. But the subsequent development of the social order in Europe had noticeably changed this value-based thought, where namesake charity and huge accumulation of wealth had

© The Author(s), under exclusive license to Springer Nature Singapore Pte Ltd. 2021
M. Varghese, *A Brief History of Creative Work and Plutonomy*,
https://doi.org/10.1007/978-981-15-9263-8_20

taken over as the norm of the industrial world. The newly rich bourgeoisies began to subjugate the members from the same class, the serfs, who were liberated after the feudal system being collapsed with the ending of the holy Roman empire, and with the advent of enlightenment movement. Majority of bourgeoisies and proletariats were the same, freed serf underclass.

Karl Marx found that one of outcome of the dialectics between bourgeoisies against proletariat, "the work" always emerged as the synthetic unity. The works of workers would remain as the absolute that both need to be depended upon, like the pneumatic spirit of Christ in the Hegelian dialectical system. Marx also found that the bourgeoisie do less work but receive maximum benefits; whereas, the proletariat get little benefit but do maximum work. The capitalist because of his control on organizing and disseminating capital became instrumental for the origination of the banking industry. The labor of the workers evolved as the supreme that could reduce the absolutism of the money power of the capitalists. Marx wrote about the history of "work" as the history of subjugation between the controllers and the controlled. In Marxian dialectics labor has a unique stance. Marx wrote:

"The modern bourgeois society that has sprouted from the ruins of feudal society has not done away with class antagonisms. It has but established new classes, new conditions of oppression, new forms of struggle in place of the old ones. Our epoch, the epoch of the bourgeoisie, possesses, however, this distinct feature: it has simplified class antagonisms. Society as a whole is more and more splitting up into two great hostile camps, into two great classes directly facing each other—Bourgeoisie and Proletariat. From the serfs of the middle Ages sprang the chartered burghers of the earliest towns. From these burgesses the first elements of the bourgeoisie were developed."[1]

Karl Marx understood that the serfs—the underclass—of the traditional Western feudal society reemerged in the industrial world first as the hired burghers who earned better and then became the bourgeoisie class who subjugated (negated) those who cannot get such favours, who became the proletariat class. The new class antagonism was severe, as it happened when one group tries to dominate the other without any ethical or moral considerations and values as being envisaged in the doctrine of "divine providence". This happened on the basis of acquiring techno-scientific knowledge and skill as the source of all exploitation activities. The bourgeoisie class would conquer "the other", the proletariat class, on the basis of knowledge acquired by learning the contours of scientific reasoning that helps techno-scientific systems. The proletariat class, because of their naivety, would follow the traditional religious convictions and beliefs as the foundation of all their conduct and should have accepted their plight as fate, or as some cursing by God. The difference was that the bourgeoisie didn't think in the same way; they would be so cunning, bruit and astute in appropriating money and power by further exploiting the ignorance and backwardness of the proletariat, which was conditioned by their astute religious beliefs especially about sin. Marx understood that ignorance about the real thoughts of bourgeoisie is the sources of all the miseries of the proletariat. He asked the communists to work

---

[1]Communist Manifesto (2016).

relentlessly in support of the proletariat and help them with education on scientific rationalism and scientific methods, so that the naïve and gullible workers would not be exploited easily. Although Christianity was the guiding religious view for the Europeans at the time of Marx that insisted "divine providence" as a way had been cunningly used to exploit the beliefs of the common men. Nonetheless, the attitude of plutonomy today is irreligious and therefore highly exploitative and abusive, and there is no charitable attitude demanded here. Marx was influenced by the religiosity of classical Greek materialism, especially of Epicureanism.

Marx, as a scholar, wrote his Ph.D. thesis on comparing the philosophical views of the classical materialism (atomism) of Democritus and Epicurus. Marx should have known about the concept of materialism and the religiosity of the co-dependent existence (camaraderie) promoted in the Epicurean philosophy. The Epicurean idea of fellowship, camaraderie, and living a disciplined life, by accepting hedonist "pleasure" moderately, and the life style of living and sharing, should have influenced the foundation of communists' ethics. He would have understood that the class difference in a society would act against such a religiosity of sharing extant in the philosophy of Epicureanism. The epicurean view is that all human beings like to survive by co-operating with each other and that could sprout happiness in a sustainable way. The Marxian view is that that is denied in capitalism and in the religiosity of Protestantism, since modern times the capitalist distorted the conception of divine providence, and found material possessions as a way to get happiness, i.e. *eudaimonia*. According to the philosophy of Epicurus, too much possessions, would damage the chances to be free; thereby instead of happiness, unhappiness would ensue. Through this wisdom, Marx observed that if it goes on unchecked and uncontrolled by relevant philosophical thoughts and actions, capitalist bourgeoisie greed would destroy human life, and finally the entire existence of humanity. It is like eating too much sugar: if sugar is eaten without any control, one may fall sick quickly and may die of diabetes eventually. It is not a strict rule, but the chances for a sugar eater to get diabetes are very high; so, every capitalist may not feel some unhappiness, but chances for him to be unhappy are very high in comparison to a middle class (burgher) common-man. He may also live in a world of ignorance until the end of his life: thinking that money is everything and die without knowing the real reason for that ignorance. The only thing that enthuse a bourgeoisie is the perpetual greed for more wealth. Realizing *eudaimonia* should be the purpose of one's life and Epicurus shown a way that inspired the Christian humanism, European enlightenment movement, etc. including communism.

In our times, the greed and ignorance of neo-bourgeoisie—plutonomy— encourage them to use Artificial intelligence and finance heavily to implement their greed for money and control. And that could destroy the importance of human labor. Marx considered work is the conduit that unified bourgeoisie and proletariat. The ignorance that flourishes on all over the world is based on technology and a false sense of security and protection from the system of techno-sciences. And therein "work" is less important. As a result, in the world of plutonomy, in a technologically savvy contemporary world where the life systems are under the control of technology, one needs only to be a part of the oligarchic system that runs and controls those systems.

It mostly ends up with those who run the financial systems. A super capitalist may not understand that he is controlling a huge quantity of dead wealth, which would destroy him and his family's life, but he resolutely holds on to it without distributing it through "work", thinking that wealth has some sort of divine providence attached to it. For Marx super capitalism is a kind of social sickness without any cure. That may be the reason why he proposed a total revolution against capitalism and tried to redefine it with a new value system redefined by materialistic dialectic for benefiting the proletariats so that the entire community will be benefited with a different value system similar to that of Epicurean systems of camaraderie, frugality, compassion, friendship, egalitarianism, etc. in an organically progressing society, where materialism plays a significant role.

The Pin factory theory of Adam Smith is a good example to define on how we unquestioningly accepted the Artificial intelligence. In the pre-industrialized period, the artisans made all things including pins, but each one could make only a few pins in a day. Apart from iron, the main resource for making the pins was the creative skills of the artisans who had production limitations. Depending on such a low productivity, he never could satisfy the high demand of the modern industrialized world. The requirements of modern world were different, it wanted to make more and more wealth by making and selling lots and lots of pins, or more monetary wealth using more easily tradable goods, to make life easy for the growing population of that time. The industrial method of job sharing was introduced aggressively. As a consequence, high production activities also could satisfy the greed of the newly developed middle class (burghers) who were skilled, educated and savvy. This middle class soon transformed as the bourgeoisie, the wealth controllers. The world systems soon developed around the presumption that with aggressive production, using techno-sciences could answer all human problems, even those relating to spiritual life, and it could make human life happy forever. Scientific rationalism enhanced the speculative views and ignorance of the masses. Notably, the psychological sciences replaced religion and spirituality by creating a huge vacuum. The scientific systems could not create the euphoria and enchantment that provided by the religious systems.

The entrepreneurs of the modern western world who were empowered with scientific knowledge conquered the world and they made products on an industrial scale and travelled around the world to sell it. The prosperity ensued have illogically forced everything to be industrialized and technologized with some speculative expectations, based on prosperity and freedom. As a consequence, overproduction and dead (unused) wealth began to subjugate everything that is profitable and tradable. The governments began to promote unregulated financial systems by increasing credit. In order to find value for the dead money, the plutocrats under plutonomy started to buy up all properties or to securitize all wealth through investment banks. Financialization of assets demanded high production that only meant economic development in monetary terms, not in providing jobs and thereby dividing the wealth.

The "pins" that we buy today are made in different centers by using cheap labor, and by using only high technology to produce more in a 24/7 schedule with less and less labor involvement is the new order of our times; over production is now the most difficult and unsolvable problem. The unused things are thrown away to poorer countries at cheaper prices which destroys their domestic production industry and the waste is left behind as unused waste, creating huge environmental problems. But the twenty-first century plutonomy would produce goods just to keep up their capital running, it matters least, whether the goods are used or not. Because of which, we have few people within plutonomy—*plutocrats, proficians, salariat*—today everywhere, who make it running receiving huge monetary compensations. As per contemporary studies, there are around 2 billion floating workers available, to work for bare minimum salary. Human labor is the cheapest part concerning production. Minimum spending, maximum profit became the norm. Either the factories are to be moved into the cheap-labor zones, or the workers are to be brought in to the manufacturing areas; manufacturing using domestic resources is getting extinct progressively. And today all production activities are set to be done with the help of AI run machines and not with the help of any kind of creative work inputs from the workers. Thus, most of the jobs available are mechanical, boring and repetitive types. The AI systems append humans to partake a certain activity. So, the workers only act as an extension of the machines. Artificial intelligence takes care of everything running with monstrous certainty and precision. Human work has no place in production activities if Artificial intelligence would copy any new creative innovation digitally, and programmatically run it. The programs are just a copy of the logical thinking of humans that would run in systems working on Nano-seconds. That is why machines can run systems automatically with much efficiency and precision than, the humans who would naturally make mistakes.

There is no scope for applying any of the creative skills of the workers in the emerging new world order. And therefore, a kind of inertia, dullness, purposelessness, etc. is overburdening the human population in the world. Human societies are going through a war within itself. Using intelligence for creativity is no longer a factor in human life. This unusual mechanization of human life is now making depression, sexual dysfunction, fear psychosis, anger and rage, suicidal tendency, etc. as the day-to-day common problems. We use some kind of comforting narrative to forget or camouflage these problems. When the possibility for such narratives extinguishes, we feel a kind of intellectual inertia and then, we run into the world of entertainment soon to be bored up in that fictitious world too. We, now, see the ineffectiveness of following both comfort and entertainment as the aim of life.

The society may achieve economic self-sufficiency by technologizing everything. Food will be created by using bioengineering; using robotics and mechanized labor force. That way we would make all products that we use. And a few who would work to enable those systems to function can find very high paying jobs. But no solution is yet in sight for solving health problems that are skyrocketing; in fact, the modern medical system creates diseases that are resulted from unhealthy lifestyles, and trying to cure them by using high technology. The psychological sciences are not able to find a way to solve serious spiritual decline problems those are considered as mental problems. Now we have more problems generated out of the spread of fear and ignorance. Actually, we struggle to survive with fear. It overwhelms and engrosses human life today. Contrarily, I have seen people who live, without fear and spiritual decline due to confusions, throughout their lives. They all did some kind of "creative work" and had enjoyed thoroughly in engaging with work till the end of their lives. Monetary profit was one of the many benefits that they sought from work. In other words, they spend their time and effort to activate the *complex body-hand-brain faculty* regularly.

Reference

Communist Manifesto: The original text at: https://www.marxists.org/archive/marx/works/1848/ communist-manifesto/ch01.htm#007//. Retrieved on 17 July 2016

Chapter 21
The Life of Carpenter Krishnan and "Creative Work"

Carpenter Krishnan was one who had known and experienced the wonders of creative work who had to live through seeing its vast decline. He is, according to Marxian definition was a feudal serf, then became proletarian in the industrial period, but then in the globalized period, become a *precariat*—part time worker. Even with his underclass existence, he lived a good life all the while, where he decided to do creative work as a part of his being. However, by definition, his son who got a modern education become a part of the bourgeoisie in the pre-globalized world, where he owned various kinds of companies; and in the globalized world order he has become a plutocrat, who holds major shares in many companies and is also controlling huge amount of financial assets through his investment companies. He is now an international investor existing at the crest of plutonomy. But even with his large holdings he is unhappy. In the fundamental conception of Greek philosophy *techne*—the art or craft of creating things from forms that are internalized, is similar to *episteme*, the process of knowing from sense experiences with the help of intelligence; these two aspects make humans different from other living beings. Contextually, for Indian philosophy *karma* (*techne*) and *jñāna* (*episteme*) can expresses the same aspects of basic human nature.

But, on the basis of the classical Asian narrative on "work", which cannot strictly be explained in the Marxian way. The idea of feudalism and serfdom cannot strictly be narrated in the pre-industrial period of the Eastern world. In Asian countries labor was divided on the basis of caste system. From the perspective of dividing wealth, in economics, the caste system can be seen as a traditionally constructed system to ensure division of wealth into the deeper layers of the social fabric. Carpenter Krishnan was born in the caste of carpenters, which means his community and his ancestors all were from the carpenter caste. They have a history of engaging in creative works of constructing houses, buildings, furniture and all those things that can be made out of wood. Krishnan learned his trade of carpentry from his grandfather who was his first teacher. After completing his primary school education of language, and mathematics, he started to work together with his grandfather, father, uncles, etc. as an apprentice. He then started to work and learn with his grandfather from his

© The Author(s), under exclusive license to Springer Nature Singapore Pte Ltd. 2021
M. Varghese, *A Brief History of Creative Work and Plutonomy*,
https://doi.org/10.1007/978-981-15-9263-8_21

mother's side, where he learned more about the advanced temple architecture, etc. He learned there the relevant classical Indian texts, such as Vāstuśāstra, and other such texts on classical Indian architecture. He then went to another place to learn more from another senior master carpenter. Everywhere, he learned everything that he could learn through doing actual works and working together with others, by using his hands and hand tools. He learned how to activate his hand-brain faculty properly. The hand-brain faculty is what defines *techne* in creative work. He generated a spiritual affinity and intellectual connectedness to what he learned from his masters, colleagues, etc. Carpentry shaped up his life. He also knew that all the people of his caste enjoyed their works and that made them to stay together as a group. At the same time, they all lived their lives in financial difficulties that they had to live with lack of money, or with less monetary gains. Money was really a problem. But in the industrial period, the problem of monetary gains reduced, where a new challenge emerged with mechanization that hugely replaced human creative work. These changes were unacceptable and unimaginable for Carpenter Krishnan, who resisted it by doing works using his hands.

In India he lived in a time of active industrialization. The transition from an agricultural based economy to that of an industrial economy had not happened quickly and fully like in the developed countries of the west, but the stress from the industrial world began to influence the Indians too. People who were trained in doing traditional works lost their traditional occupation in the colonization period in large numbers, but were not obsolete completely. In the post independent era in India, people had no work as such, or if there had been some, those were stressed by oversupply of personals; this disparity made poverty and social decadence a big reality. The presumptive thought that troubled Krishnan's son was "should I be or should I be not" follow that tradition and culture of the forefathers, where he imbibes the art of creativity, *techne.* He refused to learn and do traditional carpentry, and like many did in his day and age; he went to a modern college and learned modern architecture and construction engineering, and soon enough he could understand the art of modern entrepreneurship, which is *episteme*—acquiring knowledge. He started a construction company. He amassed a lot of wealth, his personal wealth increased into astronomical limits. Now he owns an international investment company, which is very active in the stock market, and also as an investor he owns a hedge fund. Here, he uses his engineering knowledge to manipulate things in his favour. The phenomenal growth of this son of an ordinary carpenter, from poor economic situations to that of a plutocrat of our times has not happened gradually in phases, but happened like one who wakes up and enters into one's own dream. The economic prosperity he acquired was not even in his wildest dreams. Plutonomy has this mesmerizing impact that draws support from everywhere.

However, carpenter Krishnan continued to live in his native village seeing the dissolution of his community and caste values. As nobody uses the services of the traditional carpenters, he found that his traditional carpentry knowledge would be wasted. And, he also refused to join with his son's newly found affluent life style. He rejected it out rightly, because of its artificiality, snobbishness and worthlessness. He decided to continue living in the village following traditional carpentry works. He also noticed that with all modern amenities gong around, people in the villages are least interested in doing any kind of traditional work. Due to the surge of opportunities in various other related production works, people could get a lot of money by doing little work. And mostly, everyone is in the Marxian sense behaved like a petty bourgeois that bluntly follows some kind of pompous attitude of the middle class. The new rural middle class, who all behave in the same way, live in the same conditions, see the same kind of TV shows, movies, news, etc. This kind of middle class is being conditioned by the system especially of the democratic capitalism founded on the ideals of Western liberal and conservative values, which work now like a religion. People in the postmodern globalized world order are destined to follow the values of Western liberalism and conservatism irrespective of the particularity of their culture and tradition. The world opinion would bend on to the dictates of those values.

But carpenter Krishnan was not happy with the change in the lifestyle of the people around him that, as a defense, he did different kinds of carpentry jobs. However, he found some ways to use his creative knowledge to learn more by teaching and self-learning more. In other words, he learns how to find a synergic balance between *techne (karma)* and *episteme (jñāna)*, which has guided him to live a happy life. He joined with a certain voluntary—nonprofit—organization that makes handmade toys for children. He gets only very little income from that job, but could live on with less income like a precariat of the postmodern world order.

All his life Carpenter Krishnan never found money makes him any happier. He knew intuitively that his inherited traditional work could make him really happy. He only thought of making a better toy that may get a life into it, as the perfect expression of his creativity. Or, for him work is not for finding more monetary benefits, but for getting creative satisfaction from executing a creative work perfectly well with a personal signature on it: whether it is a temple with intricate structural specifics or with a toy that demands the least of such specifics. He lived throughout his life by doing such creative activities. In his living world, Carpenter Krishnan is a contented man. That kind of happiness and enthusiasm, we cannot find with neither Joe, nor Noriyasu, nor Hillary who missed out on drawing happiness from doing certain work. Though the three were economically well off than Krishnan. They were not serious in finding any kind of creative satisfaction from doing a "work". In the Aristotelian sense as for creating on object, Krishan is—the efficient cause; working with wood—the material cause; by using the inherent skills—the formal cause; creating a particular object—the final cause, that would give him eudemonia: the spiritual flourishing and wellness. That should lead him to realize the true meaning of his being—the transcended *qua-being*. However, his son has no opportunity to receive such a blessing as he is looking towards wisdom from his knowledge, but rather looking at material possessions as the only means to achieve the transcended wisdom, which is impossible.

Chapter 22
God Versus Money

Carpenter Krishnan's son lived a life in which he pursued making monetary benefits as the sole aim of life. He viewed his life through the prism of his ability to have financial acquisitions and large-scale wealth accumulations. He is now a recognized billionaire and has everything that money could buy. He has many children. He married a few times with women from different sociocultural backgrounds. He, in fact, established his life with all sorts of support systems that should have bring him happiness. He has many houses, private jets, yachts, charities, foundations, etc. But his greed for more power by getting more and more money is a continuing process without any end. He now feels that he needs to get more and more of what he already has. He invests money everywhere. He is a postmodern VVIP: a world citizen can transcend all national boundaries. His friend circle is so wide: Presidents, Prime ministers, and all the rich and famous around the world. Even though he is into a series of boom and bust cycles with his investments, but with the availability of interest free money and the algorithm-based AI trading system have made him feel invincible with no more busts but only booms. Algorithmic systems that are being used by the financial industry to protect his investments work perfectly like an impenetrable wall.

In the pre-industrial world philosophy and religion determined the morality and ethical behavior of an individual, but today economics replaced philosophy and religion and ethical behaviors where the rationale of economics particularly displaced philosophy out rightly. There is a kind of wealth-based morality and lifestyle that has been developed in the twenty-first century. Today, the conception of "God" is revolving around wealth and money. Money controllers are like demigods who can have the invincible weapons of financial products. Because money is the force that connects and controls humans with one another, we can safely say that money has a unique position in the world of today. The conception of plutonomy is based on that, and that should have a strong bearing and accent on the exhortation of Ayn Rand: "Until and unless you discover that money is the root of all good, you ask for your own destruction. When money ceases to become the means by which men deal with one another, then men become the tools of other men. Blood, whips and guns or

© The Author(s), under exclusive license to Springer Nature Singapore Pte Ltd. 2021   137
M. Varghese, *A Brief History of Creative Work and Plutonomy*,
https://doi.org/10.1007/978-981-15-9263-8_22

dollars. Take your choice—there is no other."[1] Here Ayn Rand shows how the world would function in a highly monetized world to have power equal to blood, guns, or whips. Our existence itself would be hugely defined by money and all that goodness money could fetch. Money today is like the absolute God. In the religious beliefs of Christians, Muslims, and Jews (Abrahamic religions), God controls the world at His divine will and divine providence. But here money could replace that godly will that is independent according to Christianity. Money is the force that drives government decisions, public opinions, family relationships, etc. Today, with money you can make and break anything. Krishnan's son knows it very well that he is only scared of losing his control over money; as they feel that losing its control would completely destroy them eventually. The hegemonic power desired by the plutonomy is founded on fear and deep ignorance, both plutonomy and "the others".

Many, like carpenter Krishnan's son, are trapped into this new religiosity that is centered on money. Billionaires have a unique position in the world of today. Nobody is willing to criticize them directly or name them but talk about them and their actions as a failure of the capitalistic system. The power that they can exercise by using money and digital technology is what determines everything in the world today. Money and the faith in money, like the faith in God in the pre-industrialized world, is making man mad and crazy for getting more power through money power. There is a rat race to protect the value of money since the great recession and financial collapse after 2008, that mainly started off with the subprime mortgage collapse in the USA. The indomitability of wealth and money begun to be questioned by many: whether money has true value or an assumed pseudo value? Nonetheless, the god like power of money still exists and controls our thoughts and imaginations. Yet, why we call as monetary wealth is all-powerful? How to evaluate the true value for money? Is it only a measure of services and goods that we use where the value changes accordingly? We may have to find sensible answer to these questions.

The history of money shows us that the modern evolution and use of it is different from the way money was invented and used in the ancient world, the history of money is as follows: "Paper currency, first introduced in China in 910 CE, was used by Italian goldsmiths during the Middle Ages, but it was the invention of printing that allowed it to spread rapidly, And while the first banknotes were issued by the Bank of Stockholm in 1661 (the Bank of England followed in 1694)."[2] Initially it was printed notes against a presumed value of Gold that was the norm. But that has changed now. The valuation of money, everywhere, is based on the value of US Dollar, before it was British Pound-Sterling. Now since 1970's the value of US Dollar is created based on what is known as *fractional reserve system*. Furthermore, now the monetary system never works on printed money alone now we have what is known as digital money. According to Mark C. Taylor: "It turns out that money had been dematerializing throughout its long and surprising history, which began in Greek temples and ends in today's temples of finance, where believers in omniscient, omnipotent and omnipresent markets worship their virtual currencies. The trajectory

---

[1]Quoted from Zizek (2012), p. 209.

[2]Taylor (2014), p. 63.

of this history is characterized by the progressive dematerialization of tokens of exchange: people > animals > commodities > precious metals > paper > electrical current > data, information > e-money > virtual currencies."[3]

In a world of today money is the only power that moves everything. It is an undisputable fact. We trust money like the way we used to trust in various conceptions of God; at the same time, unlike God our faith in money is so fickle and fragile, that it can disappear at any moment. Fearsomely, we have to live with e-money and virtual currencies that can be deactivated momentously with the click of a button or the nefarious actions of a computer hacker, or in a highly likely future cyber war. The fear of today is the value and valueless-ness of money. It can buy things you want, and again one can feel that with lots of money one may get a feeling that he can control and dominate the world. The popular conception that money can buy anything and everything is now viciously challenged. The eternal status of money like the God in heaven is disappearing now. Money means trust but trust is what we lose in the case of money. The Chinese who invented paper money used to call it, the flying money. It means as we can buy things easily using money, it runs out of our hands simply. But it has another deeper philosophical message.

We live in a world of three-dimensional objects; we create wealth out it; we store that wealth in the form of three-dimensional objects as fixed assets. The most valued assets were gold, silver, diamond and other such precious metals that last long. But when paper money started to circulate, the Chinese found that those are two-dimensional destructible objects, and stays for some specified period of time: maybe for few years; so, one must be careful with paper money not only of being flying out of hands, but it may fly off from one's hand by way of its overuse or its physical destructibility. But today's digital money is zero- dimensional. It may vanish into the thin air with the click of a button, or in a financial crash as what happened for many during the 2008 financial crash. We cannot fully depend on any such zero-dimensional objects, as millions could be lost at the time of a financial crash. And it is regularly happening in the world of digital money.

References

Taylor, M.C.: Speed Limits. Yale University Press, New Heaven (2014)
Zizek, S.: Living in the End Times. Verso Books, London (2012)

---

[3]Ibid, p. 107.

Chapter 23
A Perspective from Classical Philosophy to the Millennial Apathy

Carpenter Krishnan was a person who intrinsically understood that the creative work satisfaction and happiness are more important than the satisfaction from money. He belonged to a tradition where work (karma) is a part of the day-to-day living and the spiritual life, where doing and learning from an activity continued, so long as, a human person could live. In the classical world, philosophical systems and religious views that have influenced by those systems taught such kind of knowledge which was traditionally formed. Work is a way of life. The Eastern understanding of Karma is essentially meant that. One should do "work" and should use "work" as a way to realize the internal spiritual being for knowing the qua-being—life's source which is in the Vedic conception is—Brahman—the source of everything. Learning through work is important for building one's life in the right way. The discussion on Karma Yoga in Bhagavad-Gita explains this aspect elaborately.

Why money dominates creative work, especially in the modern times, is a question that is very difficult for anyone to answer. In the classical Christian philosophy, God as the trinity is first answered that the father aspect of God is in the heaven as the totality of everything, the son aspect of God is in the world reside in the human soul, and the Holy Spirit aspect of God is the conduit that works between God and the soul that is confused and convoluted by the forces of the world. But the view of the well-known Christian philosopher Saint Augustine made it as the spiritual spectrum of life is more philosophical and rational. Saint Augustine reinterpreted it: the father aspect of God is the reality of knowledge that contains in the human soul; the Son aspect of God represent our understanding of the reality; and the Holy Spirit is the Will (freewill) that allow us to work with the reality to learn and know more about it. Augustine taught that though God has self-revelation capacity and it works in the world of ignorance (the world of temptation, etc.) but man has the freewill to use for removing all the ignorance. As for the modern thinkers, Economics would redefine this Trinitarian aspect of God into three level of interpreting wealth. The totality of wealth is the father aspect of God; the wealth one can acquire is the Son aspect of God; and the Holy Spirit aspect of God is the money that has the invincibility and

© The Author(s), under exclusive license to Springer Nature Singapore Pte Ltd. 2021   141
M. Varghese, *A Brief History of Creative Work and Plutonomy*,
https://doi.org/10.1007/978-981-15-9263-8_23

the power of its pursuance and influence on human life, which is achievable if one activates his freewill.

Saint Augustine presumed if we would use freewill indiscriminately we would "fall" into the abysmal depth of ignorance, which can be exemplified as greed, passion, and avarice that could destroy life. The fall happens from control of the "city of God" to the hellish world of suffering, fear and death. We are in that destructive phase, lest we change the conceptions of money especially its coursing power to pursue human life and culture substantially. We may be destroyed as living beings. As Aristotle implied in his ethical works, money is only a tool to get goods and services beyond which money has no special value.

But the world of today is not using any such idea of God. In our times, God is freewill, the invincible money power aspect of God. This aspect of God that subjugate the other two aspects: wealth aspect and a person's share of it to conduct a personal and social life. But the whole world irrespective of culture or tradition, worships money as God, which is more near and practical. And also, we have created mythology around the wealthy as they can behave like Gods and demigods of today. That God makes carpenter Krishnan to be a precariat and his son a plutocrat. That is what makes Noriyasu to lose his work life and to live his life in depravation of everything that he valued in life: such as his own being, his own dignity, and his own reason and purpose of live. Lack of understanding about the meaning and value of money made Joe to find his life totally uninteresting, dull and boring. He disappeared from active life at a very young age. Onto the new idea of money as God, Mark C. Taylor explains how money acts in the world of today: "During the latter half of the twentieth century, money become God in more than a trivial sense. The traditional opposition between liberal and conservative policies as well as liberal and neoliberal economics repeats and extends philosophical and theological disputes that erupted at the end of the Middle Ages and the beginning of modern era. One of the most pressing questions then, as now, concerned the relation of the individual to the group or the part to the whole."[1] The Trinitarian understanding of God is well explained in this quote. Money replaces the God in Heaven that authorizes everything; money reflects in each soul and directs it; money as freewill gives us freedom to achieve control and be acting like a sovereign.

The less than 1% of plutocrats who own enormous amount of wealth are the ones who used their freewill freely and effectively to be like the sovereign. They are everywhere and they could exert authority over the more than 99% who lacks any ability to use freewill and freedom and therefore living in poverty or near to poverty, the modern-day equivalent of Christian idea of sin. Sin here is being understood as acting against the will of God, or the dictums of plutonomy.

In a world of precarity—precariousness—a young person may intuitively feel his/her uselessness. The dull, apathetic millennials know very well that they have no way to use their creative energy to work with, and make their lives better. As Karl Marx well explained in his Communist Manifesto, a situation in which intense competition leads to mechanizations and at that point, the life of a worker would

---

[1] Taylor (2014), p.37.

become precarious, as his workmanship needs to be compromised with the superior efficiency of the machines.[2] Now these machines controls and navigates human work.

The young people of today are lost in a kind of limbo, especially the aspects relating to life. The apathy and indecision have become a part of modern life. At this point it is important to review how creative work and the hand-brain faculty were conceived and appreciated in various systems of philosophy and how modern studies on human consciousness agree with the classical notion of considering work as a means to condition life and live a life fully. The focus of the contemporary world is to create profit or wealth that would not be distributed and how that may petrify life in a negative way. The contemporary financial economics works like a black hole that astrophysics considered as that something, which enters into, never could return back from it. That something is permanently lost. The money that is going into the world of investment economics loses its value and never could retain any of its assumed value, but the only solution to that is to make more money for making up the loses. But when that happens value of money is taken from the hands of majority of the people who may have to find other ways to exchange goods and services.

When observing the history of thought that relates to work and life, the most important aspect that struck in our minds is the ineffectiveness of wealth of nation that could have made the lives of people better in a nation-state. In the postmodern globalized plutonomic world order, the wealth of a nation and its value in deciding the fate of its people is getting obsolete and meaningless. We must rethink on the thought history of work and life philosophically to discern the stupidity of plutonomy.

References

Taylor, M.C.: Speed Limits. Yale University Press, New Heaven (2014)
Communist Manifesto: The original text at: https://www.marxists.org/archive/marx/works/1848/ communist-manifesto/ch01.htm#007//. Retrieved on 17 July 2016

---

[2]Communist Manifesto (2016).

Part II
Rethinking on Human *Life* and *Creative Work*

Chapter 24
Creative Work: Freedom and Happiness

In the turn of seventeenth century, when the western world adopted modern science and technology, the industrial revolution started to catch up with its first phase there. Since then, it had created an own exclusive narrative basing scientific logical reasonings on the entire world systems. It gave a novel power and authority to the Christian western civilization founded on Protestant ethics with a deep spiritual conception of "divine providence" and other related thoughts. The capitalist economic system founded on "divine providence" used "creative work" as the focal point for creating and distributing wealth. And this authority and providential thought had matured in to as colonialism in other parts of the world. But the colonies of western political powers were treated as the resource centers to power their industries in the west. The main manufacturing of goods was done in manufacturing centers always been in the western world giving jobs to a vast number of its people. Some thinkers call this period of phase as Industry-1.0, notably when the world economic model moved from agricultural to industrial in the West. And it was the time of the birth of nation-states, where national pride took a clear shape in all aspects of life.

The industrial growth made those industrial nation states as super economic powers that they controlled huge wealth and military powers, but then, that created the situations for more greed for more wealth ending in conflicts on the basis, of national pride and nationhood. The wars in the modern world are an expression of that national pride finally making two world wars in the early half of twentieth century resulting in an unforgettable catastrophe. The so-called industrial progress of the Western world demanded a new restructuring of wealth due to huge accumulation of wealth in a few countries and entities, and unfortunately that happened after the world wars. Normally the restructuring and the redistribution of wealth had happened with the creation of big cities, temples, big palaces, or the building of structures like the Great Wall in China. But in the case of the Western civilization, the redistributions of wealth today can happen only through wars when the wealth can be distributed for financing, manufacturing of war weapons and systems, and the after-war reconstruction. Maybe the exclusive narrative on logic and reasoning that

© The Author(s), under exclusive license to Springer Nature Singapore Pte Ltd. 2021
M. Varghese, *A Brief History of Creative Work and Plutonomy*,
https://doi.org/10.1007/978-981-15-9263-8_24

started since seventeenth century is taking a paradigm shift now with the advent of *plutonomy* and demotion of *creative work* in to all aspects of human life.

Most of the western powers that participated in the world wars eventually lost huge amount of wealth and human resources. But there emerged a huge demand for finance and resources for the reconstruction of the world after the two world wars. Then, since 1950-and 1960s there was another phase of re-industrialization—industry-2.0, which gave a new boost to the national economies of the Western world including Japan. In this period banking and finance began to be emerged like an industry. The political systems in the world were divided into countries that followed communist socialist system or democratic capitalist system. Because of the lack of access to financial resources, the communist socialist system failed to accomplish the formation of a functioning socialist society, but democratic capitalism survived with the huge accumulation of financialized assets. As the third phase of the industrial movement, there started a new call for globalization starting from 1980s, which according to scholars is known as the third industrial revolution—industry-3.0. This phase should be known as the age of financialization and technologization happening in an unimaginable pace. At this period, different modern philosophical views emerged to substantiate the new world order, but one thing was denigrated and forgiven, the Christian idea of "divine providence" that gave capitalism and communism equal legitimacy and acceptance far and wide. The capitalists' and communists' values were accepted due to the acceptability of divine providence. It acted as the metanarratives for all the phases of industrialization. The conception of "divine providence" had variously been interpreted by other cultures and civilizations as the values of our times. But, today, notably in the industry-3.0 there are conscious efforts to denigrate the original spirit of "divine providence" by shrinking the opportunity to work and divide wealth through work. And thereby further disparaging the economic security for a large number of workers and their family's livelihoods. In the case of industry 1.0, and industry 2.0, human work was hugely appreciated as it was a necessary element and was a means for dividing the wealth, owing to a constant denigration to do *creative work* and the use of *hand-brain faculty*. The complex body-hand-brain system helped humans to develop creative artistic skills—*techne* and to develop knowledge leading to wisdom—*episteme*. At the time of industry-3.0, we denigrate synergy of these two further, to face a huge crisis in the sphere of ethics and morality and the providential thoughts that made capitalism to thrive. Plutonomy today follows the ghost of such ethical thoughts.

The historical progression of class antagonism has happened, in the pre-industrial western world, between the feudal oligarchy and the serfs; at the time of industry-1.0, it has progressed to be between bourgeoisie and proletariat; but, in industry-2.0, at the time of nation states, during and after the world wars, the whole world was divided into those following socialism (communism) and those following capitalism (democracy) had evolved, yet the bourgeoisie versus. proletariat narrative got subdued, but not disappeared.. The communist bloc had institutionalized workers' rights, whereas in the capitalist countries, it was labor unions that protected workers' rights. But in the case of industry-3.0, the class antagonism has taken a new turn with the spread of technological unemployment. it has mainly happened due to the use of technology, yet in definition, it includes the huge automation of manufacturing and service industries, the forceful incursion of technology into agriculture production, the shifting of manufacturing jobs to cost effective centers, etc. And as an unintended consequence the new era of *plutonomy*—the norm of the wealthy, has emerged as the superstructure, pushing workers' rights and opportunity for finding work into a corner giving birth to a new class of part-time workers (*precariats*) replacing the class structure of the earlier periods. The plutonomy today has swallowed up *creative work* completely making *precarity* a fact of life.

A miniscule percentage of superrich plutocrats that controlled the whole wealth of a nation state is now making the existence of the nation state redundant. We can see a warning in this issue from Aristotle who is the father of Economics: "By a Nation we mean an assemblage of houses, lands, and property sufficient to enable the inhabitants to lead a civilized life. This is proved by the fact that when such a life is no longer possible for them, the tie itself which unites them is dissolved."[1] When such unethical confiscation of wealth by a few happens, the structure of a nation that comprises property, land, etc. be unavailable to majority of the citizens to conduct a civilized life. That makes majority to untie with the unity of the nation. Today that phenomenon happens with the shrinkage of "work".

As a telling consequence, the major labor force become part-time workers (*precariats*) in the industry-3.0. The class antagonism has now taken a new turn, plutocrat with immense power at the global level, and the part-time workers with no power or control on the wealth emerged simultaneously. Precarity—unsecured employment or income is a growing phenomenon under plutonomy and we can call such a population of *precariats* as the economic zombies, who may take little and contribute very little to the wealth of the nations. At the same time, the Plutocrats are the watchmen of dead wealth or custodians of meaningless quantum of wealth. We can fear that the plutonomy would turn the nation states into dysfunctional entities with no control on the life of any human person. Till the time of globalization—industry- 3.0, both bourgeoisie and proletariat in some sense enjoyed "divine providence" by involving directly with the creation and distribution of wealth, but that protection would be completely denigrated in the case of industry-4.0, where complete automation would denigrate human life as nobody has any opportunity to engage in any kind of creative work that big data and Nano-technology would replace the *hand-brain faculty* with robotic systems.

The semantics of the term Plutonomy is norm of the wealthy (Gr. *Ploutos*: 'wealth', and *nomos*: 'law' or 'norm'). Contextually, it should be read as the totalitarian control of the wealthy on every aspect of human life. In a world system where the wealthy rules in accordance with their whims and fancies, what will happen to the life of normal workers who have appreciated life by engaging in creative work and with the emoluments and rewards then received. Now is the time to review that, since the founding principle of industry-4.0 is to create a super stream of data driven super highways, for to control and guide each individual, where production, distribution and all such activities would be guided by a super grid. It is not yet clear how such a

---

[1] Aristotle (1920), p. 1342.

system could evolve in a world where human life can only be defined in the maxims of finite expressions, so that the data collection systems can collect clear and certain data for the AI controlled technocracy to make decisions automatically. Such maxims are antithetical to the nature and progress of life. Thus, we may have to review the history of thoughts that explains the human nature, and the virtue based ethical and moral systems that supported human life up until now. It is argued here that "creative work" by appreciating hand-brain faculty has helped humans to build a virtue ethical system. The readings of such an ethical system is manifested as the providence of God, or providence of nature.

Reference

Aristotle: Oeconomica (Book-I, 1343a). In: Foster, E.S. (Trans. and ed.) The Works of Aristotle. Oxford University Press, London (1920)

Chapter 25
"Deaths of Despair": *Being* in the Time of Precarity

Nobel laureate economist Angus Deaton introduced the phrase "deaths of despair" to explain the precarious socioeconomic conditions of the working class of the twenty-first century, where virtues in work are not valued and rewarded well. He explained the situation of the working-class individuals in a paper published titled "Mortality and Morbidity in the twenty-first century". He presented in that paper, the concept of *precarity* and the precarious life situations of the middle class whose mobility in life got shunted due to the dwindling chances for doing "work" in the USA and other part of the western developed world. Angus Deaton and Anne Case wrote "In our account here, we emphasize the labor market, globalization, and technical change as the fundamental force, and put less focus on any loss of virtue, though we certainly accept that the latter could a consequence of the former. Virtue is easier to maintain when it is rewarded."[1] We can interpret the traumatic life and death of Noriyasu, as it is a typical case point to explain the real situation of the working class people of the industry-3.0, who are forced to live in a world that never reward human values such as the virtues of goodness and truth which are ethically defined as "divine providence", which Aristotle called *arete*—excellence in doing virtuous activities that would lead one to *eudaimonia*—human flourishing and happiness. The lack of the rule of virtue makes people like Noriyasu to fall into deep despair easily and lose any zest for life. And according to Angus Deaton and Anne Case: "mortality from deaths of despair and all-cause mortality are highly correlated: deaths of despair are a larger and growing component of midlife all-cause mortality."[2] The rewards can come as monetary acquisition as well as satisfaction and contentment from executing a creative activity; under plutonomy both are neglected.

In the case of Noriyasu, he was from the agriculture background, who later became a part of the reindustrialization (industry-2.0) of post war Japan; and who lost his job in the globalization phase (industry-3.0) due to technologization and financialization

---

[1] Deaton and Case (2017).

[2] Ibid.

© The Author(s), under exclusive license to Springer Nature Singapore Pte Ltd. 2021
M. Varghese, *A Brief History of Creative Work and Plutonomy*,
https://doi.org/10.1007/978-981-15-9263-8_25

of the economy. He lost his job in his prime-work-life time to do some work in his mid-life. but unlike many others he was financially secure because of his wealthy wife. Yet why he committed suicide? Or why had he experienced that kind of excruciating pain in his life? We may not be able to find any cognizable reason in this regard. In fact, he had no good reason to kill himself, because financially he had everything to live on till the end of his life, but at the same time, his despair overwhelmed everything else. He almost had everything that the modern world could offer. He had a traditional family back in his village; a rich, caring and understanding wife; and a lot of time and money to do whatever he wanted; and no grown up children for to be worried about. But he couldn't have been happy or satisfied with his life. Despite having all these what he didn't have was the opportunity to engage in any sort of "creative work" and to experience the virtues implied in the idea of "divine providence" or *eudaimonia-arete* for living a virtuous rewarding life. "Death of despair" is a complicated phenomenon that the modern and postmodern philosophy ever could explain as they don't recognize virtue as a necessary aspect for life; instead, they crave for freedom in all aspects of life.

Noriyasu's life in the traditional world of his village life, where he experienced a kind of continued protection that almost everyone had worked till the time, their bodies could endure it. Most of the village population used to get some schooling for a few years and then they all did some work either, in family's own farms, or in factories, or in fishing, or in carpentry work, etc. After learning the work from a senior person (senpai), most of them worked independently and retired from active work-life after going through a life cycle of doing some kind of work till the end of their lives. As a culture, the community he belonged considered work as an important part of life. The income they used to earn was not the main issue, but doing no work was an issue. An organic self-sustaining system that emerged in the rural life system in and around work is no more possible. Doing some work, talking about one's own work, learning something new, gossiping about work, etc. are the few things that people around him enjoyed. Work was the most unifying force that supported the social life everywhere around.

But, a tectonic change happened, with re-industrialization period (industry-2.0) in Japan, with a new axiom emerged in the popular culture that with money one can control and stop all the problems of life. Earning money had become the main purpose of life. Creative satisfaction from work got lowered, but monetary gains and satisfaction became the sole purpose of doing any work. The only worry of the young in the industry-2.0, period was about how to be a part of the emerging world in the post-World War-II order and to gain as much money as possible for to be happy in the future. During that period, the main mantra that was being followed everywhere was reform and reconstruct everything for monetary gain. Some countries could generate more wealth by reforming their industrial economic systems of all redundancies. This aspect of the abundance of monetary prosperity captured the imagination of the world during this period. At this period of industrialization and growth, suicide was unthinkable that one would end his life due to the lack of opportunities for doing creative works. If there were plenty of opportunities to find any sort of work, suicide is an extreme act, but that happens when people lose interest in living a life. People engage in such acts of self-destruction when they lose all enthusiasm to live a life. For a fulfilling life, one should find enough opportunities for getting the creative spirits activated to achieve a feeling of some accomplishments. Money could bring some fulfilling feelings to one's desires but aggravation of such desires would destroy one's personality. It may also be argued that the pent-up creative energy would retroactively destroy a human being through constant boredom.

To understand the nuances of this issue, we need to look into the developments of thought in our times since eighteenth century, after the advent of modern scientific philosophical thought that dominated the world. Scientifically verified thoughts dominated philosophy. There emerged a kind of tectonic changes in our social life with far reaching influences. Now we apply scientific analyses and scientific rationalism everywhere. Scientific methods allow us to create theories with the help of some chosen thoughts which are mere scientific dogmas. Such dogmas created a network of thoughts spreading to all aspects of life. For some thinkers, in the modern period, the thought that money is everything that shall bring us to absolute freedom is very persuasive and compelling. They always talk about achieving social justice through the distribution of wealth in the form of money. But a very few people think that pursuing "creative instincts" is important for experiencing a spiritually flourishing happiness—*eudaimonia*. Their thoughts are being displaced at a faster rate, and together with their abilities to think and decide on their personal lives by activating the creative instincts are turning out to be less important. Almost everyone is caught up with a feeling of lifelessness and inertness, that would lead one to despair.

Now, in the globalization period 'work' is equated exclusively for money and profit. So, when money is given freely to people, we can avoid inefficient workers' labor. Inefficient labor is a problem for high production and high profit. Technology could do all work and achieve high production, so maybe in future, nobody needs to work, machines will do everything. When machines do all the work, one question remains, what will happen to human's mental and physical health. There is an intrinsic organic relationship between one's physical health and mental health. In fact, through creative work one can harmonize that intrinsic relationship. It is found that the distinctive feature of homo-sapiens (modern humans) in comparison to all other prehumen species and other living beings is the abilities of humans to use intelligence (*nous: buddhi*) and work creatively by following logic and reasonings.

Doing creative works by activating hand-brain faculty is a way to make humans to use the reasoning faculties fully. The inactive human body function could make a very inactive brain function leading to the making of poor mental faculties. The studies in contemporary neurology say so. Doing a work with the involvement of body would enhance the formation of a stable neural structure, by activating the body-hand- brain complex, and then a robust consciousness would be built for initiating an actively functioning mind. Creative work and learning from work would create an all-important conscious space by structuring a special kind of neural circuit in the brain that guides an individual's life positively. The latest developments in neurological studies, on the relationship of 'consciousness' and the development of neural structures in an individual person, have proven scientifically that there is a strong relationship between "creative work" and "human life"; because creative work provides satisfaction and happiness (*eudaimonia*). *Eudemonia* according Aristotle is the spiritual energy generated, when engaging in virtuous action (*arete*), that propels and activates human soul (*psyche*) and helps one to experience a kind of pride and self-worth, which is unified in the metaphysical realm with the transcendental virtues (NE.1123b).[3]

References

Aristotle: Nicomachean ethics (Book-1V, 1123b). In: McKeon, R. (Trans. and ed.) The Basic Works of Aristotle. Random House, New York (1941)

Deaton, A., Case, A: mortality and morbidity in the 21st Century. In: Brookings papers on economic activity. Spring (2017). Retrieved on 13 Nov 2018 from https://www.brookings.edu/wp-content/uploads/2017/08/casetextsp17bpea.pdf

---

[3] Aristotle (1941), p. 991.

Chapter 26
Creative Work: Some Thoughts from Contemporary Neuro-science

Contemporary studies in neuro-science identified that creative work is a necessary factor for humans to live a healthy life. We can seek related details from the studies of Thomas Metzinger and others who studied the development of consciousness and the formation of neural circuits that provide a unique particular identity to an individual personality. The neuro-scientists of today could prove that learning by performing a "work activity" is the key to support the formation of a robust consciousness, for which one should use the creative energy and continue learning further from it in detail, by actually doing a work. The formation of the basic neural structure through creative work is the key for the formation of a personal self-model in the inner self, and for that one needs to do creative work. Metzinger calls this formation is a kind of tunneling process—Ego tunnel—in the brain-conscious faculty of an individual personality.

Ego is the Latin term for "I" in English. Thus, ego-tunnel indicates the formations of the "I" sense in the subjective self of a personality, and it forms like a tunnel with intricate inner walls formed by creating neural structures. The formation of Ego tunnel in each individual self is the making of a unique Neural Correlate of Consciousness (NCC) that would form as a result of doing something through working and learning. The inner idea (form) would get reformed to a higher level, yet it would not happen when one learns about the form from a book. The whole body participates in the creation of such a conscious space and it organically designs itself, step by step, in the inner wall of the ego-tunnel—personal self-model. Though the process seems simple, it involves complicated structural formations of the neural structures. Metzinger says, it is like how one learns to ride a bicycle, the process of learning involves several phases and each phase creates unique neural structures: "Note that when you learn a difficult task for the first time, such as tying your shoes or riding a bicycle, your practicing is always conscious. Yet as soon as you've mastered tying your shoes or riding a bicycle, you forget all about the learning process-to the point that it becomes difficult to teach skill to your children. It quickly sinks below the threshold of awareness and becomes a fast and efficient subroutine. But wherever the system is confronted with a novel or challenging stimulus, its global workspace is

© The Author(s), under exclusive license to Springer Nature Singapore Pte Ltd. 2021

M. Varghese, *A Brief History of Creative Work and Plutonomy*,
https://doi.org/10.1007/978-981-15-9263-8_26

activated and represented in consciousness. This is also the point when you become aware of the process".[1] In other words, when you are able to read the subroutine that is created subconsciously by practice, you are able to talk about the concepts behind the process, but until then, the subroutine remains in the ego tunnel acting automatically, because at that point the ego-tunnel activate a particular process naturally. A good dancer may not be a good dance teacher; or a housewife who cook daily at home may not make a good chef who could run a restaurant kitchen effortlessly. A scholar or teacher can study the concepts and could explain dance theoretically, but never could dance with that knowledge; or a restaurant chef need to know the formation of taste conceptually and intuitively, but not a nutrition specialist. The scholar food specialist should know the concepts and interpret it in quantity and quality after studying about it from different sources, such as housewives, chefs, etc. The skill learned through practice designs the individual personality by creating the "ego tunnel".

Contextually, in the era of postmodern philosophy, mostly the philosophical studies are focused on mind, where the mind is accepted only as a reflexive medium controlled by the neural circuits of the brain. Notably, it declines the importance of "consciousness" and the function of consciousness in the entire body. And after with the invention of computer the mind-brain faculty is considered as similar to the CPU of a computer—a data processing device—and not the "mind" that is a part of the total consciousness conditioned by emotions and rational faculties. Postmodern "mind" studies are solely focused on how mind knows something or about the foundation of it as the sources of knowledge.[2] Our psychological studies are based on scientific sampling and on proof taking where mind turn in as an object for analytical study. However, the idea of "ego tunnel" is exceptionally similar to the classical philosophies' conception of consciousness—a faculty of subjective knowledge—of an individual person. The consciousness responds and it pervades in the whole body, not just in the brain. In the case of classical philosophy, the conception of consciousness was considered as the main aspect of philosophy, because it explains "life" in its totality. The classical conception of God, Brahman, etc. comes from this understanding of a particular subjective consciousness finding its unity. The classical Greek idea of *psyche* (soul) reflects the idea of consciousness, which is created by and belonged to the creator God in the heaven—*Demiurge*. The individual soul always seeks to find its unity in a transcended realm. In classical Vedic and Buddhist philosophies, the understanding of *cit* (consciousness) is what explains life in its fullness. And an individual consciousness is submissive to the higher consciousness, Brahman. Physical body and brain condition the individual consciousness; in this case, body and mind, form an integral whole that represents an individual's conscious-space. Plato's understanding of the "idea" or of the "form" signifies the higher order of things and · we as humans have the intelligence to engage with those transcended "forms". The purpose of life according to Plato is to work freely with those God given forms and create objects that would harmonize one's life with the heavenly goodness (wisdom)

---

[1] Metzinger (2009), p. 56.

[2] Ibid., p. 26.

and beauty for living a comfortable life. We should do creative works on the ideas (forms) for knowing the perfect knowledge implied in God's eternal "forms". The Latest studies on consciousness, based on the neuro-scientific studies show that the classical understanding of consciousness is the best suited way to explain everything that is personal or subjective. Human consciousness, therefore, depends on brain as well as the whole body. An individual consciousness should be integrated to the Being of a total consciousness to understand the nature of its being.

On the other hand, the modern psychology and psychological studies reject the presence of consciousness and try to explain on how mind react to the external world of objects. For them, the mind is only a reflexive medium reacting to the external world. It is assumed that the mind is like a clean slate that reflects the external objects based on the earlier data acquired through the learning experiences. A modern psychologist may naively call the suicide of Noriyasu as a stupid act, and he may naively blame him for his lack of ability to use all the available opportunities. They take it as a typical example of following negative thoughts, instead of positive thoughts. And for them, people like Noriyasu are exceptions where majority are living happily by following scientific reasoning and the scientific way of life. As a complete solution to such psychological declines, they suggest the inculcation of positive thoughts. When many follow the path of Noriyasu or many live a hellish life with depression, frustration, and inaction, we need to look into this problem directly by abandoning the naïve discourses or the self-congratulatory attitude of the postmodern thinkers' views. Negative thoughts and suffering are a fact of life, for nobody has found any sure shot solution yet. We cannot stop that, but could control suffering by activating our body and mind. Creative work should be seen as an opportunity to resist one's declining enthusiasm for living life.

As for Noriyasu, the security and support he experienced in his village life, where he could have lived working till the end of his life, was completely denied with his life in the city. In city life, everything is defined on the basis of the happiness from money, and on exercising the power of the monetized wealth, and on a metanarrative on positive thoughts. On the other hand, the joy of life for him should have come from doing "creative works" for building a better robust consciousness (ego-tunnel) that should have resisted the mental depression that lead to his suicide. Severe mental depression is the reason for suicides in the postmodern world order. As per Japanese tradition, learning from a senior (*senpai*) is highly valued and revered and it is a necessary factor in one's own work-life, because one receives protection from the senior (*senpai*) where one continues to enrich the knowledge under his guidance. Knowledge from a creative work is what builds the conscious space. It was believed that people who might engage in any kind of creative work could draw satisfaction and contentment. In this life through long engagement with "creative work", one can build his ego-tunnel with robust resistance against all kinds of psychological declines. Note that modern psychiatry has no effective cure for diseases that comes out of mind-brain issues; psychiatry mostly can only drug a person to forget his negative thoughts mostly through psychotropic drugs.

Reference

Metzinger, T.: Ego Tunnel. Basic Books, New York (2009)

Chapter 27
The Imprint of Femininity in Creative Work

The creative energy in a human person, according to Plato, is formed in as the feminine nature, to the internal structure of one's personality. And, creativity is being expressed in its perfect form as femininity. Each personality has an element of deep-rooted femininity as an attribute determining creativity. Plato beautifully explained about this unique human trait in the dialogue, *Symposium*. The essential being of the soul of a human person is half feminine and half male. Femininity may be subdued in an individual male personality, while it is apparent in a female personality. The gender segregation is not absolute and total, but uncertain, fluid, changeable, incomplete, and inexplicable, yet it is experiential and cognizable. Plato defined the feminine characteristic as creativity, love, affection and other such distinctive aspects, we explicitly could see in a woman as her essential nature. Naturally female part of any living being is internally and physically predisposed to procreate a new life: organically would conceive a new life and naturally deliver it to the world as the divine duty of protecting and continuing life. According to Plato, for both man and woman this process of creating a new life not only satisfies the urge to reproduce but also satisfies the urge for the fulfillment of the creative energy that naturally happens when participating in the process of procreation. Sexual intercourse is the mutual organic partaking of the flourish of that creative energy which gives a feeling of harmony in unity, and creativity. The other creative work relatively differs from procreation, and the imbibed *eudaimonic* pleasure also varies. The Greek term *eudaimonia* is the internal ability of human soul (*psyche*) to engage and experience life with deep feelings of wellness and flourishing. Aristotle thought such a flourish of spiritual energy—*eudaimonia*—happens only when one attains excellence in virtuous actions—*arete*.[1]

Every activity of work also has an element of this divine mission when accomplishing it creatively. Any form of creative work has this property. In the dialogue *Symposium*, this notable aspect on creativity is what Priestess Diotima clarified to

---

[1] See Article on Aristotle's Ethics in Stanford Encyclopedia of Philosophy. https://plato.stanford.edu/entries/aristotle-ethics/. Retrieved on 18/07/2020.

© The Author(s), under exclusive license to Springer Nature Singapore Pte Ltd. 2021 159
M. Varghese, *A Brief History of Creative Work and Plutonomy*, https://doi.org/10.1007/978-981-15-9263-8_27

Socrates: as femininity, the aspect of human "creativity": "Those who are pregnant in the body only, betake themselves to women and beget children—this is the character of their love; their offspring, as they hope, will preserve their memory and give them the blessedness and immortality, which they desire in the future. But souls, which are pregnant—for there certainly are men who are more creative in their souls than in their bodies –conceive that which is proper for the soul to conceive or contain. And what are these conceptions?—Wisdom and Virtue in general. And such creators are poets and all artists who are deserving of the name inventor."[2] Diotima argues, here, that the feminine urge to conceive is, in fact ingrained in the body-mind-consciousness complex of every man (male) as much as in a woman (female) that is why a man seeks to find a woman in order to make her conceive a baby from him. Sexual pleasure is the release of the subdued procreative energy in both man and woman that is subtly embedded in both the bodies as the ultimate manifestation of the creative energy. The spirit of baby also is impregnated in the body of man subtly waiting to be delivered by part-taking a woman in love. Even though woman is the one who actually conceives and delivers the child, man too part-take and be associated with the whole process of creativity that is of giving birth to a new born child. And therefore, a man continues his inherent relationship with the child till the end of his life. Such expression of creative energy is the nature of all humans. That is what makes humans different and distinct from other living beings. On the other hand, in animals the parent—child (offspring) relationship ends at a particular point of time and then the offspring loses all nuptial relationship with the progenitors. Using creativity, in both body and soul is a part of the spiritual existence of all humans. Humans will not exist with all the traits of being human, if they do not use the inherent creative energy naturally. In Indian philosophy the conception of *Śiva* and *Śakti* is in fact similar to the Platonic idea of the existence of the synergic existence of femininity and creativity in a human personality, where *Śakti* signifies femininity and creativity. Indians call the conception of a human person is half feminine: *Arthanārīśwara*. The Godhead is in its perfect stage of being harmonizing the bipolarity of maleness and femaleness into one perfect unity. This again can be interpreted as the Indian conception of the human person beyond gender distinction.

How the emotional urges of a child are shared between the parents; the soul of a man is pregnant with the pro-creative energy that makes him to take part a role in impregnating a child in the womb of the woman he chosen to share with his love. Another aspect of the same creative energy enables an inventor, artist, carpenter, etc. to work with an idea—form—for creating new objects. The thing that enriches a person's life and the others around him is the presence of femininity as creative energy which aspires for gradual fruition. It is everywhere but humans fail to acknowledge it. Satisfying creative instinct and searching for more creative possibilities are, in fact, one of the pursuits of a human person to find immortality through the procreation of an offspring. As Diotima told to Socrates in the Platonic dialogue of *Symposium*, "I am persuaded that all men do all things and the better they are the more they do them, in hope of the glorious fame of immortal virtue;

[2]Kaplan (1950), p. 214.

for they desire the immortal."[3] According to classical Greek thinkers achieving the transcendental virtues is the way to achieve *eudaimonia* (happiness). Eudaimonia is the spiritual flourishing and the contentment one receives upon achieving satisfaction and freedom on any sort of action one does. When he does something, he seeks some form of virtue by achieving true knowledge. Pursuing the transcendental virtues of Goodness, truth, justice, beauty, unity, being etc. is the only way for one to get that sort of happiness and satisfaction in one's day-to-day life. Since soul is an aspect of God, it would pursue immortality wherever one exists. The urge to engage with creative work: the god given gift, is something that undoubtedly gives us the feeling of virtue flourishing within our souls. The satisfaction, we receive is apparent in the form of fulfilling the transcendentals, which is inherent within us. In other words, the *eudaimonic* urge we have within us is what makes us to live a complete life. Using creative energy is the best way to achieve eudaimonic virtues of goodness, truth, harmony, etc. When an artist or a writer or a poet or a carpenter or any other creative worker creates something, s/he uses the creative energy impregnated and saturated inside his deep consciousness (soul); a book, a new life, a poem, an artwork, a cot, or any other created object is an expression of that subdued creative energy actualized or got matured. It gives him immense spiritual and physical happiness. In India creative work executed with the purity of thought (*dharma*) is what makes one reaching the ultimate stage (*mokṣa*) or the union with the ultimate reality, Brahman. At the same time ignorance leads one to do unvirtuous actions ending in self-destruction, for one seeks true knowledge and cultivates virtuous thoughts leading to the thoughts of the creator God. This search for virtuous thoughts from every action is what is meant by *arete*, leading to a kind of spiritual flourish and wellness (*eudaimonia*).

However, in the re-industrialization period creativity was partially taken over by the automatized systems to support huge production, where higher quantities were compromised for quality. Thereby the humans who engaged in production never could use their creative energies fully as did in the classical period. Work in the modern times became a means to support day-to-day needs by making the power of money as the pivot of all activities; eventually, chances for work-satisfactions from creative work were substantially being reduced gradually in phases, reaching to its ultimate destruction. In the postmodern globalized world, the attack on human creativity further compromised for high profitability, which is now heightened and maligned with the introduction of the fully automatized AI systems. Contextually, satisfaction from work is considered as the highest virtue (*Mokṣa*) revered and aspired in Indian philosophy, and as *Dao* in Chinese philosophy. Humans should pursue themselves to get an understanding of the higher order of things. The scientific philosophy in modern times conclude that we can get a complete grasp of the higher order of things by using science and technology, where happiness is centered around and is related to getting power, money and freedom. In classical philosophy freedom is related with the pursuit of transcendentals: Truth, Goodness and Beauty, and the realization of which is implied in the conceptions of Greek *eudemonia*, Indian *mokṣa*, *or* Chinese *Dao*.

---

[3]Ibid., p. 214.

In the Platonic dialogue, symposium, the narration is on the internal faculty of creativity and its importance in leading a virtuous life with perfect fulfilment and satisfaction—eudaimonia. Aristotle used a different narration on this by introducing the word *arete* meaning executing an activity with excellence and with the purpose of achieving fulfilment and satisfaction leading to *eudai/monia* as the main aim of living—a virtuous life. The idea of Karma in Indian thought talks about a similar idea more comprehensively and elaborately, where "karma" acts as the internal faculty of creativity, which leads to *mokṣa*, meaning freedom, fulfilment, satisfaction and happiness. In this case too knowledge (*vidya*) supports one; not ignorance (*avidya*); bringing the synergic relationship between knowledge and karma is the purpose of living a life; and the knowledge (*vidya*) would be discerned from creative work. It is one of the defining factors of all philosophical systems originated in India. For the Indians, Karma or action is what defines human life. Everyone is predisposed with own duty (*sva-karma*). Philosophy of Karma explains how everything is related to a network of action (work) in the life of an individual. Karma comes from the Sanskrit root word *kṛ*, which denotes the ability for creative action. The Sanskrit word for hand is *karaḥ*, the main organ in the body for performing karma. Human life endeavors to fulfill actions and one has to have proper thoughts, creative knowledge, efforts to engage in actions, because doing actions perfectly is an aspect of the human consciousness. This individual specific attribute can be rebuilt by engaging in creative work, which helps the functioning of a robust consciousness. The role hand-*brain faculty* in creative work can be explained thus.

When we analyze the dullness of Joe or the trauma of Noriyasu; both had less and less opportunities to use their creative energy and skills in the assigned works (*sva-karma*). In their works, they were appended mainly to a machine, where their individual contribution or participation did make no difference. At his work, Joe hadn't learned anything from the seniors, nobody taught him anything personally. Like a machine, he did read the instruction manuals to execute his assigned works. Learning from a senior (*senpai*) is a part of the Asian work culture, notably in Japan. Initially, Noriyasu was minimally instructed by his seniors, albeit he had nothing more to do than operating the program which did most of the jobs by itself. The tradition of learning from a senior (*senpai*)and relearning it again and again by doing oneself has lost its meaning in the postmodern world. Learning and teaching about "work" related issues are redundant in today's globalized world order. In the postmodern globalized world "work" is a mockery on what the traditional work culture signified, where appreciating "creativity" was the main factor. How can someone learn anything by creating something? When a creator creates something, he would work towards the final form of the object, which Aristotle called as the *final cause* of creativity where the conception of *arete* attains fruition providing the creator with a flourishing feeling. This is what is meant by excellence in virtuous action; or achieving *puṇya* (merit) from executing own duties (*sva-karma*).

However, today different parts of a thing are made at different outsourced centers and being assembled at, yet, another location. Moreover, in his work, Noriyasu was rather guided by the automatized Artificial intelligence systems not the directions of an experienced senior employee (*senpai*). The hope that he could work and learn

more and contribute with more personal contributions was thwarted by the focus
of the company to use machines that are exclusively supported by algorithmically
programmed AI systems. The appreciation of human virtues such as, goodness, truth,
beauty, being, etc. had taken away from work. It was only for profit and greed. The
personal human relationships that existed between experienced seniors and junior
co-workers had disappeared from the work culture instantaneously. The personal
integrity of a worker to work is now worrying hugely for being watched and controlled
by a very intrusive surveillance systems that follow one almost everywhere. The lure
of Artificial Intelligence systems is so huge that we follow them madly and drawn
ourselves into a kind of matrix, from which there is no way to get out. The aspect
of creativity in work is now replaced by a system which can think itself without
any active human interface and can function like an automaton. The human values
that helped us to survive, thus far, would be relegated and discarded; we in Platonic
terms would destroy the femininity—creativity—within us, by not being allowed us
with any creative activities completely and extensively. In such a society, the value
of femininity would be declined. The dignity and integrity of being women would
be equal to that of an automaton. This aspect has far reaching deep consequences
for the natural progress of human life. A kind of thrusted asexuality is spreading
everywhere. The talk about a genderless personality that is being propagated by the
popular media and pop culture today in the Western world can be interpreted as an
aftermath of this aspect of the horrendous disregard for creativity and creative work
in shaping the consciousness of a human person.

The focus of a business enterprise today is only to make more money to satisfy the
greed for more profit of the investors, banks and governments. The aspect of social
well-being and individual happiness is also a part of mainstream social discourses,
but that only remains, as topics in social discourses as taking points. And now in
actuality such extraneous discourse could support only as a setting that would make
the exploitation of human work furthermore, by making everything into monetized
wealth such as shares, bonds and other such tradable (financial) products. Now most
of the part-time jobs are contracted by labor dispatch companies with huge financial
interests, supporting the financial industry immensely.

The paradigm shift that started since 1960s (industry-2) had changed the life
of people like Noriyasu for the worst in the twenty-first century globalized world
(industry-3). This happened against the security that he expected on work related life
he had experienced in his rural life settings, where *work and life* were closely linked to
a person's happiness and well-being. When monetary benefits destroyed the creative
knowledge and satisfaction from work, people like Noriyasu lost all the motivations
for actively getting involved with work and therein acquire creative happiness as
wellbeing. We should look at this issue differently to understand the intricate nuances
about "work" in one's life. Today, in the age of techno-sciences, also some neuro-
scientific studies on consciousness duly agree with the exhortations of the classical
philosophical view on creative work in conditioning good life (Goodness) that the
true being of an individual could be harmonized by carefully structuring the neural
circuits by engaging and learning from creative work. What the classical Greeks
believed in introducing *eudaimonia* and *arete*, are not *happiness* and *freedom* as

some postmodern thinkers try to configure and propagate, but are there in inculcating excellence in virtue through creative work. By being Engaged in creative work or by invoking femininity in the conscious, a human person could find happiness and satisfaction. The modern findings in neuroscience would agree with that view. In recent times, some neuroscientists are actively studying this aspect of creativity in human life and its functional necessity to create a robust and active consciousness.

27.1 Religion Versus Technoscience

The world order that faithfully follows technoscience, nobody ever could take up the issue of creative satisfaction as a part of living life, lest we establish a clear connection between work and the formation of consciousness on the basis of neurosciences. In our times, science is like a religion we accept only scientific principles with a kind of religious fervor conditioned by deep faith. We discard the thoughts of the ancients as archaic and worthless. This is condemnable attitude the postmodernists. According to Jacob Needleman: "We live in the same world, metaphysically, cosmically speaking, as did Pythagoras, Gautama Buddha, St. Augustine, or Moses. The same forces are at play on this plane of being called earth, influencing human life on earth implicitly. The Greeks gave the names of gods to these forces—Apollo, Aphrodite, Kronos. Today such forces are given names derived from modern psychology or science— for example, entropy, libido, and homeostasis—which, however, convey only a pale reflection of their real power on human life and the cosmic scheme. And, in our time, the forces that define human life on earth manifest themselves through money.[4] However, the modern Western philosophers think that classical philosophy is worthless junk knowledge, and preemptively reject that as an entity with no meaning with real life. They propagate that the humanity has received true knowledge only after using scientific methods, since seventeenth century, when science revealed all the real truths rationally and systematically into a kind of singularity. Nevertheless, the scientific theories on mind (Psychology) have been refuted by the latest studies on consciousness in the latest neurological studies. As Jacob Needleman suggested the cosmological conception of God representing life forces would signify more than its scientific substitutes that could give only slight theoretical tangents. We must note that the conception of God is closely connected with the inner life of humans. And if we anticipate that that protection can be replaced by money is a farfetched wild expectation, yet some superrich individuals think that they are acting like gods who can decide on the fate of the others wantonly. In Biblical terms they are doing the work of Mammon—the fallen angel, not God.

The results of studies in neuroscience are quite telling that it has been scientifically established that the life experience of a person would create the networks of neural circuits, a tunnel like formation in the brain with an internal structure, and the formation of neural-circuits from life experiences of the living environment, the formation

---

[4]Needleman (1991), p. 40.

of such neural circuit structures, is called "ego tunnel" creation. As far as the life of a person in the world is concerned, the effective functioning of the ego tunnel is important. It has been established using experiments that one creates a personal specific structure on the already existing structures through various learning activities. It means that each individual has born with an existing structure, the formation of which is inexplicable to technoscience of our time. And to achieve that, one needs to "work" creatively with the already existing structure by continuously reforming the structures with each phase of working and learning. How this happens is what helps us to understand the importance of creative "work" in our lives. We can see that completion of a "work" gives a unique meaning and a sense of fulfillment in life, which is defined as human flourishing—*eudaimonia*—spiritual bliss from Greek god *daimon*, an inherent internal ability of the human soul which one should experience as a part of living life.

We can argue that the trauma of a person who is unemployed or who doesn't work at all is a life without any opportunity to create a "personal self-model"—ego tunnel—for oneself, which eventually might destroy the integrity and spiritual worth of human life. The psychological scientists, on the other hand, are engaged in researches for creating a unified theory of mind where the sole motivation is pursuing "freewill and freedom" for more worthless pursuance of "comfort and entertainment" in order to spice up our lives. We need to look at the neurological theory on consciousness to understand our current difficulties. It is not so naïve as the postmodernists try to configure. The definition of "freedom" in the postmodern globalized world order is an objectively discernable construct that needed to be achieved as the only aim of life. However, the classical philosophers argue that it should be something one should inculcate by living a good life where creative work plays a significant role. As Aristotle explained *eudaimonia* is what conditions a person's ethical and moral life, where the lack of creative work would destroy a person's moral life, which is centered on human flourishing (*eudaimonia*). The postmodern thinkers implicitly configured that we could achieve *eudaimonia* through "comfort and entertainment", and argued fervently that knowledge, sourced from technoscience could help to perpetuate it.

References

Kaplan, J.D. (ed.): Dialogues of Plato: Symposium. Washington Square Press, New York (1950)
Needleman, J.: Money and the Meaning of Life. Doubleday, New York (1991)

Chapter 28
The Neurology of Consciousness: The *Ego Tunnel*

Darwinian theories of evolution find that human consciousness should have gone through 200 million years of evolution to reach at the present level of cognition ability and a way to experience life as the way humans do today. The human centrality we experience today is in the process of that evolution.[1] That means the reality as we perceive and experience is true and real only for the human species, and would not be the same for any other living beings. Human consciousness is a unique complex biological phenomenon, and it cannot fully be objectively discernable, but partially experiential at the subjective mental level of a human person. The idea of individual "soul" evolved from this perspective. The psychological sciences study, mind, as an object and try to define it scientifically. The mind is only a vague representation of that absolute consciousness discernable collectively. According to Indian classical philosophers, it is difficult to discern and experience the full nature of consciousness (Brahman) because we, as humans, live within the dominion of that consciousness. The conception of mind, may explain an aspect of the complex system of consciousness, but may not explain it fully. The importance of consciousness is that it makes the reality appear within itself not beyond. The apparent reality can be understood comprehensively but not as a singular entity. Singular reality signifies one unified understanding of connected phenomena where each phenomenon may not explain the whole. To address the complexity of mind and its relation to consciousness, in Buddhism, there are five aspects connected with the subjective self—including consciousness, that is always active in an individual person. It is widely accepted that human subjectivity inheres an aspect of consciousness.[2]

The one and the same reality has multiple facets and manifestations. The understandings of the reality changes always. From person to person the same reality may appear differently. So, what is presumed as reality is not eternally real. It is just an apparent phenomenon. What is known as the neural circuits relating to a person's consciousness is neither consistent nor constant, it changes as it strives to find its

---

[1] Metzinger (2009), p. 15.

[2] Varghese (2020), p. 49.

© The Author(s), under exclusive license to Springer Nature Singapore Pte Ltd. 2021 167
M. Varghese, *A Brief History of Creative Work and Plutonomy*,
https://doi.org/10.1007/978-981-15-9263-8_28

ultimate model. The neural circuit that represent an individual consciousness is in a stage of constant change. In other words, the reality we experience within our ego tunnel will always be subjected to constant reflection in our mind. The phenomenal experience, in the form of thoughts, would change like constantly changing images; for example, if we perceive a shining object it will form different images in the mind until we realize its truth-value. The shining object can be a silver piece, platinum or aluminum or even a shell. Our conscious mind invokes our sense organs to get the complete experience of the truth about the conceived phenomenon, the shining object. So, about the existent world, we can get a comprehensive view only, not any perfect cognition of any perfect object. Truth is dependent and relative. The objectivity of the object is impossible to cognize.

The term "consciousness" comes from its Latin root word *conscentia*. It means *cum*: with or together; *scire*: to know. However, modern Western philosophy understands the concept of consciousness on the basis of its use in the Medieval Christian and Islamic philosophies, where it means "moral insight".[3] And it is the spiritual space for God in man: the "soul". According to Plato: "Haven't you realized that our soul is immortal and never destroyed?" (Republic-608d)[4] The creator God, *Demiurge* had created and controlled the "soul" residing deep inside the human minds as the constant observer. The "soul" with its property of intelligence helps human minds to follow the moral life taught by the prophets. The religious philosophy, especially the Abrahamic religions, considers consciousness as an inner space, a contact point for an individual with the Ideal one: God. One needs to follow the path of that inner controller of morality. According to Metzinger, "Consciousness connected with your thoughts with your actions by submitting to them to the moral judgment of the ideal observer... Consciousness was an inner space providing a point of contact between the real human being and the ideal one inside"[5] This concept of consciousness connects the transcended reality—God and soul—that resides deep inside of the human minds. This idea of "conscious space" as soul is no longer acceptable to the philosophers who follow objectivized reality which functions within the structure of science and technology, especially after the enlightenment period in Europe. During this period any conception on God was not been fully accepted but was accepted only as the beliefs of the ancients. Yet, it is a belief that is redundant and archaic for the scientifically literate human societies enlightened with scientific knowledge and critical thinking. But there is a metanarrative of some aggressive wrathful force that might punish us for all our wrong doings with the sharpest edge of the axe that they carry to discipline everyone, so to escape that we must be vigilant, cunning and manipulative with knowledge—*episteme*.

However, even if we decline the idea of God, it is not possible to decline the idea of consciousness, because, it is the only aspect, what explains that we are livings beings. In the world of today, we depend on brain studies to learn about consciousness, or the sense of being aware, for knowing about human subjectivity. The new brain studies

---

[3] Metzinger (2009), p. 26.
[4] Plato (1953), p. 352.
[5] Metzinger (2009), p. 26.

have shown a new perspective on consciousness. And the result of which says that the mind knows only through the consciousness and that is based on the conception of the formation of a personal self-model (ego-tunnel), for it is impossible to understand anything about the formation of the individual subjectivity. The formation of the ego-tunnel is founded on the basis of human involvement in physical activity (work), because learning through experience is important for its creation.

Thomas Metzinger is a philosopher who has studied the idea of consciousness by using the findings of modern neurosciences, and also, could read philosophy properly on the basis of the neurological structure of consciousness. Those readings show us an unimaginably complex neural structure determines our inner lives, or the flow of the conscious experiences. In classical philosophy, consciousness was considered as the foundation of all the subjective experiences. However, since eighteenth century when the world began to follow scientific technological systems, the conception of subjective self with consciousness had changed to an objectively analyzable entity that is flexible for scientific studies. That method of psychological sciences has replaced the idea of the soul having divine properties. The objectification of human consciousness became a serious issue for the modern sciences to confront with, because we have to accept consciousness as the seat of memory, attention, feelings, perception, self-awareness and higher order of thoughts. And the essential feature of consciousness is that, it situates us in the world, where we live, giving us a sense of place and time. In dream stage and other such situations, we also exist in the realm of consciousness. A structure of neural correlates forms with each conscious stage but the neural structure of each of our emotional stage has not been discerned yet. According to Metzinger: "The conscious brain is a biological machine—a reality engine—that purports to tell us what exists and what doesn't. It is unsettling to discover that there are no colors are there in front of your eyes. The apricot pink of the setting sun is not a property of the evening sky, a model created by your brain. The evening sky is colorless."[6] The human conscious brain is like a machine, which creates a system, with the support of the neural structure, telling us why we experience the phenomenal world, in a unique particular way. When we experience an object, the brain creates a representation in our brains depending on various factors, which are personal and internal to an individual as well as shared; that is why, we can communicate our experiences with the entire community of humans, which each of us individually interpret through a mind language (*mentalese*) and communicate with the others through linguistic expressions. This uniquely human faculty that helps humans to use language is known as *logos*. The beauty of the evening sky we experience is, in fact, arrays of electromagnetic radiations of different wavelengths, many of them are not visible to us and they never would be visible. "What is really happening is the visual system of our brain is drilling a tunnel through the inconceivably rich physical environment and in that process is painting the tunnel walls in various shades and color. *Phenomenal* color. *Appearance*. For your conscious eyes only".[7]

---

[6]Ibid., p. 20.
[7]Ibid., p. 20.

With respect to the living external world, every person creates a Personal Self Model (PSM)—an ego tunnel. The ego tunnel determinates that each of our experiences is personal and unique. In other words, we can discern a "soul" as being explained as life by Aristotle: "That is why the soul is the first grade of actuality of a natural body having life potentiality in it. The body so described is a body which is organized." (*De Anima* 412a27)[8] The soul is an all-pervading facet in the body, yet difficult to locate in a precise region; but for a particular individual, soul could be discerned as life.

That is why the same evening sunshine, or music, or food doesn't create the same response in each and every individual. The neural structures responsible for a particular experience (conscious experience) can make nearly same neural structures in the brain of each person but, subtly, they are different to one another. The neural structures form a flow of conscious experience with each phenomenal experience, giving a feeling of a robust consciousness in the mind: This "I" consciousness is the ego-tunnel. These kinds of highly intricate and inexplicable neural correlate are what would form the robust structure of the consciousness in an individual. This inexplicable and intricately structured consciousness further enables the brain to create new neural structures and that would determine the individual personality or the "own being" of a person. According to the theory of ego tunnel, every personal experience of an individual is true and certain, and he always attempts to make perspectives and viewpoints accordingly. When individualized viewpoints conflict with one another, we get conflicting situations. So, to put it in platonic understanding of creative work, each human person uses creative work in order to structure a particular structure of neural circuit that begets one the unique particular personality (own being). The personal self-model can be related to the idea of "soul", in the classical Greek philosophy. The same conception has deep implications with regard to ancient Indian and Chinese philosophies. The conception of an ego-tunnel or personal self-modal as the foundation of a human personality is just a reinterpretation of an idea that had enriched human life for centuries. It is known differently as soul, self, *ātman*, human person (*pudgala*), mind-brain faculty, etc. This property of structuring ego-tunnel is possible for the humans only. In the classical philosophy subjective self is *soul, ātman*, etc., which is considered as the medium through which an individual self is connected with God, Brahman, etc.

References

Aristotle: De Anima (Book-1, 402). In: McKeon, R. (Trans. and ed.) The Basic Works of Aristotle. Random House, New York (1941)

Metzinger, T.: Ego Tunnel. Basic Books, New York (2009)

Plato: The Republic. In: Lee, D. (Trans. and ed.). Penduin Books, Cambridge (1953)

Varghese, M.: Nāgārjuna and the Art of Negation. Sanctum Books, New Delhi (2020)

---

[8] Aristotle (1941), p. 555.

Chapter 29
Consciousness: The Lower and Higher Dimensional Realms

We may review the observations made by Thomas Metzinger; in his studies, as he created a paradigm to understand the idea of consciousness with the formation of the neural structures, *ego tunnel*. The reflection of such a formation should be the foundation of the inner life of an individual. The idea of two consciousness levels is comparable to the philosophical idea of universal consciousness and the individual consciousness as being discoursed in most of the classical philosophical (religious) systems. The consciousness of a single individual person is distinguishable from the all-pervading universal consciousness. According to Metzinger, neuroscientists experimentally found that the structure of the *ego-tunnel* has two levels, the lower dimensional level constantly seeking for a higher dimensional level. The nature of higher dimensional level is not fully known to the individual, but the individual neural formations are seeking some kind of higher unity, as it is obvious that the lower dimensional level is the reflection of the higher dimensional realm and it is experiential to the individual personality intuitively. The images reflected on the ego-tunnel are the reflection of something that is richer, higher and more profound. Philosophers call it as the transcended realm. This explains why human experiences are uniform yet different. Metzinger opines: "Phenomenal shadows are low-dimensional projections within the central nervous system of a biological organism… Conscious experiences are full-blown mental models in the representational space opened up by the gigantic neural networks in our heads- and because this space is generated by a person possessing a memory and moving forward in time, it is a tunnel."[1] The projections in the low dimensional realm are reflections from a higher dimensional realm, which is common to every other human being that the individual personality experiences the same experience differently, yet can realize sameness collectively. The nature of which is inexplicable, intricate and complex at the individual level. We, therefore, feel and experience that there is a world out there controlling our deep conscious mind, but in actuality the deep neural system hidden as the "ego tunnel" inside the brain gives each of us a unique particular kind of knowledge about the

---

[1] Metzinger (2009), p. 23.

© The Author(s), under exclusive license to Springer Nature Singapore Pte Ltd. 2021   171
M. Varghese, *A Brief History of Creative Work and Plutonomy*,
https://doi.org/10.1007/978-981-15-9263-8_29

external world. The creation of these neural networks is a continuing process and it moves forward so long as a person is alive. The ego tunnel is responsible for all the conscious experience of knowing, acting and being connected with the living world. The higher dimensional realm is a projection that is created by the individual ego-tunnel or *personal self-model* (PSM). That is the reason why we react differently to one and the same phenomenal experience, in a personalized way. This is the reason for the constant struggles in human life, as the neural circuits never could reach to the full-blown projection reaching out to stretch in to the higher dimensional realm. Somewhere it is internally impaired. But the neurons in the brain instigate and incite us to reach to the fullest potential and to perfection. That maybe the reason why we feel that we have much more to learn, and also why we hold on to the belief that learning never ends.

Contextually the religious philosophers call the fully blown state of consciousness as the world of God, heaven, transcended realm, Brahman, Dao, etc.; and for them, human soul is eternally connected and tethered with God. Or, in other words, individual "life" with the "source of life". We are afraid of death and never want to die until we have realized the whole truth about the significance of life. Plato promoted the concept of the form of Good as the stage of full-blown state of the soul's urge to know its source, goodness—wisdom.

We may have to find answers to some fundamental questions. Why we think life in the world is full of sufferings. Why people commit suicide? Why fear dominates us so conspicuously? Why we have no ability to confront simple setbacks in life? For understanding all these, we need to understand the idea of "naïve reality" that gives us an easy "naïve view" about life, which again gives us a false sense of protection about everything. Naïve reality is what we experience in the experiential world. All work on the simple logic of cause and effect; Good and bad; true and untrue; we naively place ourselves with the easy and relaxed position when we follow only positive things by naively negating the negatives. But we forget to realize the obvious fact that a particular reality is true only for a particular time and situation, or being conditioned by time and space. At a different level of perception, it could be different, and we may have to view the situation differently depending on the situation. But we have created a reality about the world that is short lived, and we try to hold on to them with a strong grip, while the higher dimensional realm instigates each individual person to understand the external world fully. At the low dimensional reflexive experience, we imagine and create a reality, which is individual and is conditioned by our simple ignorance and naïve fears.

All human beings can perceive the world of objects in a uniform pattern, and conceive them as real, because of our sense organs have gone through years of evolution process, generating that kind of consciousness (according to Darwin 200 million years). This may not be so for other living beings. The living worlds of dogs or cows or bats or ants should be different experientially. And we perceive the world with the help of such a conscious space—ego tunnel—(personal self-model) that is actively functioning in the human brain, which is individual specific. All realities that we perceive are very naïve for us in our conscious space. We innocently believe that the world we conceive is real and true to all of the living beings, and they conceive it as the same way as we do. This is the nature of the naïve reality and is defined as: "Because it has been optimized over millions of years, this mechanism is so fast and so reliable that you never notice its existence. It makes your brain invisible to itself. You are in contact with its content; you never see the representation as such; therefore, you have the illusion of being directly in contact with the world. And that is how you become a *naïve realist*, a person who thinks she is in touch with an observer-independent reality".[2] This aspect of creation and maintenance of inner self by the way of creating an *ego tunnel* with the support of huge structures of neural circuits is a mysterious process that never be replicated. It can be argued that the conception of a transcended subjectivity is a part of human consciousness. Every individual person inherits a personal specific neural structure upon which one can create an ego tunnel (PSM) that would support his personality. The creation of ego tunnel (PSM) is fully possible only if one activates those circuits through "creative work", *(techne)* so that one can transform, the inherent ignorance, with knowledge that is imbibed from working with the form of an object. The process of development of virtue in the idea of *karma* or *arete* can be discerned from this concept.

But at the same time, those circuits are functionally same, in totality, as all human beings share same faculties irrespective of differences in race and creed. It means that a black man and a white man would share the same experience with regard to the world they live in, but not a white man and a dog. It also means that human beings can live only by submitting to nature, not by challenging it, and also can use experiential knowledge to live well by agreeing with the nature. A black man who practice (work with) his natural instincts can become a great athlete or musician or artist, but would be different from all others including black or white or any other race, because in order to change naïve formation of neural circuits, one need to understand it intuitively. The conception of the transcended something is real when a man is in distress and confusion, but that aspect become less influential when one is not in distress or suffering. According to Buddhism an individual's view point changes from moment to moment due to the influence of internal and external factors. However, the knowledge one discerned from creative work by activating the *hand-brain faculty* is what incites *eudaimonia*—the spiritual wellness.

The ego-tunnel—neuro phenomenological cave—that each of us creates upon the innate neural structures, is difficult to change. It works like the computer's operating system. We can add different software Apps and make it functional as the way we want to, but the essential nature of the operating system remains the same. Likewise, the inside surface of the cave is the operating system and must be closed for it to be fully realistic. A person in meditation can close that inside surface, but when s/he interact with the world around, it changes, like the App could do to the computer. It acts like an internal filter reacting to the external world. It works like the door of perception that Aldus Huxley explained in his book: *Doors of Perception* (1954) for describing the nature of conscious experience.[3] So long as the perception is transparent, one lives comfortably within the ego tunnel, reacting naturally to the living world. "This

---

[2]Ibid., p. 43.
[3]Ibid., p. 45.

window must be clean and crystal clear. That is what phenomenal transparency is: It contributes to the effortlessness and seamlessness that are the hallmark of reliable conscious perception...As long as nothing goes wrong, naïve realism makes for a very relaxed way of living".[4] The transparency of the windows of perception can be explained that, if Noriyasu was awarded with a promotion and with an expected salary hike for making a better family situation, he wouldn't have faced any problem of depression or wouldn't have fallen into the pit of despair and ended his life; on the other hand, he would have found more passion for living his life. In that way, he would have achieved another kind of satisfaction from doing his work for monetary gains only. Through creative work his consciousness could have been flourished and developed into the higher dimensional realm with joy and happiness. Classical philosophers are of the opinion that true happiness is possible only when one gets a feeling of the higher consciousness realm, represented as the world of gods—heaven. But in Noriyasu's case no such kind of satisfaction by doing a work was forthcoming and the financial gains were negligible. He became sad and confused for his inability to find any kind of fulfillment from work that made him to subsist in to a kind of precarious life situation. He couldn't live well, in the low dimensional realm of the ego tunnel (PSM), that had petrified and terrified him. He has no ability to restructure the ego-tunnel with more creative work-related experiential knowledge.

In his naïve realistic conscious space, Noriyasu thought that the world is safe and secure. His naïve presumption was that he was protected and being taken care of by the modern economic system, that keeps him working till the retirement age. Normally people, who work, think that the position, they hold, would bring all goodness, and that would continue to be enriching their lives, even after retirement a pension be supporting them, etc. Noriyasu knew that his forefathers never had to retire from active work-life, in old age, the family took care of them. This feeling of continuance, in engaging with one's work, is the measure of devotion to life. In normal life, we want to live like or even better than our parents' or grandparents' generation. The life in Tokyo and the Job in the American company was so clearly understandable for him as a sign of progress, and he was very sure about his future life naively as anyone in his situation would imagine. He felt very comfortable in that world. In the modern times, especially since the first industrial revolution the scientific systems and the capitalistic economy gave a sense of crystal-clear security with "work" and "life" due to the influence of the ethical doctrine of "divine providence". The security that the scientifically literate modern systems provided was unprecedented and would continue to flourish even into the postmodern globalized world order, though the reality is different. We no longer have the control on work to shape up our lives. Human creative work is the least valued commodity today, and it continues to be so, lest we rethink comprehensively about work and life as the principal doctrine.

The discourses in modern and postmodern scientific philosophy have made us to live comfortably situated and locked within the world of scientific rationalism. We, as humans, are inclined to latch on to something new to get better with our lives. And we unknowingly create a comfort zone around the new. Since eighteenth century science

---

[4]Ibid., p. 46.

and later technology revealed to us newer systems that created life easy and trouble-less. As a matter of fact, the scientific reasoning following the Newton's physical laws together with the laws on the mechanical order of life proposed by Galileo made us to follow naively all the scientific systems that are being developed ever since. The scientific world, even today peruses the Galilean worldview aggressively, and projects the external world with a kind of certainty beyond which none can think further. This was the situation since the modern times, which according to Noam Chomsky: "The concept of mind was framed in terms of what was called "the mechanical philosophy," the idea that the natural world is a complex machine that could, in principle, be constructed by a skilled artisan. "The world was merely a set of Archimedean simple machines hooked together" .... "or a set of colliding corpuscles that obeyed the laws of mechanical collision. The world is something like the intricate clocks and other automata that excited the scientific imagination of that era, much as computers do today."[5] We naively believe that the world we live in is objectively analyzable and discernable. The inner life, we create artificially for us, is drawn from such a presumed naïve world order. We turn ourselves as the software application programs—Apps—of a computer, and add or remove various application programs suiting to each situation. So long as nothing bad happens the naïve world continue to support us. And we will remain comfortable within that artificially created world. The idea of National Socialism was drawn from this kind of naïve fundamental view. The idea of scientific socialism was in fact also based on such a naïve view, but the inner contradictions with this view has changed everything, ending in the demise of scientific socialism of the communists and the national socialism of the NAZIs, etc. The scientific socialism or the systematically planned way of thinking, on strict scientific reasoning, didn't work as the way it was expected to. The later findings by scientists in the later part of nineteenth and twentieth century destroyed scientific and systematic reasoning introduced by the Newtonian worldview. But in order to remain in the comfort zone, we began to follow it with a sense of faith and religiosity by infusing Newton's thoughts in to the sociopolitical systems even though Newtonian laws are outdated now.

But, ironically, using the same methodology of scientific experiments, quantum mechanics challenged the reality-based theories of Newtonian perspective and shocked the world with a new kind of understanding about the world order scientifi-cally. As Niels Bohr wrote: "if quantum mechanics hasn't profoundly shocked you. You haven't understood it yet. Everything we see as real is made of things that cannot be regarded as real."[6] This view of Niels Bohr in the context of Neuro sciences is that we should have the naïve reality to be true, as we experience the world that we want it to be clear and transparent at, all the time. Therefore, we follow the perspec-tive of Newtonian science instead of quantum theories, which provide us a new challenge to confront with. But when the expected transparency becomes opaque or non-transparent, we feel frustrated and confused, yet we fall back into our comfort zones and we strongly seek refuge there. The same inner contradictions began to work

---

[5]Chomsky (2002), p. 49.
[6]Scoular (2007), p. 89.

with western communism and nationalism; both follow the ideals of capitalism since 1990. Like communism, capitalism is now failing to solve human problems as being expected. The emergence of plutonomy and the new systems of economic model in the postmodern globalized world order are deemed as symptoms of that failure. We now incline and pursued to be manufacturing poverty with the widespread use of AI controlled machines taking away systematically all the production works, because we love to follow naïve thoughts that are propounded by scientific revelations that we can pursue endless growth unabatedly as a monotonous process without any need to return back.

But in the case of Noriyasu the comfort and safety that he expected from the world, had discontinued, affecting his inner consciousness. It became opaque deeply. In the globalized postmodern world order, instead of more remuneration and more opportunities to engage with creative works, Noriyasu got a sudden shock on receiving the job termination order. The transparency he enjoyed in his consciousness (ego-tunnel) suddenly became opaque and a kind of deep creepy discomfort set into his consciousness. Metzinger writes about his theory on the transparency of ego-tunnel (personal self-model): "My theory- the self, model theory of subjectivity- predicts that as soon as a conscious representation becomes opaque, we lose naïve realism. Consciousness without naïve realism does exist… When the window is dirty or cracked, we immediately realize that conscious perception is only an interface, and we become aware of the medium itself."[7] At this point, Noriyasu began to realize and understand deeply, the perception and understandings that made him to follow certain patterns of thoughts. The representation of a perfect mechanical world order, Noriyasu presumed, has now become a problem for his naïve rational understandings. He now has lost that protective cover. He now fears his conscious experiences. He couldn't find any transparency in his ego tunnel. Instead of clarity and pure knowledge, he could only experience fear, or the opaqueness turn into fear and ignorance, making deep fishers into his consciousness—ego tunnel. Still he expects that things will turn around with better results and continuously waiting for restarting the comfort zone, but, which never happened for him and began to fall in to deep despair. And since despair is also a natural human emotion, people would sink deeply into the depth of it predictably. "Deaths of despair" is seen as a worldwide issue today.

The brain lesions that were responsible for the robust transparent consciousness become less functional and less transparent. A kind of blankness which philosophers like Nietzsche warned us, is dragging oneself into a kind of fearsome emptiness. It creates complicated psychological situations for any human person. Based on this view of the neurological understanding of consciousness, Noriyasu's trauma is understandable and explainable. In other words, he began to cultivate a kind of alienation leading to self-petrification ending in the destruction of his individuality. "Losing face" or self-respect is a kind of disgrace in the East Asians' culture. And he could get only a tainted picture of the reality around, which he thought would be rational and transparent always due to the rationalist perspectives of the world order. In his case, the low dimensional level of consciousness, within his living world,

---

[7] Metzinger (2009), p. 46.

was reformed with some unexpected and weird life experiences, where a kind of disconnect began to occur into his self and he could not figure out the happenings of the higher realm of the external social consciousness that was being influenced comprehensively by plutonomy.

Economic systems became plutonomy (super capitalism); works became mechanized; unemployment and precarity (part-time jobs) became the order of the newly emerging world systems. When the plutonomy emerged, plutocrats could decide on everything, and democracy slowly changed into plutocracy. Nobody seems to be worrying about it, as we follow the old value system founded on democratic capitalist values supported by a convenient narrative on "divine providence". The problem of plutonomy is like a bad dream from which everyone would like to wake up; and now it is turning out to be a persistent nightmare, scaring everyone from falling in to sleep. Yet, people like Noriyasu naively believe that the world systems would support his life and happiness by providing, more and more opportunities, for doing creative work, but the opposite is what is happening with plutonomy today. His soul was impregnated with a lot of creative ideas and a spirit of goodness to apply them for achieving greater goodness for supporting everyone else; on the other hand, the systems run using artificial intelligence dented all those chances to use any creative energy. Within his consciousness, Noriyasu had the image of a world where creative work would continue and he could prosper with more monetary profits and good lives for everybody. He never wants to know the truth about the world systems of today. The light of wisdom scares him; he prefers the shadow of ignorance. In his ego-tunnel he experienced a kind of separation of himself from the world around. Plato revealed such a precarious life situation with the example of life in a cave, narrated profoundly in *The Republic*.

What will happen when your psychic—subjective—faculties are not activated to the higher dimensional realm, it could remain within the confines of lower realm or may go further down into hell (Gr. *Hades* or Heb. *Sheol*). Plato uses the cave example to explain it. According to Jacob Needleman: "Sheol is the condition of human life proceeding with ever-diminishing human progress. It is the movement towards absence, the movement away from God-for let us carefully note that one of the central definitions of God that is given in the old testament is conscious presence [...] The Ancient Greeks had a view of hell similar to that of the Hebrews—the land of shadows ruled by the lord Hades."[8]

References

Chomsky, N.: On Nature and Language. Cambridge University Press, New York (2002)
Metzinger, T.: Ego Tunnel. Basic Books, New York (2009)
Needleman, J.: Money and the Meaning of Life. Doubleday, New York (1991)
Scoular, S.: First Philosophy: The Theory of Everything. Universal Publishers, Irvine (2007)

---

[8]Needleman (1991), pp. 34–35.

Chapter 30
Plato's Cavemen: Existence in Low Dimensional Realm of Consciousness Versus Freedom

To explain the complexities of life in the world, Plato used the example of a cave in which chained prisoners were being held to live there since birth. A direct depiction of the mythological world of shadows—hell—ruled by lord Hades. In the book—VII of *The Republic* Plato explained the situation of each of us in the world, where we predestine to live in. In this example of "cave", representing human life, Plato narrated that the normal human "life" would be like that of the situation of prisoners who were chained and forcefully made to sit inside a cave with minimum freedom of movement; who had also made to think that the moving shadows seen on the front wall were real and true, but those were projected with the support of a source of light from behind falling on certain moving objects that could be invisible for the chained prisoners. Since birth the prisoners were living inside the cave, and never had seen directly neither the moving objects behind nor the world outside.

Plato's thought evokes us to understand that the human existence in the world is similar to the situation of those prisoners: living in the shadowy world of confusion, deception and suffering presuming that there is nothing beyond the dark shadowy cave and that we have no direct vision of the real objects. They do not know the sources of the light or the real natures of the objects, that make the shadows, at all. They see only the images on the wall and repeatedly watching it again and again day-in and day-out. The prisoners have lost the internal light (consciousness) to search even for the source of the faint light, and also the real nature of the objects. Plato explains that this, kind of existence, is natural and we could respond only to what appear in front of us. Normal human nature never used to investigate the source of the light or the source of the images. It is so used to react only to what is appeared for the immediate direct perceptions.

However, Plato thought that some human souls have the innate motivation and courage to disbelieve and question the common narratives thrusted upon them. They, in order to find the source of the faint light, would venture out and struggle to investigate all that triggered the shadows on the walls of the cave. For searching the source of light, they should move out of the cave. Even though, staying inside of the cave and looking at the moving shadows was more comfortable and acceptable than getting

© The Author(s), under exclusive license to Springer Nature Singapore Pte Ltd. 2021
M. Varghese, *A Brief History of Creative Work and Plutonomy*,
https://doi.org/10.1007/978-981-15-9263-8_30

out and searching for the sources of light; nonetheless, the men—impregnated—with natural courage would get out of the cave. The soul with the light of intelligence made them to think differently from the masses who believe in and follow the shadowy world as real. Those who were staying inside the cave would be influenced only by the shadow of Ignorance; and ignorance would develop into fear, and fear made them to accept the illusory reality and could make them to suffer more. That should be the nature of the world ruled by lord Hades.

Therefore, we have to pursue the internal urge for more knowledge that could remove ignorance progressively; otherwise, because of the lack of true knowledge, our souls would take ignorance as true knowledge. As for Plato in the dialectics between knowledge and ignorance, knowledge always should dominate and lead. Because we as humans are instinctively predisposed to know more, we should use knowledge as the highest good. (*Republic* 508e, 2–3)[1] Knowing more deeply would lead us to true knowledge (wisdom) that is inexplicable, but gives us a suffering-less life. Learning and gaining knowledge is a continuous process and only knowledge can help us in facing our lives boldly. The instinct to know impels us to realize the metaphysical realities of life. According to Aristotle: "All men by nature desire to know. An indication of this is the delight we take in our senses; for even apart from their usefulness they are loved for themselves; and above all others the sense of sight."[2]

Plato used the metaphor of shadow and light to explain how the knowing process works, or how wisdom (pure and clear knowledge) leads us in to the right path. Here, he had explained it with the example of the cave on how the untrue and unclear shadowy knowledge or ignorance leads us in the wrong path. The philosophy of Plato should be understood as the dialectics between knowledge and ignorance. Plato explained that dialectic in *The Republic* with the cave example: "I want you to go on to picture the enlightenment or ignorance of our human condition somewhat as follows. Imagine an underground chamber like a cave, with a long entrance open to the daylight and as wide as the cave. In this chamber are men who have been prisoners there since they were children, their legs and necks being so fastened that they can only look straight ahead of them and cannot turn their heads. Some way off, behind and higher up, a fire is burning, and between the fire and the prisoners and above them runs a road, in front of which a certain wall has been built, like screen at puppet shows between the operators and their audience, above which they show their puppets. Imagine further that there are men carrying all sort of gear along behind the curtain wall, projecting above it and including figures of man and animals made of wood and stone and all sets of other materials. And some of these men as you would expect are talking and some not.... do you think our prisoners could see anything of themselves or their fellows except the shadows thrown by the fire on the wall of the cave opposite them?"[3] The prisoners couldn't see the objects or the people who carry the objects or the sounds produced by carriers. They could

---

[1] Plato (2007), p. 234.
[2] Aristotle (1941), p. 689.
[3] Plato (2007), p. 241.

get only the reflected images of the original things that were moving behind them. The prisoners were tempted to believe that the shadows are real and true by their existential condition. Plato narrated the situation thus: "Then what would naturally happen to them if they were released from their bonds and cured of their delusions. Suppose one of them were let loose, and suddenly compelled to stand up and turn his head and look and walk towards the fire; all these actions would be painful and he would be so dazzled to see properly the objects of which he used to see and the shadows. What do you think he would say if he was told that what he used to see was so much empty nonsense and that he was now nearer reality and seeing more correctly? ...And if he were made to look directly at the light of the fire it would hurt his eyes and he would turn back and retreat to the things which he could see properly... and not let go till he had been dragged out into the sunlight, the process would be a painful one, to which he would much object.... First, he would find it easiest to look at shadows, next at the reflections of men and other objects in water and later on the objects themselves. After that he would find it easier to observe the heavenly bodies and the sky itself at night, and to look at the light of the moon and stars rather than at the sun and its light by day."[4]

Our lives, ordinarily at any stage, is like sitting in the shadowy cave and experiencing life as drama played out in the front stage. None of us is enlightened at birth. Our understanding of the world can be related to the ones who sit in the cave of ignorance. We get so much used to such a world that is presented and seen in front of us as real and true. Even if we are free to do anything that we may want to do, paradoxically, we won't attempt to do anything to get out of the cave to achieve our freedom, normally, we continue sitting inside by nursing our ignorance, because most of us are lazy to getting out. We like to sit inside comfortably as the audience, as we can watch the drama played on stage and be engaged and entertained with what is being played out, in front of our sense perceptions. We fear the unknown and feel happy with our ignorance and illusions. But a few among us are inclined to challenge the unknown by courageously learning and searching about the source of everything by pursuing our inner instincts to know more—the true being of our prime predisposition. Inherently our psychic faculties are predisposed to fall in to ignorance, the world of hell, the world of *Sheol* or of *Hades*. Yet the Godly aspects in us is always tries to protect us from the hellish world that is so apparent to us as ignorance. The Christian doctrine of fall should be the direct depiction of falling naturally into the mythical world of Hades—Hell.

One way of explaining this situation would be that when Noriyasu was in his village, he was in such a cave of Japanese traditional rural life style nurtured by the conditionings of the traditions of the feudal Japan. Yet, he had shown the courage to get out of that self-imposed confinement determined by the traditions. Most of his friends did not have the courage to get out of the village life, because of the comfort zones provided by the Japanese rural feudal society. On the other hand, by moving into the city, for pursuing his dreams, after following an inner light, Noriyasu got educated and learned a lot about the values of city life style. He was like one of those

---

[4]Ibid., p. 242.

brave prisoners who had shown the courage to get out of the cave besieged with the shadow of ignorance.

In other words, a human person should continue learning as the shadows of ignorance follow him/her everywhere as a part of living life, because ignorance changes with the progress of life moving forward. Plato used this allegory to show us that we, as humans, are unable to know the complete state about the living world. Unless we use the knowing faculties effectively through continuous learning, we may have to live in the world of ignorance that perpetuates fear while comforting us to resist fear. And at various levels of knowing, we could only get partial knowledge even with our very decisive efforts. The partial knowledge are only mere opinions: knowledge shadowed by ignorance. The one who comes out of the cave saw partially the source of light, and he would tempt to look at it directly. The natural human nature of knowing is such that when we began to knowing the truth, we want to know more and more and then furthering the knowing process, and according to the strength of the intelligence, one would naturally stop it. This internal urge to know more would push, the ignorant cave dweller, out of the cave. At first, he could not look directly at the source of light, as his eyes would be blurred with the bright sunrays, stopping him to look directly at the sun. Therefore, he looks at the reflections of the sun and then to the moon, before looking directly at the sun. By the time, he would know perfectly well that the changes happening in the world are due to the sun. Sun is the source of life. At the same time, he knows fully well that he never could reach the sun and know about it fully well. The human knowledge has deep limitations. Here, Plato wants us to know that we never could get fully revealed knowledge about everything as we are hugely constrained as humans with a lot of limitations with innumerable constraints. Yet, we may pretend that we know everything even when we are made to sit inside the cave of deep ignorance. The ignorant people (like the chained prisoners) may accept what is seen on the wall as real and die with that faith. And blunt faith perpetuates ignorance and fear. On the other hand, the one who removed his chains and ventured in to the open world should have understood, the reason behind the shadow, would be getting a different kind of understanding about the world he lives in and also about "knowledge and life".

The one, who gets the "knowledge about life", outside of the cave, would soon think of returning to the cave because to reveal the realized truth to the people, who still live there, believing that the shallows are real because of being lived in the world of deep ignorance since birth. And he wants to help them with the new knowledge that has been identified and comprehended by him. And in this case too, when he returned to occupy his old seat, people despise him; Plato explains this unique situation: "Wouldn't his eyes be blinded by the darkness, because he had come in suddenly out of the sunlight…And if he had to discriminate between the shadows, in competition with the other prisoners, while he was still blinded and before his eyes got used to the darkness."[5] It means that when the freed prisoner came back to his old seat he couldn't see anything, as his sight is so blinded with the darkness of the cave, and the vision is weaker than that of the chained prisoners, who

---

[5]Ibid., p. 243.

sit inside that cave since birth. For them, the returnee is an unfamiliar new person, who now possess a different vision. He couldn't see or recognize anything inside the shadowy cave. He is blinded because of the lack of light inside the cave. He could not see anything properly. This is a typical situation for people who acquired new education and knowledge everywhere. They would receive ridicule from those who are ignorant and living in the cave—world of ignorance. All new revelations are destined to be declined and refuted vehemently.

Noriyasu is a person who has the typical village upbringing of the Northern Japan belonging to a family of rice cultivators and most of his family members, for centuries, were farmers who cultivated rice and vegetables. Farming was the only job they did and they knew well about. They never wanted, to know anything further, about the life situation outside their villages. They stayed put inside the cave of the traditional village cultural life. However, like the person who had shown the courage to venture out of the cave into the world of leading lights. Noriyasu made himself to know and learn more about the vibrant Japan after the Tokyo Olympics of 1964, and to participate in with the newly emerging, reindustrializing phase of Japanese city life. His aim at schools was to pursue the path of more knowledge for venturing into that new world. Unlike his friends and relatives, he opened his "ego tunnel" into the new world to become successful by creating new neural circuits with new knowledge, or painting new pictures on the wall of the "ego tunnel". The personal self-model he created with his life in Tokyo was different from others in his native village. The conscious experience from learning and knowing more about everything made him happy, inspired and motivated. However, the abrupt rupture in the progress of prospects by working and learning ended abruptly. He became so confused and uninspired, and fell back into the shadow of ignorance: A situation comparable to that of the returnee cava dweller.

A new kind of shadowy cave began to be opened before Noriyasu. Like the person who returned back to the cave in the Platonic example, where he couldn't locate a place in the cave. He was totally confused in locating his place inside the cave. He feared that the cave dwellers and others wouldn't accept him fully; in fact, they mocked him for being different. What he had experienced and known about the postmodern globalized world were not acceptable for his peer group colleagues back home, and his living world inside the city. In the city, after he lost his job and the social status, the people around Noriyasu became hostile and unfriendly. He felt a creepy darkness within his ego-tunnel (personal conscious space) that he had created with a lot of hard work and dedicated efforts. Returning to village life or finding lesser paying jobs wouldn't have satisfied him, as his self-consciousness (ego-tunnel), which was so much used to naïve realism of life in the modern world that he experienced in Tokyo's city life. He began to doubt everything and a kind of fear and ignorance entered into his ego tunnel that again painted a different scarier picture that he couldn't adjust with anymore. Fear and worry made his vision about his future blurred. The new experience made the walls of the ego-tunnel opaque and shadowy. The transparency provided by naïve realism is now redundant. Human life in the world should be focused, according to Plato, towards wisdom; according to Hebrew Bible, towards the conscious presence of God; and according to Buddhism towards deep insight (*prajñā*). It is the knowledge that we acquire through work is what make one to live in the world of goodness and truth.

References

Aristotle: Metaphysics (Book-1, 980). In: McKeon, R. (Trans. and ed.) The Basic Works of Aristotle. Random House, New York (1941)
Plato: The Republic (516-a). In: Lee, D. (Trans. and ed.). Penguin Books, London (first pub. 1955) reprint (2007)

Chapter 31
Learning by Working: How *Body-Hand-Brain Complex* Evolves as a Faculty

Philosophically understanding, creative work forms a foundation for the conception of the spiritual self-culture. Plato says creator god *Demiurge* is the supreme creator who created only "the forms" and is only one of the several gods in the Greek pantheon of Gods. His conception of God is different from the Abrahamic religious conception of God as an anthropoid personal deity and an absolutistic entity: the supreme craftsman and the supreme creator that controls everything. For Plato, the ability to use creative energy is equal to engaging closely with the God given virtues of beauty, truth, bliss and Goodness: "Plato also calls him a craftsman—in Greek: *demiurge*. The so-called "Demiurge" has two things in common with human craftsmen, which make him unlike God as He is usually understood in Christianity, Judaism, and Islam. Firstly, the "Demiurge" is working from a set of plans. Just as a house-builder might follow architectural drawings, so the Demiurge looks to the forms. He seeks to create an imitation of these, and this imitation is the physical universe. Secondly, the Demiurge does not create from absolute nothingness. Instead he fashions the universe in a kind of receptacle, without which he would have nowhere to put anything."[1] When one engages with any kind of creativity s/he is part-taking the creative aspect of God *Demiurge* as the only executor that can create only the forms. A human personality acts as the creator of receptacle that can contain and receive the forms created by god Demiurge. Thereby, one develops *techne*—craftmanship, the ability to create things creatively and artistically. The ability to create something should be seen as a way to engage with the "providence and love of God", which is ingrained, in the human soul (consciousness) as eternal knowledge. Thus, on reading Plato closely, the knowledge acquired through work (practice) has a special place in our lives as it spiritually protects us, and help us to be with the gods and heavenly wisdom. It is only the humans who can create things on the forms created by the God *Demiurge* and could get associated with the eternal wisdom behind all the eternal forms.

However, to make this point clear: we would take the story of a person who learned almost everything about swimming by reading books. This story could contrast with

---

[1] Adamson (2014), p. 182.

© The Author(s), under exclusive license to Springer Nature Singapore Pte Ltd. 2021
M. Varghese, *A Brief History of Creative Work and Plutonomy*,
https://doi.org/10.1007/978-981-15-9263-8_31

the situation of learning something by actively practicing it. A bookish learner on swimming from different books, also learned from teachers, and peer groups; yet, when he fell off from a boat, while crossing the river, he couldn't apply it into practice. But the expectation is that the bookish and theoretical knowledge—*episteme*—should be the foundation of all knowledge. However, on the occasion of drowning, the educated and literate, swimmer might be saved by an illiterate swimmer who had learned nothing about swimming theoretically, yet practiced—*techne*—of swimming by training in the water. In comparison the knowledge acquired by the illiterate swimmer was superior and enlightening. For each time he swam in water, he did learn something new, as he got a flourishing feeling with the act of swimming each time. In Aristotelian sense *techne* should be another aspect of *arete*—the virtue one imbibes from learning and doing some virtuous action that leads one to *eudaimonia*; unvirtuous action may do the opposite, pull him deep into despair, fear and ignorance.

Nevertheless, the general conception of education is of inputting knowledge into the mind of the learner like inputting data into a computer software. By following theoretical knowledge, we create only replicas of forms created by God *Demiurge*, but by working on the forms and by becoming creative on making things, we become humans; it is only humans who can be creative, on the forms given by God *Demiurge* who can create only perfect forms, not things out of them. But in the case of the creation of the neural structure for the ego-tunnel—the individual conscious space, one needs to "work" towards it, for creating it. The knowledge that is inserted into the mind of a learner requires him to practice on it creatively to forming the conscious space in the brain—the robust consciousness; in classical Greek sense, *techne*— the craftmanship that become a part of one's life. This knowledge is different from opinion that one can get from reading, etc. In the theory of ego-tunnel, Metzinger reiterated the idea of creative work: "(True) consciousness is a robust phenomenon; it doesn't change simply because of the opinion we have about it. Like the cyclist who learns to pedal a cycle using the whole body, helps the body to participate learning the art of pedaling. The art of cycling is opening the conscious space. It gives him a unique freedom. But it does change through practice (think about wine connoisseurs, perfume designers, musical geniuses).[2] The body can participate only with the involvement of human hand and here we could configure the involvement of body in the generative complex learning system the, body—*hand-brain faculty*.

This explains why "creative work" enables, a person, to live a fully satisfied life. On the other hand, when using artificial intelligence, we do the opposite. The automated machine does the creative part of any work and none can learn anything by actually executing a work. Appending to a machine is what a human person does in this case. We can only act as an entity subservient to the system of automated network of machines. As a result, doing a work by being a part of the machine, but not learning from the actual work activity, will not create the conscious space, or ego tunnel. This would make the worker act like the machine he is working with. This negative learning process would aggressively streamlined and be reduced to zero in the future, because the machines will be able to reprogram itself without any human

---

[2]Metzinger (2009), p. 17.

interface. In the case of Noriyasu, if he had creatively worked continuously on what he was educated for, he should have progressed by learning more new knowledge and should have matured like a music Maestro or a wine connoisseur, in his work-life, by self-generating a personal specific self-knowledge—*techne*. He should have created a personal specific ego-tunnel. But leaving abruptly in the middle of his work-life, his conscious space became opaque and his personal self-model of himself blurred. He could only find darkness in the end of his conscious tunnel; instead of transparency, there is only opaqueness riddled with shadowy fear. A man after completing his schooling learns almost everything by doing something, otherwise the learned knowledge is having no use and would be wasted. This kind of *master-student, guru-śikṣya, senpai-kohai, senior-junior* tradition is a part of work culture in Asia; in such cases the learner imbibes, *techne*—the craftmanship from the senior. The bookish knowledge—*episteme*—should have killed one, when he tried to apply it in practice, without any swimming practice. But if he had practiced swimming, by working on that bookish knowledge should have acted as an added advantage and that could have enlightened his consciousness with robust reflexes; at the same time, one needs somebody to put him into the water to start swimming. The education, one may acquire, is of zero value with regard to his work-life, if he just trained to be appended to a machine. Learning from work is a curious thing: One learns everyday a new thing by continuously working on a job. There is no end to this kind of learning. That is the reason why Plato considered knowledge as the supreme form of Goodness. The philosophical meaning of creative work is a curious thing that Plato thought that there is no end to learning and knowing, as perfect knowledge is unapproachable for humans; therefore, one needs to work on the god given forms by creating things out of it.

And that is the learning Plato demonstrated in his example of caveman who live in the shadow of ignorance, venturing out and getting the experience of the true knowledge about light, by actually looking at the sun; and realizing that sun is the source of all lights on earth and therefore life is dependent on sun. In fact, one who practices and learns from work is like the caveman who understood light in this way that he should learn looking at various forms of light before directly looking at the sun. Thereby, he progressively could build a robust consciousness from the natural human urge to know more, like the musical genius who tries to make the best music till the end of his life. This aspect about learning would get lost, when we use machines that can function by itself. Therefore, artificial intelligence would kill the consciousness of the humans, making us behave strangely with ignorance and fear in our minds. Artificial intelligence can be the huge monster that stands on the mouth of "the cave", stopping anyone from getting out in search of the truth. And thereby putting a bolt into the creative instincts of any discerning personality who would aspire for a satisfying work-life.

Plato, through this example, wanted to teach that the experiences of life, in the world, for all living beings is, like, that of the chained prisoners living inside the cave of fear and ignorance. The other living beings habituate themselves in living there, but humans are endowed with *logos*, the ability to reasoning, learning, using language, etc. If we won't use the faculty of *logos* (reasoning) and the inherent ability to know more, we would live like other being, living in the world of instincts only. Inside the cave, our freedoms to know and learn are limited, yet we imagine that the basic nature of "life" is like living inside a cave, and we need to feel, happy, of being alive, but when unfreedom sets in, we revolt against. Instead, a person should use the thinking faculty for forming new knowledge, then knowledge will show us a way to acquire freedom from the chains that we are tied up with, i.e. ignorance and fear. The particular "caveman" who got out, was working with the faculty of reasoning to know the sources of life and everything outside of his confined existence; his ability to reason made clear to him that the world inside is not the "true reality". On his way out, he saw different kinds of "light forms", reflecting on various mediums, making him realize that what he saw on the walls of the cave were just a kind of reflection of the light. He then understood clearly that the source of all light should be more profound like the whole encompassing "sun", to which he could not reach as it stayed far way, and unapproachable due to its unimaginably high heat. He understood that the true knowledge about the true being of sun could not be possible to know fully for humans. Likewise, he would also understand that he never could read the creative spirit of God *Demiurge* fully, as the world outside is full of things formulated by *Demiurge*. He could only attempt to read relatively better conception, as its perfect form remains unapproachable like our attempt to reach the Sun. So, the efforts to understand to know more about the source of light is as difficult as the approach to "sun".

Our knowing faculties are so limited for acquiring knowledge in its complete form, but each attempt would reveal to us with a better form of knowledge entrenched in. True knowledge according to Plato is wisdom; wisdom is the knowledge of transcended Goodness. This supreme goodness should be the nature of gods in heaven. So, knowing fully about the knowledge of Gods is also difficult. Our faculties are so limited to realize God perfectly, even though the god *Demiurge* created the "soul" with pure heavenly materials but with its existence within our bodies, the divine nature subdues, but with knowledge, we can realize its heavenliness *eudaimonia* (spiritual flourishing) through *arete* (excellence in virtuous actions) using like our eyes can recognize the "light", but unable to reach its source: Sun. God demiurge can create forms (ideas), but not objects. He also created soul that is why we cannot locate at a particular place in the body, but discernable in the living body. Plato also wanted to teach us that creative "work" is the best way to engage with the God created "forms" as that is impregnated in our souls, we can open it, like we open our eyes slowly, when looking at the sun, to realize that sun is the super source of all light's sources. We can realize that aspect but cannot know it fully, as we cannot reach there. When we engage in work we actually get closer to the soul's spirit that exists as creativity within us. Paradoxically, the life on earth is of living with an eternal challenge of, not being able to reach sun, or not being able to know the source of life, God. But through creativity, we could appease the "soul" (life) and could survive against ignorance by creating a robust consciousness that protects us from sufferings.

Whenever one engages in a creative work s/he learns something new, which moves him closer to happiness (*eudaimonia*). Knowing by doing a work—*techne*, has this spiritual meaning. It protects us from ignorance and fear. Plato conceives that God only created forms (ideas), not specific objects by imbibing forms; only humans have that ability to imbibe forms and be creative in the objective world. It is for man to create specific objects. When we create individual objects with the god given forms (ideas), we are nearing closer to God by the way of engaging with that creative spirit. Creativity is what makes humans to know their self-worth. Plato's God is philosophical God; when we become creative in any work, God will reveal to us as happiness and satisfaction (*eudaimonia*) which is heavenly embedded with the transcendental virtues; contextually, Plato rubbishes carnal pleasures as worthless. One can live a life to its fullest potential by acquiring self-worth through virtue ethical practices. But similar to the chained prisoners, we live with the shadow of ignorance and with the opinions generated out of that ignorance. And for experiencing *eudaimonia* (happiness and satisfaction) fully, we need to follow virtue ethics, which is of following-truth, goodness, and beauty- as the guiding principles of life so that the eternal Goodness would dawn upon us.

According to Plato the actual process of knowing is declining opinions (*doxa*) but searching for the true knowledge (*Sophia*: wisdom). This dialectical learning is the most important part of the philosophy of Plato. The idea of pure knowledge is the knowledge about goodness: the knowledge knowing itself: God, which had divine qualities that one must cherish it. But for achieving which, one needs to venture out of "the cave" that should help him to know the real nature of "life" in the world. Plato considers the purpose of life is of knowing about Goodness, because the search for goodness is what would sustain "life". The life in the world is supported by an eternal goodness, but since we live in the world of ignorance, we see only the shadowy world, that lacks Goodness everywhere. In Plato's example, the one who returns to the cave would make efforts to look at the images in the cave, but could not see anything new, as one could see only repeats of the same shadowy appearance day after day. The returning caveman could not see anything as his eyes become opaque because of the lack of light in the cave, and also due to the sudden darkness of the cave. And the cave-dwellers, who continues to live there, would ridicule him of being different. They never going to believe his story about the actual source of light and the source of life is the sun. In the Platonic conception, knowledge is liberation and it should be achieved through creative work and creative thinking. And that is the way to know the true nature of goodness (God). For achieving creative thinking, one needs to use the complex mechanism of body-hand-brain into a faculty through graduated practices, as the caveman did, when he physically unchained himself using of his hand and the cleaver application of his brain (thoughts) and then walked out; that is how he developed his *hand-brain faculty*.

The aspects of Noriyasu's trauma can be analyzed using Platonic idea of God and spiritual life. The conscious space (consciousness) that he had created in the ego-tunnel now became less transparent as the external situation stopped him from getting new knowledge through creative work. Noriyasu found his existence neither inside nor outside of the cave. He could not get the satisfaction and fullness that he was seeking for, because the "ego tunnel" was not transparent and clear anymore, it was opaque and a kind of fear began to creep up into his consciousness. Ignorance generates fear; fear generates trauma; and trauma made him to end his life in suicide.

The goodness (God) in him should have died as the eternal virtues in the form of Goodness, truth and harmony become redundant for him in such a situation. He didn't use his body-hand-brain complex properly anymore, but the urge to know more still existed in him alive and kicking, unlike other cavemen who accepted in the shadowy cave as the fate.

Unlike the conception of God in Christianity, Judaism, and Islam; Plato's God is not a personal deity who rewards and punishes, who grows angry, who loves his creatures. The *Demiurge* or other gods would do none of those things. The gods may be providential and generous; but in making the universe the attitude of the god is aesthetic taste than love. Demiurge does not need our love. He is divine and perfect, and needs nothing.[3] The idea of creativity as a way to engage with the divine spirit is the Platonic idea of spiritual life and when one creates things with aesthetic teste (*arete*) he would be growing with knowledge and may reach to the higher knowledge or an inkling of wisdom which helps one to realize the inner virtues leading to the flourish of wellness—*eudaimonia*.

References

Adamson, P.: Classical Philosophy, vol. 1. Oxford University Press, Oxford (2014)
Metzinger, T.: Ego Tunnel. Basic Books, New York (2009)

---

[3] Adamson (2014), p. 188.

Chapter 32
Evolution of Work and Declining Creativity

In our times both modern industrialized world—industry-1 (since eighteenth century) and the postmodern re-industrialization world—industry-2 (since 1960s), the world systems adopted mechanization slowly from a support tool, to improve the efficiency of human hand in production, to a system that destroyed the involvement of human *hand-brain faculty* in creative works. In the millennial globalized world—industry-3, under the digital revolution, the strategic deployment of Artificial Intelligence is displacing all kinds of creative work. The improved production and consumption changed the meaning of "work", from a creative act that could have given satisfaction and happiness and a true meaning to life, to an act that could give profit to humans to buy happiness in various ways. Since 1960s the thinkers and philosophers in the Western world began to think that humans achieved self-sufficiency in everything; so, that should be the time for redefining human life using scientific methods and that became the trend after the European enlightenment, because those methods had provided the humanity with the truth about everything, that controls the phenomenal world of experiences. Immortality through scientific means was one of such, set out, prime targets; yet, it was/is an unrealizable dream. They also began to think that capitalism and democracy with liberal values should be the end of history that had progressed through struggles.

The argument that supported this view should be that a lot of people who lived in poverty in the medieval Europe could find a better life of freedom through protestant reformation that changed the life under the dictates of the Holy Roman Empire controlled by the Catholic Church, and that also controlled human thoughts through their decrees. The reformation initiated by the Protestant movement of Martin Luther and John Calvin, was based on the Christian doctrines of "freedom and freewill" of the individual soul to search and find its inner essence in God. The freedom to follow God's dictates founded on love and compassion, and the fundamental rights to use freewill as an attribute of holy spirit (an aspect of God), had inspired the protestant movement for gaining acceptability everywhere. This movement conserved this

© The Author(s), under exclusive license to Springer Nature Singapore Pte Ltd. 2021   191
M. Varghese, *A Brief History of Creative Work and Plutonomy*,
https://doi.org/10.1007/978-981-15-9263-8_32

doctrine for benefiting the poor (the serfs) who were denied such rights. The reformation of Protestantism helped to create a middleclass community (burghers). The
influence of Raman Catholic church, on political decisions and on keeping the public
opinion controlled, was reformed by the protestant movement with the adoption of
Holy Bible as the sole authority for developing spiritual self-culture and for redefining
the relationship between God and man. The effort to develop human self-worth was
considered as the act of freewill, where one should be free to act, as an agent of
the "divine providence". Today the economists continuing the ideals of Protestant
reformation further, making the world of wealth into the hand of a few who would
continue the reformation started of with Protestant movement, giving plutonomy as
the supreme answer to all problems.

The protestant movement followed the method, of searching the truth, using clear
and certain evidences and scientific reasoning, or interpreted freedom and freewill to
gain knowledge about the phenomenal world, so that the innate relationship between
God, world and humans can be understood comprehensively. Subsequently, the
Western world had adopted scientific methods, so as to know the mind of God using
the faculty of reasoning, this had forced the world systems to transform and change.
The protestant movement, with the spiritual authority of Bible and the reasoning
method of science, gave voice to the serfs, and destroyed feudalism for the middle-
class society to emerge as the new class. The part of middle class (burghers), soon,
emerged as the controllers of wealth in the industrialized world, due to their ability
to learn and use those scientific systems; accordingly, the Protestantism popularized
literacy and numeracy for the newly emerged middle class to improve their lives by
learning more about technoscience. This spirit of reformation and an unstinted faith
in the providence of God and the spiritual ability to directly be connected with God
had trigged the 1st industrial revolution. During the 1st industrial revolution, the first
origination of the new middle-class society had happened over a pre-industrial society
that dialectically negated both feudalism and serfdom. However, a large section of
population had to live, on deprivation and scarcity of everything, and that a large
section was, living in ignorance and backwardness, inherited from the past under
feudalism and Catholicism. Karl Marx called the newly emerged wealth controllers:
the bourgeoisie; and called, the deprived underclass common people with no access
to any sort of wealth, as the proletariat. As the bourgeoisie had grown in strength to
be the superrich class displacing the feudal class; the proletariat (workers) got hugely
marginalized to be the new underclass replacing the serfs.

But in the re-industrialization—industry-2.0 period, a kind of irreligious secular
movement and a kind of naïve humanism emerged to replace the Protestant Christian values founded on the conception of the "providence of God". In the newly
emerged system, the proletariats' hard labor were necessary, for making the production system running profitably, and also were used them like machines; nonetheless
machines were always been in under some sort of human control. But, as a mark of
the globalized period—industry-3.0, instead of mechanization, we have technological systems that control all the productions, and the plutonomy controls the system.
Part-time workers (precariats) are a feature of this period and they have replaced the
proletariat of the industry-2.0. And alarmingly "artificial intelligence" emerged as

the controller of human life, where the contribution of human creativity turned out to be nearly zero, as AI systems could self-produce programs that can run systems automatically. This is going to take a paradigm shift in the industry-4.0—the fourth industrial revolution. A kind of automaton would control everything giving a feeling that a very intelligent individual controls everything for the entire population in the world. Such kind of intelligent system now controls the financial market and making complex investment decisions, as if it was made by an intelligent agent, but that essentially is run by big data; and when somebody feeds fraudulent data, the system takes decisions on that, and could functionally upset the entire system. Signs of that can be apparently seen in the financial industry today that the superrich plutocrats could become a pauper overnight, just because the automaton that controls the entire operation alerted the investors of some impending danger with some activities of the plutocrat that are against the rules of the plutonomy.

As on today, at the time of industry-3.0, in the place of common sense: we have scientific rationalism; in the place of ethics: we have national and international laws; in the place of freedom from fear: we have fear and ignorance solidified. Noriyasu, of the baby boomer generation, was a silent victim of the active technologization of the industry. It encouraged technology to replace human involvement with production which resulted in the intrusion of technological unemployment—especially of outsourcing of jobs and the aggressive automation of the industry using high performance technological systems, etc. The millennial precariat like Joe who has become disinterested in, about everything in life, is a victim of the, thus emerged, technological unemployment. Similarly, another millennial, Hillary, the super-rich investor, who should have enjoyed, all the goodies of money, is just yet another living victim of technologization, because of the implementation of "artificial intelligence" in financial industry where the investor is only a silent beneficiary of the system. All have lost their creativity to the machine generated intelligence performing like a humanoid automaton. Plato compares, the people who have lost, the opportunity to use their creative instincts, to the instance of someone, who is forced to exist in a self-imposed "shadowy cave" as Noriyasu, Joe and Hillary did; or to live in the world of lord Hades—in Hell.

There is no value, in knowing the source of the shadows, as it is irrelevant and they are chained from moving about freely. One has to agree with the rules allowed, in the cave that are limited. Nobody thinks about, looking around, the chances of knowing it well. They need not have to think anything new; knowing anything new would disturb them immensely. According to Plato, knowledge only can lead one to be creative and make one free and be internally courageous to pursue definite goodness; and goodness makes one to be happy and satisfied to live a complete life. When we lose creativity, to the machine generated creativity, of "artificial intelligence" systems of the 4th industrial revolution—industry-4.0, we lose our freedoms, to pursue goodness, and to the goodness generated happiness—*eudaimonia.*

For Indians, creative work (karma) is a way to attain liberation (*mokṣa*)—*eudaimonia,* Indian understanding of Karma gives us a clear picture of what work means in the life of an individual person. Indians believe that Karma could redeem a person from the shackles and sufferings of life. The Sanskrit root word *kṛ,* which is also the root word for "*karma*" and also for "hand"—*karah*. It means with the activation of the complexity of *hand-brain faculty* is what makes creative work organically possible. One of the significant aspects of Indian philosophy is the intellectual appropriation of karma progressively ending in the liberation of the soul—in *mokṣa*.

Chapter 33
The Philosophy of Karma—Exploring Wisdom in Creative Work

Carpenter Krishnan, without falling into the lures of the industrial society, continued to work, with the skill that he acquired traditionally, from his ancestors. He, like his forefathers, always had to work, for a particular consumer and made special wood-work materials (i.e. cot, etc.), suiting to the requirement of that customer. Each time, he attempted to make the best cot: the one that should be better than the previous ones that he had created for other customers with a different set of demands. His creative activity made him feel elated and satisfied throughout his life. He tried to accomplish, one creative task after another enjoying each activity with reverence and a sense of fulfilment. He always wished to look at the satisfactory faces of his customers and rather cared a lot for that, than the monetary reward he received together with it. By following such a time-tested tradition, he had grown to be a maestro in carpentry. His personal self-model had grown and matured through years of creative work. In Platonic sense, by learning something new at each time of working with material, his knowledge generated an inkling towards the divine wisdom. In the paradigm of virtue ethics, he was duly protected with the virtues of the heavens.

All the systems of philosophies of Indian origin: Vedic systems, Buddhism, Jainism, Ajivikism, Indian Materialism, etc. had given due importance to "Karma", which essentially meant to appraise a person about the activities that one should engage throughout in one's life. Philosophically all Indian systems, argued that doing one's own "Karma" is the best way to realize redemption (*mokṣa*) from the problems of life. Any action done with full dedication and commitment could redeem one from "sufferings". Contrasting with Hegelianism, as for Hegel, choosing the "right path" is the way to freedom, that was implied in the Indian conception of *mokṣa*. Hegelian conception of *freedom* could be interpreted as Indian idea of *mokṣa*. In Indian sense, it is the "freedom" that animates life. Bhagavad Gīta says "For no one can remain even for a moment without doing work; everyone is made to act helplessly by the impulses born of nature."[1] It means humans are predisposed to do work and learn

---

[1] *na hi kaścit kṣaṇam api jātu tiṣṭhaty akarmakṛt kāryate hy avaśaḥ karma sarvaḥ prakṛtijair guṇaiḥ.* Radhakrishnan (1948), p. 133.

© The Author(s), under exclusive license to Springer Nature Singapore Pte Ltd. 2021   195
M. Varghese, *A Brief History of Creative Work and Plutonomy*,
https://doi.org/10.1007/978-981-15-9263-8_33

from work that is organically embedded with human life. It is a part of being human; or existence will be worthless if we would not use this inherent virtue by not doing any kind of work: no one can escape from this feature of human nature. One should do virtuous actions (*puṇya*), not unvirtuous actions (*pāpa*) to find liberation (*mokṣa*) in the realm of transcendental virtues of truth (*sat*), consciousness (*cit*), and bliss— harmony (*ānanda*). The aspects of virtuousness and unvirtuousness of any of the action done (karma) is determined by one's assigned duties (*dharma*). Yet, by doing creative works, one can enjoy life to its fullest; because, it would build the "conscious space" –the ego tunnel—that would mature with each moment of life. It is the leading light that may lead one to freedom or redemption (*mokṣa*). As per Aristotelianism virtuous action (*arete*) leads to *eudaimonia*—freedom and happiness.

In the Hegelian sense, freedom is the freewill to choose from the choices available in the external world, in order to construct, one's own "self being" like a "work of Art", through education and good living situations.[2] In this case, freedom is like an objective entity that should be achieved; whereas in Indian conception freedom is beyond subjectivity and objectivity, because it is an aspect of the organic human life that evolves continuously with the very act of living life. The modern thought after Hegel is directly or indirectly influenced by this aspect of creating artificially, the self-being by rejecting the internal structure forcefully to experience freedom from the objective sources. This method of creating, the new man, is severely criticized by philosophers of today as we have limited options to transform our "selves" as a creation through virtuous karma. It is argued, today, that the creation, of the self being, in a particular way is meant to satisfy, some other urges, for achieving power, money, and freedom, where the principles of "divine providence" as a forgiven super-structure. A person becomes a doctor to satisfy his greed for money; he does the job, because the money in curing diseases is good business, and for him getting the power and money is the only purpose of curing diseases; if he faults the legal system would punish him. But according to Indians, the urge to cure diseases for a doctor is innate as for being a doctor (*dharma*), because it provides him an opportunity to perform an activity (karma) that would bring virtue (*puṇya*). Karma is the spiritual principle that drives and makes a person happy; and the monetary benefit, he could get out of it, is just one aspect of the benefits of executing his duty. One always should crave for the inner freedom that one should get by doing the duty diligently. Doing the duty (*dharma*) is more rewarding than the monetary benefits. As being discussed, most of the finding in contemporary neurological studies supports this view that humans achieve, a kind of inner peace and a deep knowledge about his "self-being" by learning something through "work".

Notably, the contemporary neurological studies on consciousness suggested, that an "ego tunnel" had been made when one learned something by executing something through an action (work). And by executing "the action" in the most perfect way, he would get satisfaction and happiness. A kind of satisfaction would be followed that is similar to that of a driver, when he drives with utmost precision and attention, would get an extraordinary precision. The text Bhagavad Gīta, says "on work and its

---

[2]Malebou (2004), p. 81.

benefit" that work is important for attaining satisfaction and happiness. Gītā says: "Therefore, without attachment, perform always the work that has to be done, for man attains to the highest by doing work without attachment."[3] If a doctor does his duty, without a deep sense of attachment, to the monetary benefit as the sole aim, according to Gītā's Karma theory, he would receive the highest happiness of doing a benign duty.

The neuroscientists, who work on consciousness, express almost a similar viewpoint of the Gītā, with a different tone and accent. It is the highest sense of joy, happiness and fulfillment what happens when an individual does the work (Karma), with a sense of involvement, but not with a sense of greed for material benefits. The contemporary philosophical studies on consciousness by neurologists would agree with the view that an "ego tunnel" would be drawn in the conscious space when one involves completely with the action. According to Thomas Metzinger: "Consciousness is an inherently biological phenomenon and the tunnel is what holds it all together. Within the tunnel, the choreography of your subjective life begins to unfold". And how it unfolds, he reiterates, "Owning your body, its sensations and its various parts is fundamental to the feeling of *being someone*. Your body image is surprisingly flexible. Expert skiers, for example, can extend their consciously experienced body image to the tips of their skis. Race-car drivers can expand it to include the boundaries of the car; they do not have to judge visually whether they can squeeze through a narrow opening or avoid an obstacle—they simply feel it. Have ever tried to walk with your eyes closed, or in the dark, tapping ahead with a stick as a blind person does? If so, you've probably noticed that you suddenly feel a tactile sensation at the end of the stick. All these are examples of what philosophers call the *sense of ownership,* which is a specific aspect of conscious experience—a form of automatic self-attribution that integrates a certain kind of conscious content into what is experienced as one's self".[4]

It says that though the conscious space is detectable, with the neural circuits formed in the brain, yet for creating it, the whole body should be participated: the body is mind and mind is body. The consciousness permeates the whole life of an individual and it could be realized by executing a work properly and, there, one could feel an unusual feeling of pleasure and happiness, and a sense of ownership; like a Race-car driver enjoy racing as an experience of the expansion of the horizons that he moves in; or it is like the feeling of an expert chef who could visualize the final taste of the food he prepares, or a carpenter could see the final form of a cot on the wood he yet to work on, or the sculptor see the final form on a rock. At the cave temples in Ellora, the sculptor should have visualized the entire temple before carving it on hard rock. The consciousness pervades everywhere: within the body as well as outside of the body. Invoking that consciousness is the purpose of creative work, but when distracted with greed one never could execute an action with complete dedication. One of the several perils of life today is losing of the *sense of ownership* with one's

---

[3]*tasmād asaktaḥ satataṃ kāryaṃkarma samācara sakto hy ācaran karma param āpnoti pūruṣaḥ.* Radhakrishnan (1948), p. 138.

[4]Metzinger (2009), p. 95.

own self-being. The doctrine of Karma is meant to work with the *sense of ownership* on own consciousness (*cit*) for to be with the transcendental virtues meant in the conception of Brahman as [sat, cit, *ānanda*].

References

Malebou, C.: Future of Hegel, New York: Routledge (2004)
Metzinger, T.: Ego Tunnel. Basic Books, New York (2009)
Radhakrishnan, S. (ed.): The Bhagavad Gīta. HarperCollins, New Delhi (1948)

Chapter 34
The Karma Theory and the 200 Million Years of Consciousness Evolution

The foundational thought that extend to the entire discourse of Indian philosophy is a deep and detailed discussion on consciousness. We exist on the foundation of consciousness as living beings. The Indian conception of consciousness (*cit*) is unique, and it extends to various aspects of life including "work life" (*karma*). In the case of Vedanta (i.e. *uttara mīmāṃsa* and *pūrva mīmāṃsa*), a careful and subtle deployment of consciousness is done, very profusely and smoothly. Both these Vedanta systems would discourse on how to organize the methods that could enhance the conscious space (consciousness) in an individual person. In other words, how the active development of neural circuits is done, through the internal presence of a robust consciousness, to experiencing a sense of living life for a human person. In the case of *pūrva mīmāṃsa*, the use of the way of karma is employed, while for *uttara mīmāṃsa*, it is through knowledge (*jñānā*). It is only human beings that can have fully developed consciousness space by structuring a robust neural circuit in the brain. The notable feature of human consciousness is its ability to process sense perceptive information into knowledge that can turn in as deep insight—wisdom (*prajñā*). In the parlance of classical Greek thought it is knowledge through creative actions—*techne*; and knowledge through intellectual analysis—*episteme*. In both case the structuring of neural circuits would happen differently. Contexually these two conceptions are similar to *karma* (techne) and *jñāna* (episteme).

Indian philosophical systems, in general, consider that the purpose of life, is to find ways for experiencing the "life" (*ātman*—soul) within one's self-consciousness. It is known as self-realization: the knowing of one's own deep consciousness. Soul means life. It is the factor that situates, the human individual personality, uniquely that each personality varies from one another. Such that each person's duties and actions (Karma) differs from one to another; and when the soul develops into perfection for an individual, a kind of integration with the universal consciousness would ensue. It is called liberation (*mokṣa*), because an individual personality could experience the uniformity of that one consciousness. The purpose of life in this view is developing the consciousness to its full-blown perfection. It means one could transcend one's own limitations, like an expert skier experiences a feeling of the fullness while skiing,

© The Author(s), under exclusive license to Springer Nature Singapore Pte Ltd. 2021
M. Varghese, *A Brief History of Creative Work and Plutonomy*,
https://doi.org/10.1007/978-981-15-9263-8_34

or a Race-car driver stretches himself to the limits unconsciously, by making all the aspects of body and mind into the focus of one singularity. This singularity is beyond subjectivity and objectivity: The "One" that is been alluded both in the philosophy of Advaita Vedanta and the Neoplatonists like Plotinus.

The driver experience that the car, he drives is an extension of his body. The Gīta verse, on "work" can be rephrased as that humans are predisposed to engage in doing "work". In other words, life means work. The process of developing self-awareness through creative work may be the single most human trait that enable him to live a satisfied life. The Socratic and Hellenistic thinkers call this human trait as divine *eudaimonia* (bliss, flourishing, happiness). We may note that In *Eudemian Ethics*, Book II, Chap. 1, Aristotle proposed his conception of eudaimonia as an activity, or a range of activities where one uses reason than a mental state. The intellectual and moral virtues thus evolved are not based on innate talents or quickly acquired form of knowledge but are traits unique to a personality who develops it through long habituation, reflection and social experiences.[1] It means for experiencing *eudaimonia* one needs to use creative activities (work); however contrary to Aristotle's exhortations, the modern world since Hegel think that it is a mental stage adducible only through the grace of God, only by following the right path shown in the Bible; whereas for Aristotle it is cultivated through long habituation and reflection. Still, the affinity towards "biblical dictates" as authority is, endemic to the postmodern culture too, but accepting only the scientifically verified decrees, not the wisdomic teachings of the Bible

As for the Indians Karma determines one's ethical perspectives. It is said that when a human person lives his life, in the world, he has to move about and do things to survive, or one needs to work to earn a living by using his skills. Indian belief, on this, is that each of the actions would bring, merits (*puṇya*) and demerits (*pāpa*), to the agent's personality. Each action brings an "action-result data" to the consciousness of the individual. Similar to the neural structuring of the *ego tunnel*. The unit of which is known as *apūrvas*—the unit of action-result data.[2] The semantics of *apūrvas* means "unlike before" where the inner consciousness (*ātman*) receives, a new propensity with an action (karma). He receives a unique ability by executing a work that makes him stronger and closer to the source of life. An action makes a minute change in the consciousness of the individual mentally and physically. And the subjective self builds a structure that could change a person's life. But it should be an organic development. The inner consciousness (*ātman*) can change its inner conditionings in this way.

Indians explains the conception of Karma, by interpreting it into certain terms giving meaning to the concept. These terms that represent the concepts are just terms to make us understand the inexplicable nature of karma. These terms are only for referential purposes. In simple terms, every action has a result that is dependent on the person involved, in doing that action. All actions can have effects on our souls (*ātman*) and we also are born with the acquired karmas from our previous lives. To explain it

---

[1] See, Aristotle: Eudemian Ethics (Book II, Chap. 1). In: McKeon, R. (Trans. and ed.) The Basic Works of Aristotle, p. 991. Random House, New York 1941.

[2] Dasgupta (1975), p. 405.

better in the parlance of modern science, we may look at the scientific studies about human brain. It is said to have evolved after an evolution of 200 million years for assuming the present structure with a distinct form of consciousness. Each individual brain carries a unique particular nature, as a part of the, ever continuing, evolution process. Or, each brain carries a certain set of data. The conceptual formations of Karma are divided in a humanly conceivable term. At the time of birth, we are born with certain data (*sañcita-karmas*); It gets updated with new data (*apūrvas*), and the consciousness would evolve simultaneously. Which defines the unique particular nature of each individual with an own being (*svabhāva*) that constantly changes but some inherent properties remain the same always.

This notion on karma suggests that it carries data from the past and constantly updates, here and now, for to be carried forward as the life advances. We could define Karma's traditional classification that it has three divisions, *sañcita karma, prārabdha karma* and *āgami karma* or *kriyamāṇa karma* to explain the Karma theory. A person is born with *sañcita-karmas* that would be having all the accumulated karmas from the past, which can be discerned by observing the unique particular nature of a personality. A person shows it with certain inborn characteristics, tendencies, aptitudes, inclinations, desires, etc., which creates a foundation for his distinctive personality. All those aspects are embedded in a human soul. On the basis of the Darwinian idea of evolution, the idea of *sañcita-karmas* should be a particular instance of a human brain-body, that has undergone 200 million years of evolution constantly, thereby we can explain that an individual human brain is an aspect of that transformation showing unique particularity; at the same time, commonality with other living beings, because certain aspects of *prārabdha karma* inherent and common for all humans.

It is inevitable that, a part of the *sañcita-karmas,* need to be matured. It happens on the passing of each moment. Those karmic elements that should be matured in this life will produce consequent results; the name of the set of matured karmas is *prārabdha karma.* One has to live with his *prārabdha karma*—both inherent and acquired. The freedom one has in the present life is conditioned his/her *prārabdha karma:* The updated data that happen on moment to moment. But one can do such actions that would change *prārabdha karma,* using what is called *kriyamāṇa karma* or *āgami karma.* One can use this aspect of karma to change his/her life. One can reprogram the process of updating of data, and has tremendous freedom in doing that. The creativity aspect of human life is centered in the *kriyamāṇa karma* and how we update it with good *karmas.* One has to use intelligence to employ *kriyamāṇa karma,* which gives a person tremendous happiness and is founded on actions that one performs "here and now", which one constantly learns and updates. The soul–life—flourishes when one does a "work" using intelligence (awareness) with complete involvement. This can be interpreted as *mokṣa, nirvāṇa,* etc. the Aristotelian idea of *Eudaimonia* can be explained in the similar vein that the human soul is imbedded with *euddaimonia* which helps one to find virtue by executing an action (*arete*) excellently.

Whether a person does something or not, his *sañcita-karmas* would mature into *prārabdha karma.* The nature of *prārabdha karma* is like a covering (sheath) on one's spiritual body *karma śarīra,* but through *kriyamāṇa karmas,* one can rework with the *prārabdha karmas,* to modify that karma sheath of the spiritual body, and by doing so, one could achieve the freedom—*mokṣa*—in the form of happiness that flourishes as satisfaction. The *karma śarīra,* can receive *apūrvas* which would act as merit-units that could modify the spiritual life, whereas demerit that would decline the value of spiritual life. This is the conception of *puṇya* and *pāpa* in Indian philosophy. *Puṇya* karmas are those actions (works) that give happiness; *pāpa* karmas are those actions that should be avoided, or that could inhibit the progress of merit (*puṇya*). The actions that generate merits (*puṇya*) would structure the consciousness with positive-*apūrvās*; whereas demerits (*pāpa*) would help structure the consciousness with negative-*apūrvās,* which would drowse the flourish of happiness. It can be explained as that the karmic body, moves from one life to other, with the consciousness. With one's life, one needs to make good use of *kriyamāna karmas,* the good/bad effects of each action, would revive the spiritual life of a person, for this life and the subsequent lives. Good actions that give subsequent results (*apūrvas*—the unit of work-result data) would give satisfaction to a person and one would feel like the skilled skier or musician or chef or dancer who could live life fully. When one does no action, s/he would solidify the *sañcita-karma* sheath into *prārabdha karma* and could be imprisoned oneself in the isolated self-being, and either may end up with fear and ignorance; or, may live in the naïve realistic world of dreams and imaginations, or may push oneself into the shadowy world of Hades—hell.

The contemporary studies on the evolution of consciousness, we can find that an evolution chain that is being happening for 200 million years in the brain-consciousness of a personality, and each individual person is a part of that chain and should co-evolve with that process by doing the available actions (*karmas*) by applying the inborn creative instincts. We cannot exist without doing any actions or could not recuse ourselves from doing any actions. And we are predisposed to do actions—work, as being living beings. The more one updates the data of the *sañcita-karmas,* the soon, one gets the freedom to redeem from the conditioning aspects of *prārabdha karma;* or one can challenge one's own fate. When human life on earth is explained, it is like: born with *sañcita-karmas;* live with *prārabdha karma;* but constantly reform and update with *kriyamāna karmas,* which is the way to reach freedom (*mokṣa*) from the unfreedom that may be generated out of *prārabdha karma.* We explain *prārabdha karma* and the role it has on a person's life, in the world, is that of him/her being a part of a process that has been set out almost 200 million years ago and continues with one's present life. That is how a personality inheres unique particular as well as universal natures.

References

Aristotle: Metaphysics. In: McKeon, R. (Trans. and ed.) The Basic Works of Aristotle. Random House, New York (1941)

Dasgupta, S.: History of Indian Philosophy. Motilal Banarsidas, Delhi (1975)

Chapter 35
Karma and Dharma as the Foundation of Indian Moral Philosophy

In the Indian context, explaining the idea of "*dharma* and *karma*" is necessary for relating the Indian conception with what is known in the Western understanding of religious philosophy. For the Abrahamic religions (Judaism, Christianity and Islam), faith is the pivot of religiosity. There is nothing beyond the faith in God; one needs to always be with God, so long as one lives, because God is the only reality that is eternal. Religion can be defined as per the explanation given by Roman philosopher, Cicero is connected with *lego* "read", and. *re* (again).[1] It means, read again, in the sense of choosing and following the written—the understood path. The Greek concepts of virtuous life and eudaimonia are ingrained in this conception of redemption of following a path. The Abrahamic religions are bound by holy books: Torah for Jews, Bible for Christians and Quran for Muslims: one who follow these religions needs to follow, with utmost faith, the written words as the spiritual guide, and should read and follow them diligently. And having unstinted faith and a will to surrender completely to the God's path is the only way for redemption. The conception of "faith", in Abrahamic religions, is similar to the conception of Karma and Dharma in the Indian context.

Nonetheless, the Indian notion of religiosity, primarily, warrants us to understand Dharma and Karma. The Indian traditions, in general, use the term "*dharma*" instead of religion. For example, the popular Indian systems such as, Vedic (Hindu) systems, Buddhism, Jainism, etc. in principle actualizes various conceptions of *dharma* in their spiritual discourses, even though each interpretation of *dharma* may differ. Though there are some religious schools in India subtly subsumed the Abrahamic conceptions of faith into their religiosity. The religiosity, of the followers of Indian religions, is rooted in prime idea of *dharma*. However, *faith* as constant attentiveness (*sraddha*), or knowing well (*saṃjña*) to the teachings of other master teachers and thinkers are also central to all Indian systems. But it should aid one's dedication in executing the assigned karma.

---

[1]Müller (1889), p. 33.

© The Author(s), under exclusive license to Springer Nature Singapore Pte Ltd. 2021
M. Varghese, *A Brief History of Creative Work and Plutonomy*,
https://doi.org/10.1007/978-981-15-9263-8_35

The term dharma has several meanings in Indian philosophical discourses. The meaning, we deal here, is teachings, duty, way of life, ethical values, etc. From the etymological meaning of the root world *dhr* means "to hold", "to bear", "to wear"," to have", etc.[2] From these, we can say that dharma is the elements that which hold a personality together in one's worldly life. Or, it forms the basis of a person's life in the world. For example, the Buddhists call their traditions as Buddha *dharma*; the Hindu religion is Veda-*dharma—sanādhana dharma,* founded on eternal values; the teachings of Jain monks—Jain Religion is *Jaina-dharma*, etc. It means these ways of following "life" can successfully hold a personality together till the end of his/her life providing a virtuous life. Each tradition has the ability to instruct and guide, a person spiritually, until the end of his/her life time. In classical India *dharma*-based systems were used for explaining all aspects of life. The freedom to choose a way of life (*dharma*) came with responsibilities, as one should make sure, that his way of life, would not infringe into the ways of life (*dharma*) of others, which was considered as sacrilege. If one restricts others from their dharmas, it could bring extreme demerit (*pāpa*), to one's consciousness, that could restrict one to pursue a virtuous life. Mostly people tried to avoid such situations. The extreme demerit (*pāpa*) could bring bad rebirths with a lot of struggle and tribulations. But fatal sins could be nullified with good actions and with pure knowledge. What happened for Aṅgulimāla, is a good example to explain this. Like all other religious systems acquiring a virtuous life is the purpose life. If we can't get virtuous living we crave for it.

Aṅgulimāla became a Buddha Bikkhṣu, after learning about the sins (*pāpa*), he committed of killing lots and lots of innocent human beings and other living beings. Aṅgulimāla was a dreaded individual who enjoyed killing and killing become his habit. By stopping others from executing their life's karmas and duties (dharma), Aṅgulimāla lost his track on executing his own karma. Or, he lost his duty to be a part of the humanity that supports each other's survival. To keep a count on the number of people he killed, he made a garland (*māla*) of thump finger (*aṅguli*) and worn around his neck. People were scared of him and avoided offending him. A system of fear began to have firmed up around him. The Buddha knew Aṅgulimāla was an extremely unhappy individual who would like to get out of his pitiful existence as a living being. That was the reason why the Buddha was not afraid of the scare of Aṅgulimāla, because Buddha knew, Aṅgualimāla was living in the world of extreme ignorance and fear. When Buddha showed the depth of his ignorance, Aṅgulimāla followed Buddha without any resistance.[3] All bad karmas are propelled only by ignorance. When the ignorance has gone, his sins also disappeared. Therefore, one must live according to the teachings of his own dharma (*svadharma*) and karma (*svakarma*) to protect from self-destruction. As being a part of a process that started since 200 million years ago, humans could not endure with substantial amount of fear and ignorance; either one would destroy himself or harm the others nefariously. It is only through following the transcended eternal virtues, humanity could survive with knowledge that leads to wisdom, though we live in ignorance ridden knowledge

---

[2]Varghese (2008), p. 132.
[3]Bodhi (1995), p. 603.

that exists only in fear. One should find truth, goodness and harmony in life through the *dharma-karma* axiom. Indian conception of *dharma-karma* as the basis of their religiosity should be understood in this manner.

References

Müller, M.: Natural Religion. Longmans Green and Co., California (1889)
Bodhi, B. (Trans. and ed.): Majjhima Nikaya (MN 86). Wisdom Publications, Boston (1995)
Varghese, M.: Principles of Buddhist Tantra. Munshiram Manoharlal, New Delhi (2008)

Chapter 36
Pan Asian Caste System: Way, to Divide Wealth Through "Work"

Indian caste system is based on the discernment of karma. Caste system that was practiced in ancient Asia is interpreted as an efficient way to divide wealth, between the members of a particular social group—caste, and it is based on the principles of *dharma-karma*. In another interpretation it is taken as the agent's spiritual purity and that is been adopted into the narratives of certain communities. We discard the purity argument as a worthless discourse; but the mainstream discourse on caste system is only based on this unworthy decadent discourse. One of the reasons for this debauchery is because caste segregation, in India, is equated with racial segregations which was part of European ethnocentrism. Conversely dharma is understood as an individual's way of life (*svadharma*) and the social privileges, rights, duties and actions that one could accord. This system provides a living space, for everyone in the civil society. Which is like, sets of instructions that are given, as guides, to *kings, scholars, teachers, merchants, farmers, workers* of different kinds, and even to outcastes like, *fakirs, sanyasis, prostitutes, vagabonds,* etc. The dharma for the rulers, the Raj-dharma (king's duties) that a king is required to follow as a part of his reign. The ruler should make sure that he would, impartially act, in the establishment, sustenance and maintenance of *karma-dharma* of each subject: the (citizen's) personal dharma (*svadharma*). It is not just in India, but also in the other Asian traditions like Chinese and Japanese, the caste divisions had been followed as a means to divide wealth in the society.

In the Chinese tradition, for example, there existed a caste system that worked in for accomplishing the same purpose of dividing the wealth, where discharging assigned duties of a person by the social convictions, were supposed to ensure good life for everyone in the society. This process of social engineering worked like a machine: the hierarchical division starts from *scholars*, to *farmers*, to *artisans*, and to *merchants*; each of the four groups of people had their respective duties to perform in the civil society; then they can enjoy the assigned privileges. Those who studied in order to occupy positions of the highest rank—the decision makers were called the *shi* (scholars). Those who cultivated the soil and distributed the produce like grains were called *nong* (farmers). Those who had manifested skill (*qiao*) and made

© The Author(s), under exclusive license to Springer Nature Singapore Pte Ltd. 2021
M. Varghese, *A Brief History of Creative Work and Plutonomy*,
https://doi.org/10.1007/978-981-15-9263-8_36

utensils were called *gong* (artisans). Those who transported valuable articles and sold commodities were called *shang* (merchants).[1] The communities in a country were divided based on these assigned duties. These caste divisions are essentially similar to the Indian idea of *dharma-karma*.

In the Japanese tradition, there were such a kind of caste division, maybe, following the line of Confucian tradition for dividing wealth. By this system, society was composed of (*shi*): rulers and samurais; (*nō*): the farming community; (*kō*): the artisans; and (*shō*): the merchants. Samurais were placed at the top of the social hierarchy because they followed an order that sets a meta structure of high moral standard of living (*Bushido*). They were the scholars, protectors, and rulers: The *Bushido* system, they followed, was to accentuate the ideals of high standards of being the ruling class, so that they should work towards the benefit of everyone, which is similar to the *rāja-dharma* of the Indians. This is the life of dedication and self-sacrifice. Farmers came second because they produced the most impor-tant commodity that would support: food; and also engaged in the most important activity of working with the nature. The third division is the artisans as they produce essential goods that may make life comfortable and the artisans always engage in creative activities, and now the industrial workers and industrialists would fall in this category. The Merchants were at the bottom of the social order because they gener-ated wealth by trading, without producing any goods. This method of division has a social engineering aspect that worked successfully for centuries.[2] The richest caste was merchants but they were at the bottom of the hierarchy; yet all other castes had been depended on the wealth created by merchants through trade. In India division of caste in the pan Asian sense was: the scholars (Brahmins), the ruling class (*kṣetriya*); the merchant class *Vaiśya*; the artisans famers and workers (*śūdra*). But in certain sections of society practiced untouchability based on caste hierarchy and therefore, for the modern society it is considered as a kind of social decadence and taboo.

The aim of a person's life is to fulfill his own *dharma* (*svadharma*), defined by his caste duties (*svakarma*), and execute it through the most befitting way without interrupting the lives of others. There were also people who were outside the system, who are deemed as out castes: a kind of lumpen folks, for example, menial-workers, dead-end-job workers, all kinds of cleaning workers, sages, wanders, prostitutes, trans-genders, outsiders, foreigners etc.; and they were supported, with care and compassion, by the caste based social system. The rulers (royal authority) should ensure that the system functions in an order with stability.

Like the *dharma* of a king is to help everyone; a scholar is to tell the truth that benefit everyone, not to benefit only his own kind; and a teacher should teach any suitable student who seeks knowledge from him; a merchant should sell things to everyone with a sense of common wellbeing. Truth spirit (*satyagraha*) and an unstinted commitment on following it impartiality should be the virtue one needs to follow in his social life. One should be diligent in learning and executing his assigned *dharma* though right knowledge (*Jñāna*) and right actions (*karma*). That should be

---

[1]Barbieri Low (2007), p. 36, 37.
[2]Totman (1981), p. 135, 136.

the aim of one's life in the world. Indian religiosity finds truth (*satya*) as the eternal dharma that protects everyone. And in Indian context, that is the essential transcendental virtue—like goodness in Platonism. Truth is what everyone seeks for, and it is the essence of Indian religiosity: *sanādhana dharma*. Mahatma Gandhi famously said that his religiosity is based on *sanādhana* dharma virtues; that should be on the pursuance of the eternal truth (sat) leading to deeper consciousness (cit) and to bliss, harmony, happiness (*ānanda*). The Vedic systems (Hindus) used to follow *dharmasastras* (or *smruti* texts) as the guide for executing the assigned duties on the basis of the maxims of truth that everyone should be given a proper situation for executing the *dharma-karma*. It is similar to the constitution and laws of a modern nation state, but in the ancient times, it was connected with the caste duties and the actions of an individual person. Manu *smruti* was a popular text that had been followed in ancient India; but the liberal *dharmasastra* texts like: *Kautilya smruti*, *Narada smruti* etc. were also very popular in the ancient times.

The foundation of Mīmāṃsa system of Indian philosophy is exclusively founded on *dharma- Karma*; and according to them, the perfectly executable karma is there in conducting a ritual called *Jyothiṣṭoma-Homa* to its all puritanical perfections.[3] It means, there is no other karma, for humans to perform, in the world than this most sacred karma, which needs deep knowledge and systematic practices to achieve the required perfection because there is no act beyond this that one can perform to achieve perfect merit (*puṇya*). In the Vedic (Hindu) tradition own *dharma* (*svadharma*) is determined by one's caste duties which is normally unchangeable. So, one gets the education on it, from his elders and the texts written by the elders and gurus: the Vedas.

The Buddhists have, also, followed the teachings of the Buddha and the monastic scholars for understanding the nitty-gritties of identifying one's own actions (*svakarma*). The educational systems in Buddhism are founded on educating everyone in the society about his/her own duties (*svadharma*) by the monastic scholars, which are pedagogical and instructive in nature. The Monks are trained to help common persons to find their *dharma-karma*. Buddhism promoted secular education to help everyone to find own *dharma-karma* by acquiring knowledge about it from the compendium of Buddhist teachings found in the *Tripīdikas*. The trained monks should explain it to the common followers. However, there were intellectual disagreements between Buddhists and Vedic (Hindu) Brahmins on the question of caste system as a pivot of identifying one's own actions (*svakarma*). Buddhism vehemently criticized the Vedic systems' (Hindu) adherence to caste hierarchical system and the puritanical notions associated with their attitudes towards inferior casts in the strongest terms.

We can find the dialectical disagreement of the Buddhists on caste duties, from the opinion of the third century Buddhist scholar, Āryadeva, who severely criticized the adherence to certain practices for accruing pure merit (*puṇya*) by the Brahmins (higher caste Vedic people). The Vedic Brahmins believe that ritualistic practices are important and, if followed with diligence, would earn them spiritual virtue (*puṇya*).

---

[3] Varghese (2008), p. 137.

The Buddhist declined such practices as non-sense and criticized the value of such practices than giving them an upper hand over the people who are not permitted to practice them. From the interpretation of the following quote, we can discern the nature of aggression and bitterness in the perspectives of the Buddhists on the Brahmins views on *dharma-karma:* " A dog which swam across Ganga should get equal purity (*punya*) supposed to have acquired by a Brahmin.; if *dharma* accrues by bathing in holy waters, then the fisherman-folk will be the gainers, not to talk of the fish and other organisms which reside in such waters, day and night."[4] Buddhists reiterate with this view that one should be given the freedom and education to choose the preferable work without altering the societal factors; then only one can achieve true freedom from work. But if one is forced to do the work of the forefathers without any rational understanding like the one who nonsensical archaic activities like bathing in Ganga, etc. he would be wasting his valuable time in life to get knowledge and be well informed, so that he could achieve spiritual merits (*punya*) for freedom from sufferings (*moksa*). That is why Buddhist monasteries become schools of secular education and leaning in the ancient India, as they encouraged learning of all kinds of thoughts that lead to true-dharma (*saddharma*) to learn about *dharma* that humanity need to know for conducting a fruitful and meaningful life that could lead to *nirvāṇā*—freedom from sufferings.

This makes one to know convincingly why carpenter Krishnan was a happy man until his death, though he was poor economically. He followed his true-dharma (*saddharma*) of creating things experimentally creative, even though the situation demanded him to follow a different life style. Contextually, when we evaluate, the benefits of work, between monetary gains and work satisfaction, carpenter Krishnan chose creative work satisfaction, as he was habituated by activating hand-brain faculty. But his son chose a different life style of following monetary gains and satisfaction, as the ultimate aim of doing any "work". Krishnan followed the *dharma-karma* (way of life) followed by his forefathers; whereas his son followed the methods of modern economic sciences, where monetary gains as the mark of all successes. Carpenter Krishnan still has a challenge to get accomplished that of creating, the best usable object, that would make the user perfectly happy. But, for his son, there are no such challenges to be accomplished, except an unnatural and exaggerated greed for getting more power through money. He thinks and believes that he is in control but couldn't have realized or understood the problem of the accumulated dead wealth. He never experienced the activation of hand-brain faculty as his father did. Work should have given immense happiness to a person as it is embedded in the consciousness of humans. That is the reason why most of the ancient high cultures upheld work as the main aspect that protect and sustains human life.

Why people, like Krishnan, find happiness and comfort in doing creative work than following comfort and entertainment as the only purpose of life? Money and wealth can bring comfort and entertainment easily. Krishnan's son thinks so, wealth and power are the only way to bring happiness; work is only a means for that. We may look at the analogy that is usually given, in Indian philosophy, to explain how

---

[4]Ibid. p. 242.

karma is the means for acquiring freedom (*mokṣa*), and why everyone should follow it diligently.

The process of acquiring merit from an action can be explained with the instance of a hunter (bowman). Imagine a 'bowman' stands with a quiver of arrows, is taking aim, and shoots arrows at a target. He has already shot an arrow at the target: that has gone out of his control; and he aims with another arrow to be shot at a new target: that is within his control. Here the karma theory explains that the bundle of arrows, in the quiver, hung on his back is called the *sañcita-karma*; the arrow he already has shot at the target, is *prārabdha-karma*; and the one arrow, that he is about to shoot from his bow is *kryamāna-karma*. Explaining this further, the shooter has perfect control in the case of the *sañcita-karma* and *kriyamāna-karma*, but in the case of *prārabdha-* karma he would have no control at all: it has gone out of his control. No living individual can be free of his *prārabdha-* karma, because he has to live with it as a part of his living life. That is how Indians explained the intellectual and cultural predispositions of an individual person on the basis of his/her karma. The present "living life" is an opportunity for an individual to reform and restructure his consciousness through works that could provide him some creative happiness and would restructure his karmic body (*karma śarīra*). A person should cherish the facets of *kriyamāna-karma* highly, because it is the area of his creative work instincts. According to Indians and Asians, a human person should draw creative happiness and a sense of belonging from his, living, life. The modern men accept only good results, i.e. *prārabdha-karma* that gives comfort and entrainment; if not they would send a torrent of arrows to the target and would destroy it completely, because people are so habituated to get good results only, and would think only emotionally not rationally when good results hardly come by.

Human being has freedom to reform his karmic centered character and alter his ways with present actions, but the results of the actions of the past, which already had taken place, is a part of his consciousness and he ought to experience the consequent effects. The consequent effects of *sañcita-karma*, that are a part of the present life of an individual can be reduced or even nullified, with knowledge-adduced from creative work and that could evoke and arouse his consciousness progressively. There were several dialectical arguments taken place between various schools of Indian philosophy on the ways to remove the karmic influences (*sañcita karma*) on whether it is through knowledge (*jñāna*): Upaniṣads and Vedāntā; or only through virtuous actions (*karma*): Mīmāṃsaka, etc. But those of the *prārabdha*-karma actions, those already committed in this life cannot be changed by meditations alone because it is connected with the norms and rules of the present life. One should constantly learn about right actions that could benefit him. Impulsive actions are detrimental and could destroy the purpose of "life".[5]

From the perspective of creative work in the case of Krishnan, his birth in the carpenter's family (caste), his initial education from his father and elders of his family and community represents: the *sañcita karma*. The learning that he received

---

[5]Pandey (2010), p. 15.

through doing the job as a working carpenter represents: *kriyamāṇa* karma (*āgami-karma*); his social position as a carpenter that he had acquired by doing actual work represents: *prārabdha* karma, on which, he has little control. He can only perform the carpentry works based on his acquired inherent skills and the knowledge he has gained from each creative work. At the same time his son uses his *kriyamāṇa* karma to reconstruct his *sañcita karma* to acquire a new personality—*prārabdha* karma. Though he has born in the carpenter caste, he could work with his acquired skills (*sañcita karma*), and learned skills (*kriyamāṇa karma*) and redefined his *prārabdha* karma as a master carpenter, instead he has chosen another way of life. He is now an investor and financial expert. However, how his new identity, shapes up his karmic body (*karma-śarīra*) conditioned by *prārabdha* karma is beyond his control. It is a mystery. If luck helps, he may get a great name instantaneously, or may get it after many years, but if not, he may not be recognized by anyone at all. But the development of his consciousness through creative work is not assured in the industrialized world systems. It ignores the development of a personality organically, as it should have if he followed his traditional carpentry work. Even after he has redefined his identity (*prārabdha* karma) as an investment specialist, he may not get any creative work happiness as his work is not creating anything of maintainable value, by becoming a part of a highly manipulative business structure. The investment based current economic system is based on unsustainable fraudulent methods, which can crash any moment of time.

On the other hand, by executing the knowledge (*sañcita-karma*), his father Krishnan, like a musician, develops certain inexplicable skills that is internal and impossible for words to elucidate; but that would help him to live a well-lived "life". The death of carpenter Krishnan was not an event noticed by many; but it would be like the passing of a life that is well lived. He disappeared like a migratory bird retuning back to its abode without any trials and tribulations.

When comparing with the contemporary constitutional systems of Governments, the rules that bind a person to the state is *sañcita-karma*; the freedom that one can enjoy within that system is *kriyamāṇa-karma* (*āgami-karma*), the authority, the state can execute on an individual person, upon his actions, is *prārabdha-karma*. The state can reprimand him or punish him on any violations of the rules of the constitutional laws. One of the issues of the constitutional system is that the government could not watch over all the violations; in case, if all violations are to be caught and punished, then the state would turn into a police state, running thousands of jails, that would work on scare and fear only; whereas, if violations are unchecked, the society would become corrupt where a kind of lawlessness ensues constantly. This aspect throws out a big question whether modern legal system is competent enough to control human consciousness without injecting it with fear, petrification and scare. This aspect is contextually relevant when people are set, to live a life for monetary profits as the aim of life, they fall into the path of lawlessness. The state is eventually turning in, as an executer of fear and scare using various nefarious methods.

The philosophical understanding of the Gīta verse which says that one has an authority only to execute Karma in the best possible way without caring much about the results, as results are out of our control mechanism allowed in the systems of karma, because the system of karma works on the framework of "co-dependent co-evolution" of various other factors. Humans have limited control and authority over the living world. But one can live well within the space designated for humans to perform. If an actor or performer tries to achieve the perfection like another famous actor or performer, s/he would end up imitating the methods of that another person. But if the actor in this case uses all his potential allowed to perform to the best of his abilities, he could achieve own perfection indicated in *prārabdha- karma*, for he could subtly enter into the system of co-dependent co-evolution process.

In the contemporary modern world, almost everything can be copied and be created as Artificial intelligent systems, and that could destroy the chances of doing any kind of creative work. We unknowingly destroy the purpose of life, thinking that human work has no significant role in defining life. By denigrating creative work, today that we make artificial intelligence systems looking towards making more and more monetary profits, is something that should worry everyone. We can predict that if this contemporary trend continues the existence of humanity would be in danger. A kind of fatalism would ensue to human life.

References

Barbieri Low, A.J.: Artisans in Early Imperial China. University of Washington Press, Seattle & London (2007)

Pandey, R.R.: Concepts of karma and saṃsāra in Indian and Japanese culture. In: Mayeda, S., Shimoda, M. (eds.) Spread and Influence of Hinduism and Buddhism in Asia. Originals, New Delhi (2010)

Totman, C.D.: Japan Before Perry: A Short History. University of California Press, Berkeley (1981)

Varghese, M.: Principles of Buddhist Tantra. Munshiram Manoharlal, New Delhi (2008)

Chapter 37
Creative Satisfaction Versus Monetary Profit

As we have discussed in detail about the Plato's view on work and comparing it with the modern scientific worldview on work, we can easily understand that the complexities that we create with regard to work and life in our times are issues that would concern us seriously in future. The Greek God *Demiurge* is responsible for all perfect *forms* (*ideas*); and the human artisan (creator) can work directly with the *forms* and creates things for the human kind. The artisan can challenge himself to create the perfect form that is always beyond his limited understanding. Yet, according to the Socratic philosophers, God *Demiurge* cannot create anything using his creative skills. It is for the humans to use the inherent creative skills to make things including own offspring. In the case of an artist, he can only copy those God's forms of things created by the artisan. Plato reiterate the creator artisan, the one who works directly with the forms generated by god *Demiurge* can get the full satisfaction of creating the objects, and the creative challenge is the satisfaction he gets out of working with the eternal forms. The artisan, however, never could create the perfect "form" on a created object: it always remains, as an eternal challenge that never be accomplished fully, yet s/he is the one who can create a form fully into a thing and, therefore, be closer to the world of Gods, heaven: not an artist who only copies those forms created by the craftsman creator: The hierarchy of creative happiness is: God > Artisan > Artist.

In other words, the Platonic teaching on work (karma) has three levels. It is the god (*Demiurge*), the artisan (*carpenter*) and the artist (*painter*). Plato wrote: "… what the activity of representation is, on the basis of this example…. We have seen that there are three sorts of bed. The first exists in nature. It was made by god…. The second is made by the carpenter….and the third by the painter…So painter, carpenter and god are each responsible for one kind of bed." (Plato, Republic, Book X).[1] God *Demiurge* originally conceived the *Form* from his infinite wisdom; the craftsman—Artisan works on the form and creates things, e.g. the bed. The carpenter actively engages with the god given forms; but the artist can imaginatively create the design

---

[1] Plato (2007), p. 338.

© The Author(s), under exclusive license to Springer Nature Singapore Pte Ltd. 2021
M. Varghese, *A Brief History of Creative Work and Plutonomy*,
https://doi.org/10.1007/978-981-15-9263-8_37

of the form using trigonometry, or can only copy what the craftsman made objects on the basis of a mathematically discernable proportion. The artist conceives things from his imagination. In the Platonic conception, carpenter is a person who engages, with the eternal god given *Forms*, and tries to make, the best, with each mode of creative work. A carpenter who creates (works on Forms) objects such as beds is more meritorious than the one who imagines over the created forms or the one who designs it on a drawing board. The dialectics between work happiness and monetary (gain) happiness began here. The one who imaginatively uses the form get only a kind of indirect happiness; whereas, a creator would get a kind of creative happiness of working, with his creative skills, by creating object on the god created perfect forms. An artist lives in the world of imaginations, whereas an artisan lives in the world of actual objects and could use his skills to mold the material objects (wood, or clay) into the shapes of forms (cot, pot, etc.). Artisan creates, but artist copies.

The industrial scale production gradually removed the carpenter and the happiness he may draw from actually making the things using materials. And it debilitates one from getting creative happiness. As in the case of Karma theory, acquiring creative happiness is the most important purpose of life. The industrial scale production copies the designs of the things created by the artisans, and make things by using machines in multiple numbers. Today the Artificial intelligence systems can copy any creative design and be realigned it to produce things based on the specifications of an end user. Using algorithms, the modern system can collect data from different artisans and also can analyze data from consumers and artificially structure the best desired product. The opportunity to engage with creative work is almost removed from our lives. We could only use copies and imitations. We may have to fit ourselves to a uniformly created design structures conceived mainly by AI systems.

In the modern and globalized world, when monetary profit is the pivot to all human activities, the philosophy of life is centered only to maximize, as much wealth as possible, and that is, the new norm, having been followed and recopied everywhere, from villages to huge metropolises. We systematically ignore and decline deliberately the kind of creative happiness that we can earn from doing creative works. We presume that the created wealth will trickle down to all levels of the society through work; but since work is scarce due to technological unemployment caused by technological systems, the assumed trickling down effect is not happening at all. The postmodern version of unemployment is generated and promoted by outsourcing of manufacturing to other countries, by using of high technology to reduce human labor, and by using AI systems, for managing more wealth at the shortest possible time.

The created wealth would only horde into the vicious net of the financial industry; especially would move into the hands of investors, financiers, stockholders, bond holders, etc. where it would assume new values as tradable financial products. Most of the businesses are financialized and being controlled by investors and investment banks, not factory owners and farm land owners. All, the available wealth, are financially securitized everywhere. It has found that the wealth of top 1% is equal to that of the rest of 99%. It is an awkward situation for both the groups. The 1% cannot use up all the wealth they hold; and the 99% don't have enough wealth (money) to use. The acceptance of trickle-down theories assumed mythical accep- tance in the globalized world. Almost all academic classes, mass media pundits' thoughts, etc. propagate, the magical power of wealth creation and the consequent trickle-down possibilities, who act as partisan public opinion makers. Maximization of profit together with the endless creation of wealth is what is being propagated and being followed by economic pundits and thinkers of today. In order to maximize the wealth and profit, all human activities began to be mechanized, with the help of high precision technologies that are only copying the *forms* of all objects (cot, pot, car, airplane) and creating them automatically without much human "work" being allowed to be involved. The artists (engineers, programmers, system analysts, etc.) create *forms* imaginatively; and technologically enabled, artificial intelligence (AI) systems create objects—things, but the prospective users have no money to purchase them. Even if free money is given they may not use it up; they try to save it for future use, or ignore the value of money, as it is not earned or gained.

Here, notably today, AI replaces as what Plato considered as the job of the arti- sans, who may generate creative happiness: an essential ingredient for a flourishing community, as per the ethical doctrines of Aristotle on nationhood, where the wealth of a nation should be shared properly for benefiting its citizenry. The *carpenter,* in Plato's example, is now replaced by the AI systems; whereas, the artist is a few system analysts who imaginatively copies the cot that may have been created by the carpenter. The artistically created copy of the cot is standardized, in order, to increase its production. The line that differentiated artisan and artist is now very narrow and thin. The artisan (carpenter) used to study deeply the requirements of the customer while creating a cot; whereas, today the customer learned to sleep on any cot available in a readymade store. Or the customers should teach themselves to sleep on any standardized form of bed. The process of copying matures the limit of the from, the geometrical structures created by the artists in Plato's example, would turn out to be the standardized mathematical model that a machine can read. The computer-generated designs then become the resource for innumerable AI enabled systems globally and produce things automatically.

In the case of a traditional carpenter like Krishnan, who learned the designs from his masters, and created cots accordingly. He acquired an individual skill to artistically draw the designs for others and could produce the usable objects. Now machines can do all that has been done by carpenter Krishnan and his folks. With the introduction of self-programmable systems, now machines displace all analysts and programmers with systems that read the end user specifications. At the time of the 5G and fourth industrial revolution, most of the machines are expected to be self-programmable and it could make almost everyone technologically unemployed.

Krishnan is now a precariat, earning a meager income; but his son is a plutocrat— rake in cash. Krishnan has the skills, of accomplishing a work well; his son has the skills to make money, when the situations are favorable, but he does no work at all, everything is done on his behalf by AI systems. Both are trying and searching to find what make them happy. Krishnan tries to find ways to continue living for enhancing his carpentry skills, by working as a carpenter though voluntary works; though it pays him less, he is happy of doing the work well by enhancing his creative skills, by regularly activating the complexity of hand-brain faculty. But his son is, yet to get a way, to find some satisfaction, worrying with the thoughts of the surging amount of dead wealth. Now he is a part of the new herd (race) of plutocrats and running a plutocracy with his huge wealth for finding ways to invest the unused dead wealth.

The Artificial intelligence supported mechanized work culture is spreading widely. It is applied on almost everywhere and onto everything. We are hugely dependent on them. In fact, all the junior level jobs are being replaced by some kind of machine-generated alternative or outsourced for getting it cheaply done. Which should be considered as technological unemployment. The human interface in life is replaced, by mechanized alternatives, and it is becoming universal: a universal phenomenon, rising in such a severely alarming rate. Most of the creative aspects of work are done by artificial intelligence-controlled systems making human work redundant. The classical philosophical views and the modern scientific studies on consciousness show us that the use of artificial intelligence will have alarming prospects for the continued existence of human life, but nobody seems to be concerned.

The primary issue, that should worry everyone, is the substantial reduction of hand-brain activities. When human work is appended for supporting the procedures of AI systems, human brain would become ineffective. It leads to a situation, in which, humans have to live in with constant fear and suffering. Keeping oneself in creative work is what keeps one alive. In the ancient world most of the civilizations that survived like, the Indians, the Chinese, the Greeks, the Romans, the Mesopotamians, the Mayans, the Africans, etc. have been supported by creative work as a way of life. Those who declined this all-important aspect of life have also declined and could not survive the sway of time. Now the situation is so dire that creative work is what is being systematically destroyed by Artificial intelligence. The modern interpretation of Aristotelian concept of *eudaimonia* in ethics is unfortunately wrong, and his ideas that the nation-state as the regulator of the wealth of a nation is not valued anymore in the era of postmodern globalization. Plato and Aristotle upheld *eudaimonia-arete* (spiritual flourishing through virtuous actions), and declined the pleasure from sex, entertainment, etc.; where now we have to live like the inferior animals that never could experience the happiness comes out of doing creative works.

Reference

Plato: The Republic. In: Lee, D. (Trans. and ed.). Penguin Books, London (first pub. 1955) reprint (2007)

Chapter 38
Comfort and Entertainments Versus Creative Work

The value of comfort and entertainment, in the case of millennial generation, is losing its meaning. Even for an economically backward precariat, like Joe, can get all kinds of gadgets for entertainments. The smartphone itself is a substantial gadget, which keeps him connected to all kinds of entertainment and other such service facilities. Additionally he can get cheap foods at anytime, anywhere. Now it is going to be possible for Joe to order his breakfast just thinking about it. The wearable technology that are easily available everywhere could process our thoughts using the power of algorithms. As the artificial intelligence may control the thoughts, so does the social security support systems: the new world order could provide monetary support and assistance from lots of social security schemes by public and private charities. If one can eat fast foods made, from the food products made by the factory farms run on artificial intelligence systems, using most advanced genetically modified technologies (GMO), we may not have to produce any food at all using traditional farms and farming methods. The economic system is now run on investment-based methods and systems, and it is penetrating into all the activities of human life. And machines and artificial intelligence will do a major part of the work with least involvement from humans. Therefore, by becoming a consumer may help a person to eat and survive. A substantial part of profit from the artificial intelligence-controlled systems would go in to the government and that money can be used for making free comfort and free entertainment available for everyone to enjoy. In the dialectics between comfort and entertainment versus creative work, for deciding the happiness indicator: we must admit that comfort and entertainment would rule the system. The value of creative work is demoted vehemently everywhere, with deafening statement such as—when technology is available why shouldn't we use it and find happiness equally be available for everyone.

By just becoming a consumer would help the system to create more and more. The economic system, that may help production, is no longer a harmonized system of production and consumption, but the production will be hugely done by mechanized systems that would decide what is to be consumed. If some kind of nonparticipation

© The Author(s), under exclusive license to Springer Nature Singapore Pte Ltd. 2021

M. Varghese, *A Brief History of Creative Work and Plutonomy*,
https://doi.org/10.1007/978-981-15-9263-8_38

happens, the whole production system would come to a standstill. And unused wealth and dead money would be a serious problem for the world to confront.

We can explain the modern phenomena in this way: during the time of feudal societies of the pre-industrial Western world, the feudal class had everything, and the serfs class had nothing except sufferings and worries. The serfs were being subjugated by religious faith, conventional beliefs, naïve realism and fear. Then, the society during sixteenth century reformed by invoking the protestant Christian values on the principles of equality and fraternity of the entire human race, where opportunities had opened for everyone for a better life situation. The bourgeois class, during the industrial period, replaced the feudal class, of the preindustrial world. The bourgeoisie became as the controllers of all the wealth. This new class was derived from the erstwhile feudal as well as the serfs, who could use all the available opportunities to better their life situations. Nonetheless, as a characteristic feature, bourgeoisies were cleaver, crooked, skilled and educated, and they grabbed everything leaving the rest—proletariats with nothing but sufferings and worries. Then came the era of extreme capitalism heightened with the use of technology where machines did all the works; in which case plutocrats—the superrich who make less than 1% of the population to control everything; whereas, *the others*—more than 99% could live only by eating tasty fast foods and by engaging free entertainment on their internet access devices. The *precariats* (part-time workers) who become major work force replacing proletariats: part time jobs become the main source of work for those who want to work. Nevertheless, we today think, like the thinkers of the early part of twentieth century that human society today is progressing well with science and technology and more technological innovations are the solutions to all human problems. The globalized world of today is the dream project of Western philosophers like Karl Popper that called for the formation of open societies where freedom and equality should be assured for everyone. They may have thought that the Western world has achieved a state of perfect Goodness, perfect justices, perfect harmony and perfect prosperity, and that shall be disseminated to everyone, so that the entire world could enjoy the benefits of being managed by technoscience. This may be possible with the introduction of universal basic income; where machines would do all the work and provide for all the wellbeing to benefit everyone in an open society. How will it affect the basic human nature and the urge for being creative in doing "work"? Will humanity survive in the emerging world order of free "comfort and entertainment"?

Now, large majorities of people in the world are living on social security of some kind provided either by their governments or by other charitable organizations. Nobody has any realistic idea how their future would look like, but everybody eagerly presumes that a perfect life much better than the life of today is plausible in the future. The faith in scientific systems is holistic, complete and certain. A kind of zealotic pressure on society is being developed everywhere for providing charity and assistance for those who are poor. The poor who don't have any sort of economic freedom or those who are hugely indebted are in the majority, compared to those who have some kind of economic freedom; they are in the minority. The splendors of science are the sole power that decide everything, we presume and believe and submit to the view that science is the answer to all our problems. Until nineteenth century, there were some distinct differences between natural philosophy, and religion and philosophy. Later natural philosophy evolved into physical sciences, and religion and philosophy into humanity studies. But in twentieth century after modern and postmodern period, in the globalized world also, thinkers combined human science and physical sciences into one. For example, economics or politics were subjects taught as a part of ethics (philosophy), now they are taught as sciences. As a result, humans began to think that technoscience could fulfill all their needs including on ethics and morality. We expect to use artificial intelligence and surveillances systems to enforce ethical issues. Today there is a dialectics emerging between human life and AI, where AI controls human life.

The British Eugenic society, which was formed in the second half of the nineteenth century, was instrumental in initiating a kind of racially motivated thought process and it had been dominating the world order ever since. The ideas of nationalism and socialism did have a strong bearing on this kind of racism. The dominant western nations followed protestant Christian value of providence to legitimize it. This had motivated other cultures to follow their own version of nationalism. The Islamic world, the Chinese world, the Indian world, the Jewish world had developed their own version of nationalism and socialism. Most of these movements though founded on religious beliefs were less religious but more political and racial that those were based on the hierarchical superiority of the white race or more specifically, on the basis of the Anglo-Americanism. The race-based nationalism found ways to denigrate those who were not following the same views and ideologies. The first and second world wars were a consequence of racism-enhanced by ultra-nationalism. However, the post-world war societies give less credence to racism: the racial superiority views are rejected everywhere now, at least from public discourses. Yet, today the racial superiority ideals are the foundation of economics; and economic and political interests are dominating our thoughts. Our emotions and passions are drawn towards fulfilling the need of such interests, that will seek power and control through the magical power of money.

We knowingly allow such mad chases of going after money and power to ascertain somebody's superior place in the world. Superrich—plutonomy, now, is a transnational phenomenon. People want to join with the newly evolving superior class and they do any nefarious activities to get onto more wealth and power. The spirit of Eugenics was to find the perfect human beings that could control the world affairs. Such anti-human views are being supported by the systems of Artificial Intelligence. Anyone, who can get an access to it, can get immense control on the world affairs. But a kind of apathy relating to life and existence is creeping up everywhere.

When humans are not being able to use his brain and body to do daily activities and improve himself with creative knowledge, the classical philosophical understanding of life warns us that we would not be humans anymore. Contextually, today Joe is so hooked on to the technological gadgets for interacting with everything at any time. He has nothing new to learn or to do. He forgets about the nature of the world he lives in. He thinks that what is seen on the cyber space is real and he scarcely moves out of his house, or any other such comfortable abodes. Those who are supposed to be concerned about the welfare of young people like Joe are least concerned and least interested. The Protestant Christian ideals of providence and good life for everyone are not the motivational mantra of the Plutonomy controlled world of today. A kind of ignorance driven fear is controlling our thoughts all the while.

The human estrangement with the "living world" is not just because of machine generated work culture, but it may also be due to the lack of sharing of the work. Humans may have invented work not just to create things, so that they can live well, but may have found an ingenious way to engage themselves with some creative activities so that they could find satisfaction and contentment in living life. As a part of the modern scientific culture, we always attempt to achieve less work and maximum profit and when the profit margin increases the importance of work and creativity would be overlooked completely. We began to draw a kind of satisfaction and pleasure from making lots of money, because finding happiness and contentment is important for living. Wealth creation and sharing it with others is a part in the process of enhancing the wealth's value. In the globalized world, one major problem is of sharing the profit with others. Mechanization using AI destroys jobs and also devastates a justifiable way of distributing the wealth. The huge increase in profit is getting accumulated into the hand of the plutocrats, who hardly able to use even a minute part of the income. Since the wealth is hardly been distributed, it drains into non-productive activities. The increase and spread of the financial industry should be seen from this perspective. "Work" was a way to share the profits accumulated legitimately to *the others*. But AI replaces *the others* viciously. "Work" has a unique ability to keep humans happy and contented. We today hold a regressive and disparaging conception of life.

Joe did many works in his "precariat life", but he didn't learned anything from those work experiences. He was just an operator to those artificial intelligence systems that he worked with: just pressing switches—on and off. Almost all such systems work, with less and less involvements of humans. So, making convenient life for everyone with least human input and involvement is the new mantra that is being propagated in the ever-aspiring craze for more and more, by the technologically ambitious and greedy world order existing in the vicious net created by plutonomy.

Chapter 39
What AI Replaces from Our Lives

Why we need to be worried about the incursion of AI into our lives is a very important knowledge about human life today. We can explain the woeful situation of Joe, who faces a kind of self-destruction, by using the ego tunnel theory of Thomas Metzinger, through which we can illustrate, how creative work would help us to have really enjoyable experiences in life. The lower dimensional realm in the individual self (ego tunnel) creates an intrinsic connection with the higher dimensional realm with the objects of human experience. Philosophers call this as the phenomenal experience. We experience fully the objects of the world, when we engage in creative work that shapes up our *self-being* (ego tunnel). The ego tunnel of each individual is the low dimensional formation of a higher dimensional realm. The higher dimensional realm is universal, while the low dimensional realm is particular to the experiences of an individual. Plato calls the higher realm as the world of gods: heaven—city of gods. The Platonic philosophy essentially uses knowledge as the channel that connect constantly with the higher realm of Gods in the heaven. Human life in the world revolves between higher and lower realms of existence. An individual self, craves for establishing its intrinsic connection with the higher one.

Contextually, Metzinger's studies, using scientific methods, are based on the recent findings in neuro-sciences on consciousness that agrees with the classical ideas of consciousness. According to Metzinger: "*Phenomenal shadows* are low-dimensional projections with the central nervous system of a biological organism.... Shadows do not have an independence existence ...., (it is) just a shadow, a low-dimensional projections of a higher dimensional object "out there". It is an image, a representation that can be described as a region in your neural state-space ... This state space itself may well millions of dimensions; nevertheless, the physical reality you navigate with its help has an inconceivably higher number of dimensions."[1] Relating to every object we perceive, we are, in fact, getting only a low-dimensional shadowy image of a higher dimensional object. This explains how one and the same

---

[1]Metzinger (2009), p. 22.

© The Author(s), under exclusive license to Springer Nature Singapore Pte Ltd. 2021

M. Varghese, *A Brief History of Creative Work and Plutonomy*,
https://doi.org/10.1007/978-981-15-9263-8_39

object or experience makes different reactions in different individuals. Each experience may be similar but not exactly the same, which again opens up the possibility of a unified thing behind every experience. Humans are predisposed to live in the world of particular phenomenal experiences. The creative experience from work would lead us to the unified experience and a subtle insight (wisdom). Relating to, these two projections: the universal and the particular. We have classical philosophy stating that there is God at the higher realm and we, as humans, experience the world at the lower dimensional realm with the support of virtues such as Goodness, truth and beauty. As Plato says in his dialogue *Temeas*, the master craftsman—creator God-Demiurge created "forms" at the higher dimensional realm, for the humans at the lower dimensional realm to work with, on those forms to receive happiness from creating objects out of those forms. Plato's idea of creative work is for experiencing and knowing the truth about the world that is unique. Yet, what the AI aspire to take over is the sacred invincibility of the higher dimensional realm. We need not be creative and need not be working anything within the lower dimensional experiential world to realize the magnanimity of higher dimensional realm. Joe is in a situation where he has nothing to achieve and nothing to work with. The AI supported emerging world does everything for him. And in such a kind of life *eudaimonia*—the knowledge about human self-worth is least forthcoming.

Reference

Metzinger, T.: Ego Tunnel. Basic Books, New York (2009)

Chapter 40
Group Work in Daoism: Enchanting the Higher Consciousness Realm

Through philosophy of Daoism, we may argue, that there is a constant engagement for establishing an organic relationship between the higher dimensional realm and the lower dimensional realm. This classical Chinese philosophical system, promotes work and group work, as the best way of life, for moving towards finding the deeper meanings of life. The philosophy of Daoism, according to Lao-Tzu, is: "Tao (Dao) is the origin and the goal of the world and all things, hence also of the thinker. The philosophy tells us first, what Tao is; secondly, how all being proceeds from it and moves toward it; thirdly, how man lives in Tao, how he can lose it and regain it, both as an individual and political society. Thus, in Western terms, it deals with metaphysics, cosmology, ethics, and politics."[1] This Chinese system of philosophy could explain life, without resorting to any metaphysical doctrines, as in the case of Jewish, Christian, or Islamic philosophies or the theory based modern scientific philosophical interpretations of life since Galileo. The distinction between the worldly life and transcended life dissolves into a unity with Dao. Dao shows, the world, in which humans live in with its entirety. Dao is the higher dimensional realm, the unity—source of life—and the lower dimensional realm—individual life—and all the particularities of life in the world. We live in the "living world" and everything related with life is: Dao. It means experiencing "life": Dao, working towards realizing the higher dimensional realm "the source of life": Dao, and working towards Dao by realizing it through knowledge: Dao. One lives through Dao; however often, one loses it when not working towards for getting it. Constant engagement with Dao leads one to keeping it with oneself. It can be compared to the conception of *being* and *qua-being* in the Aristotelian philosophy, or as *ātman* and Brahman in the Indian philosophy.

We can reflect this, unique, understanding of Dao from the perspective of neurological studies. Dao is same for all, at the same time, different in each particular case. The same kind of effort may not earn the same result. Each effort, each individual, or each result varies even though each arrive at comparably same destination and

---

[1] Jaspers (1957), p. 88, 89.

© The Author(s), under exclusive license to Springer Nature Singapore Pte Ltd. 2021
M. Varghese, *A Brief History of Creative Work and Plutonomy*,
https://doi.org/10.1007/978-981-15-9263-8_40

conclusions. This is because each individual effort is designed by a *neural state-space* that has millions of dimensions. This complicated process is inconceivable, but it is a part of living life. Nonetheless, it all indicates a higher realm, which is to be the same, when we move towards it. This is what is called as Dao. We can get a feel of it when "working and learning" together with other people, we can get the experience of Dao. The individual experience is one of the *neural state spaces* and it is momentary. When we work in a group, we could get a feel of the higher realm. We could only prosper when we feel that we are closer with the unity.

Therefore, as for work, Daoism says we all belong to a network of different sorts of work, and work is Dao—the way. And the end result of work is also Dao—the heavens. The man who is not a part of the network of works also is a part of Dao, as he has to seek and look for Dao. But, then, how can we define Dao? According to Lao-Tzu: "I do not know its name; I call it Tao" ...... We look at it and do not see it; its name is The invisible. We listen it and do not hear it; its name is The Inaudible. We touch it and do not find it; its name is The Subtle (formless)."[2] The philosophy of Daoism is simple to understand yet it is difficult to define. The complicated world of narratives and definitions that we use, for understanding everything, could make it difficult for us to know it well. However, for a classical philosopher, it is similar to the idea of Goodness in the philosophy of Plato, or Brahman in the Vedic Philosophy. The most important thing is that we need to work towards Dao for knowing it well, and when we know it, we would live in Dao fully. Dao signifies "life" that is working towards the "source of life".

Why work is important for realizing Dao. Doing is a process that leads us to Dao. Then we will not have the problem of knowing it well, we merge with it. The problem of knowing it slowly subsides, as the duality—subject and object—weakens and lessens. This is how Lao-Tzu explains it: "The great square has no corners. The great implement (or talent) is slow to finish (or mature). Great music sounds faint. Great form has no shape".[3] All definitions need perfect forms which Dao rejects. It is similar to Plato's thoughts on God of love that is not perfect. The imperfection in God of love makes us to see the progress of goodness in Him.[4] And being with that imperfection we could realize the love in us; similar to the case of working with the things of the actual world, the neural circuits forms an individualized conscious space, the personal self-model—the ego *tunnel*, which functions by itself but always in search for something beyond. It is like a driver who drives instinctively; a musician who captivates his audience automatically; or a wine taster who valuates the wine he tastes, intuitively, with utmost precision. The conscious space, thus created, is Dao, it moves in Dao, and moves towards Dao. The efforts of creating Artificial Intelligence (AI) that replace humans are a farfetched dream of the technologized world to bring Dao under perfect control. The *neural state-space*, which is responsible for the personal self-model never could be copied or replicated. When once it is

---

[2]Jaspers (1957), p. 88, 89.

[3]ibid, p. 89.

[4]Kaplan (1950), p. 212.

recreated it loses the original human nature, and humans may find it difficult to be adopted to the refashioned form.

However, to realize Dao, we need to work towards it: step-by-step. Creative work is the most important thing to realize and to appreciate Dao. In the case of carpenter Krishnan, he was searching for that shapeless form till his death, where he would be merging with the form (Dao), with happiness by knowing the purity of that form. Maybe he has seen that formless shape (Dao). Philosophically the principles of Dao are similar to the doctrines of Karma and Brahman; contextually, it is constructed on the foundation and on the logical tools of Indian philosophy, where the approach and basic principles are typically different. As for Dao, everyone in the community should work for achieving the Dao through work, and the work only, would give us, an understanding of the Dao, that is dormant and underdeveloped in each person.

According to Dao the ruler should be a sage—a sagely minded person; and as a principle, the sage ruler, should not do any "work". Everyone should feel "Dao" in the sage ruler's presence, but it should not be evident to anyone. He should not be seen, but should be known to anybody, that he is there—protecting everyone. The sage ruler is not seen as an intelligent person who knows everything and could solve all problems, but a superficially unintelligent person that takes right decisions subtly to the benefit of everybody, as his "acts" may not create any controversies with his decisions. An apparently brave, intelligent and distinguished person cannot be freed himself from the self-image of having been so. The Dao sage ruler should avoid a self-image that shows outward attention and attraction. He will appear only when the situation duly demands for, his active presence. According to Lao-Tzu: "If the sage wishes to be above the people he has not place himself below them in words. If he wishes to be at the front of the people he has to put his person behind. Thus, when he is above the people they do not regard him as heavy when he is in front of the people, they do not regard him as harmful… He makes them work, but does not initiate them, he makes them complete their tasks and does not reside with them. Well, only because he does not reside with them, therefore they do not depart."[5] The conception of Dao sage ruler is that he should ensure the harmonious progress of life, where each should "work" on as a part of a larger unit or group; each person's work should progress to the whole—the group; and each should have the opportunity to accomplish well to fulfill the purpose of life—learning and knowing his potentialities by producing things that could protect each other's life purposes. In context, the Greek idea of stoic sage—represented in the ideal life of Socrates, who strive to make everyone's life to be moral and ethical, where he acts as a model for others to trust and follow.

The philosophy of Daoism has developed, as a continuation, of the ancient Chinese view of life. It says that, mostly, the problems of human life are originated out of "order and disorder". It is a feature of human life in the world. In modern terminology, it is because of social and political disorders.[6] Daoism sets to bring order to the society not by force but by making people to engage in all kind of creative

---

[5]Moeller (2006), p. 18, 19.
[6]ibid, p. 17.

"works". The aim of one's work is to bring order and harmony. All those works that bring disharmony should be avoided. The regions and countries where Chinese culture is being followed, this mission of one's life, working towards bringing, order and harmony, is highly valued. In other words, Chinese philosophy believe that at the *higher dimensional realm* (heaven) there is perfect order, harmony and peace; however, the humans, who live in the *lower dimensional realm* (living world), should "work" towards bringing order harmony and peace in the "living world"; much in the same way as conception of the virtue ethics of the classical Greeks. Each of us should strive to make the world a well-ordered, harmonious and peaceful place for everyone to live in. The sage ruler is a unique person, who holds no self-interest. And by the very act of declining his own self-interest, he would discourage the self-interest of all the people under his watch. He only acts as a conduit between earth and heaven. He has no ambitions, because knowledge of Dao is not acquired from outside; it grows up from within—within the human spiritual self-being. Lao-Tzu says "One may know the world without going out of doors. One may see the Way of Heaven without looking through the windows. The further one goes, the less one knows".[7] The ideals of Dao sage ruler are philosophical. Unlike the Confucian ruler who is the benevolent protector of all, the Dao sage ruler lives in emptiness, lives like a child with natural innocence, lives in a vacuum that is waiting to fill up, and lives in the realm of emptiness, *śūnyata*—the zero stage—with a potentiality to receive a real value. When value is added to zero, it receives that value, like $0 + 1 = 1$. The Dao sage could naturally understand the problems of the people near him and would help each of them to solve it by themselves by receiving virtuousness.

The Dao sage's humane compassion has the propensity to fill the vacuum created by suffering and ignorance. His self-interest-less-ness annihilates all self-interests; as vacuum sucks in, all around it. His deep consciousness understands all forms of suffering. And he tries to remove all ignorance including the ignorance of self-interest of everyone around. As self-interest would spring from deep desire and greed, and those who follow up to maximize it would fall into the disease of desire and greed. But, Daoism negates, all desires, as counterproductive to harmonious life in the "living world", because it considers desire as a sickness without any cure. But, Dao can destroy all cravings, passions, desires, etc. by generating self-awareness in a person. It is based on a belief that at the realm of the personal self-model or *ego-tunnel*, each person would be transparent and it could reveal the apparent reality as it is. Since, the apparent, disharmony and disorder are revealed, one can do his part to bring harmony and order. The ruler is only a facilitator for getting everything done in order to bring order and harmony everywhere. And he could see the flourishing of innocence in everything, in every aspect of life, because he has no self-interest at all.

He tries to reduce the self-interest of all the people, as it is known that following self-interest is the cause of worries and sufferings. He interferes, when to destroy the bourgeoning occurrence of self-interests. He only helps others to do their jobs, and he oversees that whether they execute it diligently and sincerely or not. Peace

---

[7]Jaspers (1957), p. 88, 89.

and harmony should be the order that is necessary, so the wars should be short and decisive, and should be over, at the quickest possible time for bringing in order and stability. Lao-Tzu teaches on this: "I desire without desire and the people turn to simplicity by themselves".[8] The sage ruler has no self-interest in ruling or in political matters. His only self-interest is to eliminate his selfish interest".[9] Contrarily, the modern and the postmodern scientific philosophy and capitalism promote: "self-interest maximization" as the pivot of all human "work" and all other such activities. To achieve self-interest maximization, humans should have to enhance all kinds of exploitation activities and should continue to live with disharmony, fear, self-petrification, and meaningless long wars. So, for the survival of humanity even today, it is better to ditch "self-interest" maximization methods.

The sage ruler represents emptiness. Which means he has no identity of his own; he has no distinct own-being or own nature. He assumes the identity of the needy, and the deprived, and the frightened and, the petrified; and always stays with them. However, for others he appears as an insignificant stupid person, but when the situation warrants he would advance above all conditionings and help to restore order and harmony back into the society. And he would be helping everyone to be a part of the network of the society of workers. A ruler or a leader would dedicate his life to protect the lives of those who follow him. The spiritual tradition calls for the harmonizing everything with one's life, for which everyone should work harmoniously and pleasantly, so in that sense, Dao is the way and the aim. The Japanese conception of *The Way of Bushido* or *the life of a Samurai* is influenced by this classical Chinese conception of humanity, leadership, and dedication.

There is a common saying in Japan that a *Bushi* (Samurai) would appear, at the end of a given feast, with a toothpick, before his followers and wards, pretending that he had eaten fully: even though he was hungry; he would eat only after ensuring that, everyone in the gathering of followers had eaten well. Traditionally, the ruler or leader (*Bushi*) would eat only at the end, and everyone knows about that. But, in ancient Japan, at the time of scarcity, famine, starvation, etc. people craved for food. The ruler should not worry, the others, about his helplessness or deficiencies. He should lead them with hopes, expectations and aspirations. This is because of the fact that Ignorance, fear and worry could kill the motivation to live a life with dignity and the duty of a Samurai is to instill courage and the resolve to fight against all the odds, especially relating to survival.

---

[8]Moeller (2006), p. 77.
[9]Ibid, p. 63.

References

Jaspers, K.: The Great Philosophers, vol. II. Harvest Books, New York (1957)
Kaplan, J.D. (ed.): Dialogues of Plato: Symposium. Washington Square Press, New York (1950)
Moeller, H.-G.: The Philosophy of the Daodejing. Columbia University Press, New York (2006)

Chapter 41
The Way of Samurai (Bushido) and Creative Happiness

In the modern Japan, especially after the World War II, mostly the company top executives, used to follow the traditional Bushido Ideals of dedication, commitment and leadership. The strong adherence, to Bushido ideals, had made Japanese mode of capitalism a unique system in the world, delivering excellence and perfections in everything that they did. The hierarchy-less command structures, of Japanese business systems, made the business enterprises to function as one unit. The self-interest of the company is the unified whole of all the workers' "self-interest". The CEO would also be doing all his personal works like cleaning own table, or preparing coffee for his guest, or doing all work-related errands all by himself or spending leisure time with the ordinary workers, or standing at the end of a queue in the company cafeteria. One may not see the presence of the owner of the company anywhere conspicuously; but he should ensure that everything functions well, under his command. He would come, in public only if the situation demanded his presence. This could be understood as, a kind of, the continuation of following the ideals of the Daoist sage ruler. The motivation to work was not entirely based only, on the benefits one may get, from satisfying the urge and greed for profits and other such benefits, but also, from the satisfaction he would get from doing a "work" fully well.

According to this view, the worker, the work, the satisfaction, the monetary profits etc. are all Dao, which would bring harmony and order into the society. In the Daoist tradition, work satisfaction is very important, especially when someone shares work with others by setting up it in a harmonious way. The community should work as a harmonious unit. Most of the Japanese establishments function on the basis of this principle until the 1990s when the Japanese economy financialized, in line, with all the other OECD countries. The era of globalization and economic financialization fundamentally changed the ideals of the work culture being followed, in line, with the bushido ideals. In the new system that followed by OECD countries profit superseded societal wellbeing and harmonious life around. One reason why Noriyasu lost his job was because of the financialization of Japanese economy for creating more profit for the investors or those who are the beneficiaries of the contemporary economic system. But by denying the opportunity to work is equal to bringing disharmony

© The Author(s), under exclusive license to Springer Nature Singapore Pte Ltd. 2021
M. Varghese, *A Brief History of Creative Work and Plutonomy*,
https://doi.org/10.1007/978-981-15-9263-8_41

and disorder to life and society. The greatest satisfaction, a leader would get, is by dedicating his life for the welfare of the others, making others to work and enjoy their day-to-day life, by continually engaging with creativity, which is instinctively human. In the model of industry-3.0, where digitalization revolutionized the process of profit making through investment, and it is the prime motivation for all kind of economic activities. The work satisfaction and harmonious life that the workers enjoyed were purposely distressed to create chaotic situations, so that the companies would have to depend on the financial industries' dictums. The importance of workers participation in production and services are demoted with the use of AI systems, and the demands of workers for better living conditions and better pay is relegated to a bare minimum stage.

Dao says all things flourish but each would quietly return to its root. This returning is like entering into an absolute tranquility. It is called returning to destiny. To return to destiny is known as Dao. Everyone by becoming a part of the network of works would be able to realize the Dao, which is nothing, but the way of creative work he has done by learning more and more in one's life. One progresses through work, which shows him "The way" or "Heaven" or the eternal happiness. The Brahman conception of the Vedic-philosophy accentuates this view with characteristic differences. Everything is nothing but Brahman, instead of Dao, but one has to struggle with ignorance (*māya*) in his life for realizing Brahman; for Daoism *māya* of Vedic-philosophy is also Dao.

In the machine generated work culture also there is a silent ruler who looks like the sage ruler of the Dao. The networking of the whole "work" system, and allocating the individual works, and sharing the emoluments are all done precisely and clearly using the techno-scientific systems, which includes AI, and also of modern and postmodern managements systems. But what is lacking is the human presence, like the sage ruler of the Daoism, or like the samurai leader who leads everything with complete submission and dedication, where the new techno systems work on dehumanized systems functioning on created norms of the plutonomy. But under the Daoist systems, human work with hand is appreciated and considered as a way to keep the consciousness—Dao—stable and active, or to keep the ego tunnel active and functioning. In the case of machine generated systems human creative activities are miserably negated and declined. Machines take over all creative activities, leaving humans to live eventually like machines. The progress of human consciousness, by engaging in creative work, would be nearly zero as the progress of Artificial Intelligence dominates the world systems.

According to Indian classical physiology, human nervous system that spreads all over the body from the brain finds its endings in hands and legs. It is also proven that to keep the brain healthy, one needs to use the hands and legs effectively and efficiently. Mahatma Gandhi, when he introduced handicraft-based traditional industries as a way forward for the Indians, believed that one may find happiness, when using hands for creating goods that may eventually be used by the entire community. He understood that creative happiness is very important for the individual human survival. Based on the latest studies on neuro-phenomenology, we have seen earlier that the neural structure of *ego-tunnel* is built on the already existing structures in the brain; and it is clearly based on how we efficiently use our day-to-day experiences, through creative work. If those experiences are not progressively moved from the lower dimensional realm of the individual entity to the higher dimensional realm of unity, the neural systems built as the conscious space would develop negative responses and would make reactionary repulses, such as mental depressions, suicide tendencies and other such psychic issues. The accent on virtue ethics in philosophy is meant for helping normal human persons to resist those negating tendencies.

It can be explained in simple terms, a person who learns driving, by reading a book may be able to master all driving techniques rationally, but his neural structures won't transform with this kind of learning as it is not learned through practice. When driving a car on the road, he will not be able to move the car independently and properly, if it is not learned by practice. The bookish knowledge could have created a pseudo conscious space, but not created an ego tunnel that have transformed the neural structures. The bookish knowledge may work as just an additional knowledge faculty only. The hand-brain faculty, involving the entire body, is what performs the act of driving. The machine generated work situation in the world of today uses, human work minimally, only for helping the networking of machines; like a cashier at a convenient store. When the store cashier receives money and issues receipts, a new network of automatized operations is initiated subsequently. The money will be updated into the bank accounts, which will go into various accounts, and the profit amount is automatically separated into various other accounts, using such networking procedures. And a different kind of procedure is initiated to the suppliers, as that they will be alerted, and the suppliers using another automatized system will replace the thing that was sold. In all these processes, nobody uses his intelligence or any creative activity. Artificial intelligence replaces all the bodily responses that enable a person to experience happiness.

In the beginning of the human civilizations, those who could use tools, have used them for accomplishing some impossible tasks, yet those implements only act as the extension of human hands, where hands were used very actively and efficiently with the help of tools, but at the time of reindustrialization (industry-2.0) and globalized periods (industry-3.0) the use of hand tools reduced, and it has been taken over by machines and then by automatized systems, making the humans subservient to the machines. Since the profit is created not out of the active participation of the involvement of the beneficiaries, they also would not get a chance to enjoy the fruits of creativity. The social system would disintegrate and eventually finds own destruction at the end of the tunnel, but our hopes are that we may find hopeful aspects at the end of the tunnel, instead the tunnel is leading us of the shadowy world of Hell, the dominion of lord *Hades*.

Almost 200 years ago, Karl Marx warned us about the anomalies of mechanization that, if not be careful, it could degrade and denigrate the value of human work; he implored to the communists, if they won't protect the interests of common workers and their creative skills, a kind of machine mentality may ensue in the human societies. Mahatma Gandhi, on the other hand, implored, his followers, to follow the wisdom of the spinning wheel. The freedom movement he initiated in India against the British imperialism had another dimension of deteriorating phase of work and life due to the illogical use of science and technology to gain profit at the expense of human creativity. He wanted to inform us about the kind of creative happiness and satisfaction, one could earn when engaging with creative skills. He challenged the might of industrial Britain with this simple act of defiance. He, in fact, mocked at the British Empire on their unending greed to attain satisfaction through earning money. Their greed again pushed them to participate in to both world wars and that again made them to engage in oppressive colonialism in India, Africa, and North America.

Maybe Gandhi with his deep understanding of Indian culture and tradition understood that human work is what unites people that helps them to share the joy of creative work with everybody else. Making the thread using a spinning wheel requires utmost attention and deep creative thinking skills of the worker. By doing that, one may incite the neural circuits and eventually would have created an internal conscious space, which would help one to live well by getting creative happiness. The logic of Gandhi's thoughts about creative work inspired millions of Indians and thereby spinning wheel become the symbol of resistance against the British rule and the mechanization of human life.

In the case of Carpenter Krishnan, he continued using his traditional skills for making his life to a satisfactory end as he lived in the world where creative happiness become a regular phenomenon. The happiness he could get from work was a feeling of him being involved fully. Though he couldn't get any monetary benefit from his works, in the end, he was a satisfied man. He could experience the pleasure that was only reserved for the gods in heaven; or his conscious space (ego tunnel) became more and more transparent with the higher knowledge as shadows of ignorance faded away. Noriyasu on the other hand, followed a different style of life where he created a new conscious space (*ego tunnel*) that has become opaque and he himself got confused of his real existence; he was pushed into the world of deep sadness and depression of not getting the higher knowledge through working and learning. His mind never could achieve transparency and self-control. Whatever progress, he could achieve, was abruptly ended and being curtailed by the greed for profits of the company. A kind of purposelessness and depression ensued and it prompted him to end his live in a suicide.

We decline human creative work for achieving more profit with a fear of poverty and deprivation spreading fast; we produce goods and wealth with a presumption that we can achieve economic freedom by doing that; but we cannot distribute the wealth created without human involvement by (creative) work. Distributing free money is not the solution for keeping human life healthy; the wealth created by using AI would transfer into the hands of a few plutocrats. Plutonomy is sustained by merely machine minded people who live in deep ignorance about the wants of life. We cannot find a rightful balance. We are simply taught that to follow "good", we need to negate "bad"; or for accepting "right", "wrong" should be negated. Wealth is good; poverty is bad. We live in a world of such a conundrum formed in the milieu of either/or binaries. Artificial Intelligence is created out of this kind of puzzle of choosing the one choice that we need to follow brazenly by negating the opposites.

Chapter 42
Artificial Intelligence and the Making of Zombie Societies

The millennial generations live, entirely, in a machine-dominated and machine-controlled world. Instead of learning and knowing the ways of the working of nature, they need to prepare themselves for the new ways of living together with machines and also in competing with/against the machine-minded world. Normally a young student attends school or university starts his work-life by doing part-time jobs, from the very young age, as a part of the student life in most of the OECD countries. Most of them work on, as the entry-level, labor jobs mostly, at service industries like, restaurants, department stores, bars, etc. Most of the student population today borrows money to pay their educational expenses from the banks. A part of the earnings, of such part-time jobs, would go for paying off such loans. The purpose of student-work culture was meant to help them get an introduction to the work culture of the industrial world order, into which they have to work at various levels: from executives to normal workers. Student part-time jobs should have helped a few generations of students to learn about the ways to compete in the industrialized world where people have to use machines in every aspect of life. This is a part of life in the so-called developed countries. The young generation of today is only just getting appended to the artificial intelligence systems, but not getting any new skills. Instead of learning from such jobs, they have an aversion to work from the very young age. Now, the part time student workers are used as under paid labor force, who in future, should live as the underemployed precariat in their whole life, and should have to compete with the much more-lowly paid migrant labors.

It is not the quality of the work that matters but the work itself. When the machines were made, it helped to enhance the hand skills like the spinning wheel; but when machine itself could think and automatically manage itself, the freedom that humans enjoyed by working with different workers with different working skills have also become strained and become retracted. The machines no longer are under the control of those who handle them. Machines are automatized as being a part of a wider network and by doing so machines control our hands. The networked artificial intelligence system would control the worker implicitly. We are controlled by a mechanized system rather than we control it, and are, itself, being progressing towards a

© The Author(s), under exclusive license to Springer Nature Singapore Pte Ltd. 2021
M. Varghese, *A Brief History of Creative Work and Plutonomy*,
https://doi.org/10.1007/978-981-15-9263-8_42

kind of technological singularity. The user can access to the singularity and get any kind of tasks to be accomplished. There is no one controller for those systems, but a network of human greed controls it by using fear, intimidation coercion, etc. Out of fear we feel we need to be disciplined in almost all aspects of life.

The plutocrats without their active involvement with any activities would become richer and richer. The modern algorithmic systems with the active help of artificial intelligence systems keep up and manage the wealth of the rich by creating more and more unusable wealth. Plutocrats are hoarders of dead wealth; or their role is similar to undertakers who refuse to bury the dead bodies, but instead watch over dead bodies without knowing the alarming fact that under his watch over time, each body gets rotten up and spoils the whole place with strong stench. And the dirty smell from the rotting dead bodies would annoy everyone more so the undertakers. Plutonomy now spoils all the available wealth around the world, as the avenue for distributing wealth through creative world is being destroyed systematically. They posit plutocracy instead of democracy, because they know very well that the nature of human lethargy and complacence, but their effort to create artificial heaven and act like the ancient Greek or Indian gods. That is the true extend of their ignorance. They are also humans who are influenced by lethargy, ignorance and apathetic like the millennials of today. They now are drugged by stench of the dead wealth they hold.

The workers involvements in creating wealth are nearly nil. It is more frightening than what we may think. The implicit purpose of education today is, turning out, to be making, a part of the world order where economics plays an important role. That part is a borderless one, and it is growing very fast at the expense of the others. It is very difficult to make them understand that they are just a part of the world where they can exist only for few years, like all others in the world. And that small period of time, if they destroy the world by making the world fall into the technological singularity using super-efficient AI systems that servers none, helps none, but destroys everyone and everything without any hope of returning.

The typical convenient store part time worker's situation in Japan can explain this situation well. A part-time student worker like, Joe, who goes to work in a convenient store is sent by a dispatch company, who has received the calls on the smart phone, and who is permitted to do a certain kind of job, for a specified period of time. He takes the address and goes to the store; gets the employee tag from a designated place. By doing this, he can work at the store for the allotted time. His only activity is making sure all the machines works properly and if the customer pays by cash, he needs to collect it, otherwise the customer himself could pay by card based on the amount shown on the monitor. Since he has a lot of leisure time, and he can play some games on his smart phone. Joe does nothing creatively just watching over only, which would bore him soon enough.

For the emerging life in the twenty-first century, a person needs not have to worry much about the growth of his consciousness or self-model—*ego tunnel*; he could get as much comfort and entertainment as possible. This may create alarming social consequences; one may fall deep into the world of depression and mental sufferings. Since the use of hand and body in work is less and less important: less and less forthcoming; the attention and concentration in doing a work is not necessary at all. The consciousness is never active and it is replaced by the act of Artificial Intelligence. Into that emptied space of consciousness, bringing various kinds of fear is easy and natural, which would destroy the natural life of the individual persons. An individual person can survive only by communicating actively with his living environment. If that freedom is denied, one would not survive long. During twentieth century an individual citizen was mandated to follow the rules of a country, now all the rules are delegated to a surveillance system, which may be watching everyone everywhere.

The emerging model of man is an amoral, asexual, asocial, insensitive personality whom some philosophers named as the Zombies, or a walking dead man, or a spiritually dead man. According to Metzinger: "In classical antiquity as well as in the scholastic philosophy of the Christian Middle ages, *conscientia* typically referred either to moral consciousness or to knowledge shared by certain groups of people—again, most commonly of moral ideas, interestingly being truly conscious was connected to moral insight.[Isn't it a beautiful notion that becoming conscious in the true sense could be related to moral conscious? Philosophers would have a new definition of the entity they call a *Zombie*—an amoral person ethically fast asleep but with eyes wide open]."[1] This kind of zombies are being seen everywhere in our times. The brain and neural circuits are not incited by any kind of creative work and therefore the conscious space—*ego tunnel* is not being created. A kind of fear would be generated by emotions such as passion, greed, anger, delusion and wrath making everyone inactive. We can see people who are engrossed in verbal quirk, and vilely argumentative everywhere by hating each other.

The precariats (part-time workers) never need to see the senior employee or any such persons in the store. The store can manage by itself. There is an unseen "system manager" manages the affairs of the store and watches everything that is happening inside. The same system manages many stores. One never needs to use his creative activity in any manner, nor one could learn anything new. The worker's consciousness would never build a personal self-model (PSM) or the conscious space. It is blocked or made opaque, as s/he only read the instruction manuals as a guide to the work. Nobody scolds them; he needs not have to report to anyone. His smart phone would direct him automatically from one to another, and when he is not able to do or to find any job he would be naturally directed to the social welfare schemes from which he can get sustenance and support. Comfort and entertainment are the two aspects that controls human emotions in our times, especially with the precariat-millennials. Whereas, lack of proper wealth distribution and injustice were the factors that controlled the industrial world; while, in the pre-industrialized world poverty and subjugation had spread because of the control of the feudal oligarchy on the serfs.

In the feudal period and industrial period, comfort and entertainment were available only to feudal lords and their chosen supporters, but never been accessible to the serfs. The so-called happy lives of the feudal lords were hugely dependent on the hard works of the serfs. But, after the industrial revolution, the erstwhile serfs formed a major part of the newly created middle class (burghers) and they were divided into

[1] Metzinger (2009), p. 26.

a new class system that of the bourgeoisie and the proletariat. According to Marx, bourgeoisie had all privileges and powers because of the newly created industrial wealth, whereas proletariat had nothing to lose, as they have no access to wealth; at the same time, their work was absolutely necessary for the industries to function. Therefore, unionization and industrial unrests were highly feared and were severely declined by the capitalist bourgeoisie. The antagonism of capitalism versus communism and the succeeding history of the world conflicts could be understood in this way.

But, in the context of the millennial globalized world, where super-rich plutocrats use technology and other such means to further decline the importance of work the dwindling working population marginalized into part-time workers, the precariats, who have no control on their lives or could change their precarious state; but at the same time, working class people could access to minimum comfort and entertainment, because of technology as they can find a lot of free sources for subsistence. Artificial intelligence and networked systems ensure comfort and entertainment to majority of people as the potential consumers. The plutonomy, of today, needs consumers' data to attract investments from the community of super-rich investors. Now investors can use algorithmic systems to protect their investments from all kinds of loses. And the artificial intelligence systems ensure security by giving a feeling that everyone is being constantly watched. The resource for artificial intelligence is data; data is sourced using various methods. And the same data is used to control human activities. We live in a world of fear and ignorance. The presumed protection is different from the protection provided by a Daoist sage ruler because he is human and compassionate and his religiosity is to help humans to work and better their lives. The artificial intelligence systems run on created programs, which are intentionally created by other humans who hold parochial views and perspectives. The creation of plutonomy and their huge control over undistributed wealth controls everything in the world. The bourgeoisie who powered the capitalist system now getting extinct and a new dialectics is being emerged as between plutocrats versus precariats. The wealth division is now nearing to zero.

But unknowingly, we are made to believe that that is similar to the sage ruler in the Daoist system or the king in the classical Indian system. The Daoist sage or the Indian king would control the masses with compassion and a deep sense of duty. In the case of Indian system, the ruler oversee that the subjects would live well by helping them for discharging their own Karmas as being a part of the network of works (karma) as his kingly duty (*Raja Dharma*). In both cases the ruler is a human person who act, intelligently and compassionately, according to the demands of the situation. But, for the AI (artificial intelligence) systems, the controller is not a human person, but a highly networked mechanical intelligence system that could manage the human affairs like a machine. It is created to exploit as much wealth as possible and help another system of investors to enjoy the monetary benefits that is been accorded from small individual businesses.

In the case of a small business like a store, that is run by an individual creates a system of economic and human relationship around, and like a ruler, should have run the store to benefit everyone involved. But with the systematic change that happens through AI, the whole situation, has taken a tectonic shift towards centralization and control and that it is working on a self-generated singularity. This singularity acts like a single command and control system, but in actuality, there is none controls, but everyone tries to make maximum advantage of any plausible emerging situation. The tectonic shift can be seen in human life too. Aggressive individualism and self-censorship under the influence of fear is what determine our choice and preferences. It acts like singular entity but in actuality it is run by algorithms giving a feeling that a single system is in operation.

In the case of a modern store, as and when the part-time worker completes his work and replaces his tag in the slot, his work hours are calculated and the payment is automatically deposited into his bank account. He may not see that store again in his life, as he may go to another place, a restaurant for another day's work. He is not committed to any particular work or to any particular owner. He is free to do anything he wants to do, but since there is no unfreedom, the very idea of freedom loses its meaning. Freedom for him is getting unconnected with the rest of the world. He is largely unconnected with his peer group, family, community, etc. On the smart phone or other such network-accessing devices, one could connect to any kind of information and a simplified way to understand that information. Learning something new for removing ignorance is now impossible. Knowledge is not dialectically working against ignorance. And also, one needs not use his hands to learn something new, and therefore, the personal self-model (ego tunnel) is not created at all. A part-time worker like Joe, today, plays games or visits some internet sites that would fill his ineffectual lazy mind with some activity. He is fully awakened but not to the world he lives in. His vision about the world is opaque. The consciousness that should have been active is now dysfunctional and lazy. His life is devoid of real-life experiences like, family, marriage, social life, love, care, etc. The superstructure of networked systems controls all humans viciously. The very idea of the generation of consciousness by the structuring of neural circuits, through creative work is impossible in the world of today. Nobody does any creative work. In other words, his ego tunnel is not opened fully. He lives in a dead world where he loses the appetite, and desire to live on. The user interfaced, AI run, systems of future, or the internet of things, would have the capacity to destroy life as we experience today.

One of the many concerns that should be taken seriously is the fast incursion of a technological singularity, or the smart grid, that would rule the world without any centralized authority, supervising all production, both agricultural and industrial, and the service jobs. The apathy and disinterestedness towards aspects of life by the millennial generation is an indicative of humanity's future. It is not that the singularity would rule over the world, but we might turn in as machines-minded to live in the new world order. As a symptom of this prospect is that we today try to hide our emotional states and attempt to act, like everybody else. People today are hell bend on following others, and impatient to accept opposing views, even though we understand them as true. We lose the capacity to work against adverse situations. As human creative work has been systematically declined, we are only able to work as an extension of machines; not the machine supports the creative works of the humans.

In fact, it is possible for someone to equate the act of technological singularity to the acts of the Daoist sage ruler. The inhuman nature of interaction never could be equated to the wisdom of the sage ruler. The technological systems only can monitor and enhance the efficiency of services and productions; yet, the experience shows that it retroactively turns humans into machine minded and act only on specific instructions. In a situation where natural human rationality reigns, the situation progresses on the basis of wisdom and compassion and a deep feeling of security; whereas in the mechanical rationality, we will be afraid of our own mistakes and fear others anxiously, because we are not competing with other human beings, but with technological systems where we certainly will fail; therefore we fear everything, and should live without knowing the winning spirit, or *eudaimonia*, as in Hellenic ethical concepts. But the technologically formulated systems would outwardly show a kind of perfection, which is alluring and fascinating to everyone. It generates immediate attention to people as they have the freedom to choose what they want to do, *here and now*. For example, if a person is poor he can ask to the social security service for financial assistance; if someone feels sexually excited, he/she has multiple choices without violating anyone else's freedom, that one can seek the services of an escort services, etc. that are plenteously available. Application of artificial intelligence in sex industry is an ever-evolving phenomenon from sex toys to sex robots with unmatched allurements. And there are dispatch companies that would provide rental services on all sexual related fun activities. Moreover, it is possible to hire a mother, sister, friend, husband, or wife for a day. A variety of such services are being provided in many OECD countries.[2]

The sage ruler of Daoism is not like the unknown controller who controls the part-time workers (precariats) of today, like Joe. The sage ruler, is absent from the public as his presence is not apparent, he only appears when the situation demands his presence, but he oversees everything with the spirit of compassion and wisdom. He is there for everyone to execute their own duties, and everyone would receive his patronage and help. The ruler should give all of them moral direction and the ways to improve themselves in getting work satisfaction and monetary gains. The worker needs to improve himself to move on to the next level, otherwise he may have to stay with his less accomplishments, but none never lose the chance to work of being a part of the community. His efforts would be utilized so long as the network of workers and jobs would go.

In Indian context the king's duty (*rājadharma*) is of protecting the dharma of all others in his country, but not of imposing his will for maximizing his self-interest or gains. If some did so, all people would decline such kings and rulers. The Daoist sage ruler tries to reduce the voracity for maximizing the self-interest of everyone in the community by helping to generate situations that could gain true satisfaction by doing some work, so that the greed for gaining monetary benefits would be reduced to a bare minimum. By pursuing self-interest maximization as the goal, modern business doctrines demand all workers to seek happiness by earning as much money as possible. Here monetary benefits negate work satisfaction, where happiness should

---

[2]https://blog.rentafriend.com/rent-a-wife-or-rent-a-husband/retrieved on 20-06-2020.

be drawn from seeking more comforts and entertainments. But the irony is that none can get a lot of satisfaction with lots of money. The available options for entertainment for a superrich plutocrat are there, available for a part-time worker (*precariats*) too. The presumption of those who promote self-interest maximization, as a way of life is that maximum monetary profit would make a person secure and happy and lots of insecurities are there of being a person who may not have any access to wealth. Such narratives are based on the wishful thinking about the mystical power of money. This implicit expectation made plutocrats to stockpile huge amount of money with whichever way possible. In reality more than 90% of people live without any access to wealth is a serious problem today. The proper application of human intelligence, in matters relating to money and the financial industry that is being profusely developed everywhere. AI creates a conundrum that is difficult to solve easily.

Mahatma Gandhi expressed a similar view when he upheld the ancient Indian views on karma as the pivot of protecting life; especially, the king controls all the systems for maintaining order and good life. The king or the state in this conception is constituted to protect and preserve the dharma of the diverse groupings and to guarantee the harmonious functioning of the organic groupings in the society. The dharma of an individual directs his caste duties that the Vedic tradition of Indian society followed, where the hierarchical social order has been duly made functional. But, the critiques of the Vedic systems, the Buddhist rulers in India too followed the non-hierarchical-caste based version of Raja-dharma.[3] The spirit of both systems was to provide work to the individual as a part of his/her living life, where doing own designated jobs (karma) were the criteria that decided the formation of an organic structure, which functions by itself. According to this view division of labor (work) is the key to the progress of life in the society. The challenge of a worker is reacting to his mistakes day by day and learning and correcting own mistakes. He never ends his learnings. He continues his learnings so long as the activation of the *hand-brain faculty* permits.

The modern technological systems are so perfect that it only utilizes minimum resources to maximize profit; it is a misrepresentation of facts. It, in fact, utilizes maximum energy resources to automatically run the huge mechanical systems; whereas it underutilizes human work substantially. It creates severe stress on natural resources and would destroy the nature and environment. Using human resources would substantially reduce the use of energy sources like, electric power etc. and could be able to protect the problem of production and the use of it. Like all resources, if a source is underutilized it would eventually get destroyed by itself. On the other hand, the systems that have been developing, in the era of globalization, is substantially reducing the distribution of wealth. The created wealth using artificial intelligence is moving into the hands of investors, shareholders, etc. Ironically, the distribution of wealth is done through a newer mechanism pivoted by the financial industry. Investors are free to buy and sell their properties through stock market and if they

---

[3]In the Indian context for the Vedic systems, caste system, denoted a hierarchical system where society divided on the basis of caste difference, as the castes in the higher levels are spiritually pure and therefore higher in their status which was not the case with Buddhists, Jains and others.

are willing to take more risk they could buy financial products like, CDS, CDO, SDR, SPV, or similar financial products that are abundantly available everywhere. The investment culture has taken a system of its own and prompt investors to invest in almost everything without any active participation. In the pre-industrialization period human energy was used to the maximum, in the industrialization and reindustrialization period, some kind of balance was maintained in utilizing the machine and human energy; in the globalization postmodern era, the mechanization of everything is at the zenith and utilization of human energy is declined substantially, and soon it would be zero.

In the reindustrialized world, the work culture, on the other hand, warrants us to be a part of the network of workers to use our creative energies to the maximum. At that time, earning satisfaction by earning a profit and utilizing the human potential were effectively done. The two aspects of profits are what make work interesting and rewarding. Carpenter Krishnan has born into the caste of carpenters and his family follows the tradition of making houses and furniture for the entire community. He is a part of the network of carpenters and also a part of the network of artisans, and also a part of the community, and the society at large. He is a part of the wider human community. His identity is defined in different ways. The dual profit he earns from his work is what makes him a living human being. In the traditional system the salary for work used to come as things, such as food, etc. which was shared with the community at large. The food and other immediate things were available even when one was not working actively. One aspect of profits that was highly revered, was the honor and respect. One could be happy and he disseminates that satisfaction to the community where he lives, which was revered in the community and society very well. He could enjoy a kind of protection that money cannot buy. On the other hand, people who possess financial products would not utilize even a small part of their wealth for living their lives. And the kind of respect they may get is not reverential, nor respectful, but scornful and contemptuous to a very large extent. Plutocrats live in a self-induced isolation in the world of their own.

When Artificial Intelligence replaced human work, the benefit from work reduced to wealth accumulation, not by distribution through creative work, and it moved automatically into the hands of investors making them the superrich class. Financial industry now creates a superstructure that directs all human activities. The creative work has now absolutely been taken over by a system of self-programmable methods of Artificial Intelligence. The exhortations of the plutocrats the system of Artificial intelligence can get more financial support. This is due to the stress of unused money that has been becoming the biggest concern for the plutonomy to deal with. They are ready to finance any activity in order to use the unused money. By investing such money into all kind of assets again creates more unused dead money. Any kind of wealth that is generated anywhere in the world automatically transfers into the hands of the investors. It all happens without their direct knowledge as Artificial intelligence manage them automatically.

During the industrialization period, the bourgeoisie who used to exploit the labor of the ordinary worker (proletariat) used partial mechanization to increase production but largely dependent on the committed hard work of the workers. The revolt of workers for more share of wealth created conflicts and those conflicts helped the workers to demand more and more. Though the worker could not use his creative energy fully, if he could have been a part of the culture of innovations and advancements indirectly. A system that may have developed in Britain or Germany should have implemented into the working environment of Japan or the USA in the reindustrialization period. The workers had to relearn the systems and recreate those original systems. The worker's involvements with creative activities were appreciated. But, today on the other hand, Artificial Intelligence copy it, and the machine made in one place can copy automatically all those systems without any human involvement. Convenience, comfort, more time for entertainment, etc. are the reasoning given on support of implementing the Artificial intelligence systems everywhere.

The workers' creative energy that is waiting to bloom would largely be wasted when creativity is being taken away from normal human life. Today we see less people marrying and making family like in the industrialization period or earlier periods before eighteenth century. In twenty-first century humans consider love and relationships as mere entertainments. The Platonic teaching on creative energy as a manifestation of human pleasure, happiness, or flourishing (*eudemonia*) is draining out of human life. We now move into the world of hedonism, or seeking pleasure as the main aim of life. It is not the Hedonism of Epicurus, but that of a person who seeks only low-level pleasures and gets bored of it sooner. Today we follow hedonism without any aim, morality, etc. but for Epicurean sense hedonism means respect the pleasures of life and use it to live better and to live in a community by sharing and co-operating with each other with a sense of camaraderie, so that one could maintain the spirit of it till the end of life. The influence of Artificial intelligence into our lives is like existing inside a matrix. We don't know that we are inside of it and whatever we do will enhance the strength of it.

Reference

Metzinger, T.: Ego Tunnel. Basic Books, New York (2009)

CPSIA information can be obtained
at www.ICGtesting.com
Printed in the USA
LVHW041038151121
703362LV00004B/106